D1226700

THE
BLACK
MAN
IN
AMERICA
Since Reconstruction

EUGENE SMITH LIBRARY
EASTERN CONN. STATE UNIVERSITY
J. EUGENE SMITH LIBRARY
CONN. STATE UNIVERSITY
WILLIMANTIC, CT 06226
WITHDRAWN

THE
BLACK
MAN
IN
AMERICA

Since Reconstruction

edited by
David M. Reimers
NEW YORK UNIVERSITY

THOMAS Y. CROWELL COMPANY • NEW YORK • ESTABLISHED 1834

First Printing, May, 1970
Second Printing, July, 1971

Copyright © 1970 by Thomas Y. Crowell Company, Inc.
All Rights Reserved

Except for use in a review, the reproduction
or utilization of this work in any form or by any electronic,
mechanical, or other means, now known or hereafter invented,
including photocopying and recording,
and in any information storage and retrieval system is
forbidden without the written permission of the publisher.

L. C. Card 74-117435
ISBN 0-690-14634-5

Designed by Ruth Smerechniak

Manufactured in the United States of America

9-19-96 ell

TO
Katherine & Rebecca

PREFACE

This collection of essays is designed primarily for supplementary reading in the second half of the general survey courses in American history. I have concentrated on two basic areas: the post-Reconstruction South and urbanization. First, I have chosen essays and written introductions to depict the conditions facing black Americans in the late nineteenth and early twentieth centuries and the black response to those conditions. Second, I have concentrated on the emergence of the ghetto after 1910 and the black response to changing conditions, especially the development of black nationalism and the civil rights movement.

In viewing the post-Civil War black experience, one can see Reconstruction as a critical period, an era which deserves extended treatment. Instructors would probably want an entire book devoted to Reconstruction; hence I have aimed at the post-Reconstruction period.

In the 1960s the mood of black America underwent changes which are still in process. Anything written about the late 1960s would be dated quickly. I have selected essays not to analyze the current scene but rather to explain the background of the civil rights movement and black nationalism as they appeared in the 1960s. An instructor might turn to the current black writers and commentaries to indicate the current situation. Hence, in reading the last several selections one should remember when they were written. They are good summaries and analyses of the preceding events, but may not necessarily foretell the future.

D. M. R

Contents

ix

PART 1

THE SOUTHERN SYSTEM OF RACE RELATIONS AND THE BLACK RESPONSE: 1877—1915

THE
SOUTHERN SYSTEM

The years following 1890 were a particularly wretched time for black Americans. Political disfranchisement, rural poverty, discrimination, segregation, and violence were daily features of life for southern blacks. One hundred black Americans were lynched during the first year of the new century. The white South, with northern compliance, nullified many of the modest gains of Reconstruction and carved out a new status of second-class citizenship for blacks.

Not that Reconstruction and the immediate post-Reconstruction period were a golden age. The Civil War did destroy slavery and trigger a mild movement for racial justice, and

Reconstruction produced the Fourteenth and Fifteenth Amendments and the first civil rights legislation in American history; however, the Radical governments of the 1860s and 1870s did not end segregation and discrimination. Blacks and whites did mix in some public places and on some public carriers, even during the years immediately following the overthrow of the southern Radical governments. Yet segregation was widespread. Separate churches, schools, trade unions, lodges, and family life were the norm. What happened in the two decades following 1890, as the selection from C. Vann Woodward's *The Strange Career of Jim Crow* shows, was that the system of segregation became more rigid and was buttressed by a rash of legislation.

Politics fell into the same pattern. During Reconstruction, blacks participated in, but did not control (not even in areas where they constituted a majority) southern state and local governments. They were still involved in politics in the 1880s and 1890s. The last black congressman of the time, George White of North Carolina, ended his term in 1901. Increased violence, intimidation, and fraud began to drive blacks from the political arena. John Hope Franklin's selection in this volume discusses the final step in the process, the "legal" disfranchisement of southern black voters and the virtual nullification of the Fifteenth Amendment.

Perhaps the postwar period's greatest failure was in the realm of economics. Some black leaders saw the need for a fundamental economic change to follow upon the abolition of slavery. They advocated land redistribution, education, and other schemes in order that the freedmen might acquire financial independence and mobility. Black education did become a feature of the postwar South, and was one of the real achievements of Reconstruction. For most blacks, however, the economic realities were grim and the quality of education was poor. Some journeyed north and west, as in the famous trek of thousands to Kansas under "Pap" Singleton that began in the late 1870s. Others sought out the cities, northern and southern. But in spite of these migrations 90 percent of black Americans still lived in the South at the turn of the century, and the vast majority lived in rural areas. For the black farmer this meant a life of farm tenancy and poverty; three-quarters of the black farmers were tenants of some type at the turn of the century. Hortense Powdermaker's essay, written in the 1930s, describes the plight of the tenant up to that time. Even those who owned land suffered. Their holdings were small, and after 1900 the boll weevil brought new problems. Of course, freedom did bring increased family stability and made possible the growth of an educated black middle class, but achievement of this status was not possible for the typical turn-of-the-century black American.

Along with the caste system, poverty, and racial violence went the doctrine of white supremacy. Guion Johnson describes some aspects of this ideology and some recent changes in southern white attitudes. As in the other instances noted above, it is important to realize the continuity with the past. A belief in white supremacy has been held by most white southerners since the seventeenth century. The post-Civil War spokesmen simply gave the concept a new form to justify the late nineteenth-century southern white "solution" to race relations.

The same years that witnessed intensified white racism were the years of Populist and Progressive reform. The Populists briefly flirted with an interracial alliance of poor whites and blacks, but eventually the white Populists lost their faith in such an alliance and accepted the new caste system. Some Populists, like Tom Watson of Georgia, first urged racial justice and then adopted white supremacy as their creed.

Some white Progressives sympathized with the plight of black Americans. White liberals helped found the National Association for the Advancement of Colored People and the National Urban League, and individual Progressives protested against racial discrimination. By and large, however, the Progressives accepted racism or were indifferent to the plight of the blacks. Southern Progressivism was for whites only. Some Progressives rode to power in the South on the doctrine of white supremacy and a program of Jim Crow and disfranchisement. Southern Progressives made strides in building a public school system, but blacks paid the price, for the system was more unequal in 1915 than in 1900. In South Carolina's public schools in 1915, for example, $1.13 was expended for every black child and $13.90 for every white child. This was a ratio of twelve to one; it had been six to one in 1900.

In the North, the Progressive years were marked by a deteriorating status for blacks. Segregation and discrimination were standard in northern cities, and civil rights laws passed in the late nineteenth century often went unenforced. Racial violence occurred in the northern cities as blacks moved in from the South. The last serious attempt of the period to enforce the Reconstruction amendments was made in the 1890s when Henry Cabot Lodge's "force bills," providing for federal enforcement of the Fifteenth Amendment, were introduced in Congress. Enough northern Senators joined with southerners to kill these bills. Moreover, northern judges sanctioned the southern laws nullifying these amendments. The simple fact was that the crusade for racial justice of the Civil War and Reconstruction era, never a strong movement to begin with, was played out by the turn of the century, and the North was willing to indulge its own racism and to allow white southerners to set racial policies for the South.

The failure of white northerners to support civil rights for the blacks can be attributed to several factors. In brief, abolitionists and others who had struggled for racial equality died or retired, and there were few to replace them. Many northerners became disillusioned with Radicalism and corruption or wearied of trying to create democracy. Northern politicians who hoped to build a Republican party in the South turned to southern whites for support. Theodore Roosevelt, who sometimes supported civil rights, at the 1912 Bull Moose Convention threw his lot in with the lily-white delegations from southern states in an effort to win Progressive white votes from that region. Some northerners wanted stability in the South in order that they might invest there, and they were willing to allow southern whites to set racial standards if that was the price of stability.

At bottom was the fact that most northern whites were racists. The movement for equality of the Civil War and Reconstruction did bring change, but it did not eradicate notions of white supremacy from the northern mind. This racism was clearly brought to light when blacks moved to the North in the early years of the new century. In 1900 New York City had an ugly race riot, and the racial explosion of 1908 in Springfield, Illinois, was quelled only by 5000 militiamen.

The racism of the late nineteenth and early twentieth centuries also had intellectual support. Anthropologists, biologists, psychologists, political scientists, and historians offered "scientific" evidence to support white supremacy. Anti-Negro bias probably reached its zenith during these years. It was written into the school curriculum. The film *Birth of a Nation* supported a racist interpretation of Reconstruction by glorifying the Ku Klux Klan and picturing black men as rapists. Magazines increasingly painted blacks in a derogatory light, and songs such as "All Coons Look Alike to Me" were popular in New York City.

American imperialism at the turn of the century added more ammunition to the cause of white supremacy. One of the justifications offered for overseas imperialism was the concept of the "white man's burden," and white southerners were quick to point out that if this concept was valid for a bloody conquest of the Philippines, then white supremacy in the American South was also justified.

All of these forces were apparent in the South as much as elsewhere. But the fundamental fact is that the whites there had never intended to grant blacks equality or even much say in public affairs. After all, the Confederacy had fought a long, costly war in defense of slavery. The free labor system the white South desired can be seen in the "black codes" enacted by many white state governments just after the war. These laws clearly were prejudiced against the freedmen and were meant to keep them in a second-class status. Some whites did work with the Radical black politicians during the Reconstruction period; but most were hostile to black rule or black participation and were willing to use fraud, terror, and force as well as regular political processes to overthrow the Radical regimes.

Once back in power, southern whites did hesitate before eliminating blacks entirely from politics or passing many Jim Crow laws. But by the 1890s those who had accepted some civil rights and some political participation for blacks gave way and racism won out. The Populists who had defended blacks became disillusioned when black votes were manipulated against them. Southern conservatives were alarmed when the Populists attempted an interracial alliance of the poor against the rich; hence they, too, were willing to nullify the Fifteenth Amendment. By the turn of the century only a handful of defenders were left for the southern blacks.

Deserted by the North and pressured by the intensification of racism in the South, the blacks were left with little hope and power to resist. There were black troops in the United States Army, but they were stationed in the West to help the white man control the Indians and not in the South to ensure the right to vote. The black middle class was too small and weak to resist the economic pressures, and the mass of blacks who were poor farmers were in no position to make an effective resistance. Hence the triumph of racism.

1

Capitulation to Racism

C. VANN WOODWARD

Within [a] context of growing pessimism, mounting tension, and unleashed phobias the structure of segregation and discrimination was extended by the adoption of a great number of the Jim Crow type of laws. Up to 1900 the only law of this type adopted by the majority of Southern states was that applying to passengers aboard trains. And South Carolina did

SOURCE: C. Vann Woodward, *The Strange Career of Jim Crow* (2nd rev. ed.; New York: Oxford University Press, 1966), pp. 97–102. Copyright © 1966 by Oxford University Press, Inc. Reprinted by permission of the author and publisher.

not adopt that until 1898,[1] North Carolina in 1899, and Virginia, the last, in 1900. Only three states had required or authorized the Jim Crow waiting room in railway stations before 1899, but in the next decade nearly all of the other Southern states fell in line. The adoption of laws applying to new subjects tended to take place in waves of popularity. Street cars had been common in Southern cities since the eighties, but only Georgia had a segregation law applying to them before the end of the century. Then in quick succession North Carolina and Virginia adopted such a law in 1901, Louisiana in 1902, Arkansas, South Carolina, and Tennessee in 1903, Mississippi and Maryland in 1904, Florida in 1905, and Oklahoma in 1907. These laws referred to separation within cars, but a Montgomery city ordinance of 1906 was the first to require a completely separate Jim Crow street car. During these years the older seaboard states of the South also extended the segregation laws to steamboats.

The mushroom growth of discriminatory and segregation laws during the first two decades of this century piled up a huge bulk of legislation. Much of the code was contributed by city ordinances or by local regulations and rules enforced without the formality of laws. Only a sampling is possible here. For up and down the avenues and byways of Southern life appeared with increasing profusion the little signs: "Whites Only" or "Colored." Sometimes the law prescribed their dimensions in inches, and in one case the kind and color of paint. Many appeared without requirement by law—over entrances and exits, at theaters and boarding houses, toilets and water fountains, waiting rooms and ticket windows.

A large body of law grew up concerned with the segregation of employees and their working conditions. The South Carolina code of 1915, with subsequent elaborations, prohibited textile . factories from permitting laborers of different races from working together in the same room, or using the same entrances, pay windows, exits, doorways, stairways, "or windows [sic]" at the same time, or the same "lavatories, toilets, drinking water buckets, pails, cups, dippers or glasses" at any time.

[1] For first-class coaches only, and not until 1900 was the law amended to apply to second class as well.

Exceptions were made of firemen, floor scrubbers, and repair men, who were permitted association with the white proletarian elite on an emergency basis. In most instances segregation in employment was established without the aid of statute. And in many crafts and trades the written or unwritten policies of Jim Crow unionism made segregation superfluous by excluding Negroes from employment.

State institutions for the care of the dependent or incapacitated were naturally the subject of more legislation than private institutions of the same sort, but ordinarily the latter followed pretty closely the segregation practices of the public institutions. Both types had usually made it a practice all along. The fact that only Mississippi and South Carolina specifically provided by law for general segregation in hospitals does not indicate that nonsegregation was the rule in the hospitals of other states. The two states named also required Negro nurses for Negro patients, and Alabama prohibited white female nurses from attending Negro male patients. Thirteen Southern and border states required the separation of patients by races in mental hospitals, and ten states specified segregation of inmates in penal institutions. Some of the latter went into detail regarding the chaining, transportation, feeding, and working of the prisoners on a segregated basis. Segregation of the races in homes for the aged, the indigent, the orphans, the blind, the deaf, and the dumb was the subject of numerous state laws.

Much ingenuity and effort went into the separation of the races in their amusements, diversions, recreations, and sports. The Separate Park Law of Georgia, adopted in 1905, appears to have been the first venture of a state legislature into this field, though city ordinances and local custom were quite active in pushing the Negro out of the public parks. Circuses and tent shows, including side shows, fell under a law adopted by Louisiana in 1914, which required separate entrances, exits, ticket windows, and ticket sellers that would be kept at least twenty-five feet apart. The city of Birmingham applied the principle to "any room, hall, theatre, picture house, auditorium, yard, court, ball park, or other indoor or outdoor place" and specified that the races be "distinctly separated . . . by well defined physical barriers." North Carolina and Virginia interdicted all fraternal orders or societies that permitted members of both races to address each other as brother.

Residential segregation in cities, still rare in the older seaboard towns, developed along five different patterns in the second decade of the century. The type originating in Baltimore in 1910 designated all-white and all-Negro blocks in areas occupied by both races. This experiment was imitated in Atlanta and Greenville. Virginia sought to legalize segregation by a state law that authorized city councils to divide territories into segregated districts and to prohibit either race from living in the other's district, a method adopted by Roanoke and Portsmouth, Virginia. The third method, invented by Richmond, designated blocks throughout the city black or white according to the majority of the residents and forbade any person to live in any block "where the majority of residents on such streets are occupied by those with whom said person is forbidden to intermarry." This one was later copied by Ashland, Virginia, and Winston-Salem, North Carolina. A still more complicated law originated in Norfolk, which applied to both mixed and unmixed blocks and fixed the color status by ownership as well as occupancy. And finally New Orleans developed a law requiring a person of either race to secure consent of the majority of persons living in an area before establishing a residence therein. After these devices were frustrated by a Supreme Court decision in 1917, attempts continued to be made to circumvent the decision. Probably the most effective of these was the restrictive covenant, a private contract limiting the sale of property in an area to purchasers of the favored race.

The most prevalent and widespread segregation of living areas was accomplished without need for legal sanction. The black ghettos of the "Darktown" slums in every Southern city were the consequence mainly of the Negro's economic status, his relegation to the lowest rung of the ladder. Smaller towns sometimes excluded Negro residents completely simply by letting it be known in forceful ways that their presence would not be tolerated. In 1914 there were six such towns in Texas, five in Oklahoma, and two in Alabama. On the other hand there were by that time some thirty towns in the South, besides a number of unincorporated settlements, inhabited exclusively by Negroes. In August 1913, Clarence Poe, editor of the *Progressive Farmer,* secured the unanimous endorsement of a convention of the North Carolina Farmer's Union for a movement to segregate the races in rural districts.

The extremes to which caste penalties and separation were carried in parts of the South could hardly find a counterpart short of the latitudes of India and South Africa. In 1909 Mobile passed a curfew law applying exclusively to Negroes and requiring them to be off the streets by 10 P.M. The Oklahoma legislature in 1915 authorized its Corporation Commission to require telephone companies "to maintain separate booths for white and colored patrons." North Carolina and Florida required that textbooks used by the public-school children of one race be kept separate from those used by the other, and the Florida law specified separation even while the books were in storage. South Carolina for a time segregated a third caste by establishing separate schools for mulatto as well as for white and Negro children. A New Orleans ordinance segregated white and Negro prostitutes in separate districts. Ray Stannard Baker found Jim Crow Bibles for Negro witnesses in Atlanta courts and Jim Crow elevators for Negro passengers in Atlanta buildings.

2

"Legal" Disfranchisement of the Negro

JOHN HOPE FRANKLIN

In 1890 some Southern whites were celebrating what may well be described as an uneasy victory over the individuals and groups that favored the enfranchisement of the Negro. Many Negroes had, of course, retired from politics. Some had retreated at the point of the guns of white supremacists, while others had found it impossible to cope with the economic pressures, fantastic obstacles at polling places, and a variety of petty "legal" nuisances. Even with the sharp decline of Negro

SOURCE: *Journal of Negro Education*, XXVI (Spring, 1957), 241–48 (footnotes omitted). Reprinted by permission of the *Journal of Negro Education* and the author.

participation in politics, there was hardly justification for Henry W. Grady's claim in 1889 that the Negro "as a political force has dropped out of consideration." In a moving tribute to him at the time of his death one writer credited Grady, the "Spokesman of the New South," with "literally loving a nation into peace." In his claim regarding the ineffectiveness of the Negro as a political force Grady was literally *wishing* the Negro "as a political force" out of the picture.

The situation at the end of the eighties required more than wishing, however. Negroes were still voting in many parts of the South. Between 1876 and 1890 their voting strength had been cut in some Southern states by as much as one-half, but it had not been completely wiped out anywhere. Negro voters remained so considerable in some areas, especially in the Black Belt districts, that they posed a real problem for white candidates for public office who vied with each other for Negro support; and it was not unheard-of that a white candidate for one office had to join forces with a Negro candidate for another office in order to be certain of victory. It was this situation that made it possible for Negroes to continue to hold office during the eighties. In Mississippi there were seven Negroes in the legislature in 1888. In the same year there were eight Negroes in the Virginia General Assembly. They held numerous minor offices in many parts of the South; and in 1890 there were three Negroes in the federal Congress. These conditions merely increased the anxiety of the Gradys who wanted to be rid of the Negro factor in politics.

Other factors added to the obvious anxiety of whites regarding the role of Negroes in Southern politics. In 1889 the Republicans not only inaugurated a President but regained control of both houses of the Congress. In an early message to the Congress President Harrison called for a law providing for federal intervention to police elections. Henry Cabot Lodge had advocated such a law for several years, and it was the growing sentiment favoring such legislation that impelled Henry W. Grady to go to Boston in December, 1889, to speak against it in his last public address. If the federal government was to offer its strength to protect the remaining Negroes who were exercising the franchise and holding office, there was a real danger that the Negro would become an even more important factor in Southern politics. All the favorite arguments against federal intervention were advanced. Ever-present was the claim of corruption and venality. The Negro, himself an active corrupting element during Reconstruction, had become, after the "overthrow," an irresistible temptation to the white man to corrupt himself by buying the Negro's vote in order to make him "safe."

As if the anxieties created by these conditions were not enough, there were others that were caused by the most distressing developments of an entirely different kind. The position of the Southern farmer in the eighties had steadily deteriorated. The small group of well-to-do planters and businessmen at the top, whose political strength had increased, were growing stronger as a result of their association with Northern industrialists and financiers. As the South became industrialized the merchant and industrialist ascended the economic and political ladder and moved toward a position of dominance. At times they merged their interests and identity with the planter who could offer them social position if nothing else. The economic changes did not substantially improve conditions among either the masses of Southern whites or the Negroes. Most of them remained agricultural workers, and the long years of depression in the areas of cotton production following the panic of 1873 caused suffering that bred unrest. The dissatisfaction that transcended racial lines tempted Negroes and whites to join forces to seek through political action some relief from their ills.

The radical agrarian movement in the South attracted discontented elements of both races, who maintained separate organizations. At the same time they achieved a wide area of agreement as far as goals were concerned. Many of these goals were to be reached through the candidates who sought public office under the banner of the Populist party or some coalition of radical agrarian groups with one of the regular parties. Even as these biracial combinations developed, they had within them the seeds of their own destruction. The whites involved in such combinations were largely the upland yeomen and landless element whose antagonisms toward the Negro went back to the antebellum period and whose association with Negroes, even for the common good, was of the most tenuous and indefinite nature. They needed only to have their confidence shaken or their racial antipathies aroused to cause them not only to desert their Negro allies but to turn against them with great vehemence.

The successes of the early agrarian efforts were impressive. In 1888 Negroes and whites considered the question of promoting a strike for higher wages among the cotton pickers. Within a matter of months they were organizing for political purposes. In the last decade they achieved a surprising degree of success in certain areas of the South such as Georgia, Virginia, and North Carolina. The conservative element in the South had reason to be apprehensive. They denounced Populism as radical, fanatical, and un-American; they seized every opportunity to undermine this frightening turn of events.

President Harrison's call in 1889 for the enactment of legislation for the federal control of elections gave the conservative South its first real opportunity to undermine the biracial political movement. When Henry Cabot Lodge introduced such a bill in June 1890, the Southern whites began to call for a closing of the ranks. They recalled the "horrors" of reconstruction days and declared they would never tolerate such treatment again. They implored the dissident whites to return to the party of their fathers and uphold the honor of the South. And even as Populists began to bid for power they began to suffer from the defections of those who were easily persuaded to return to the fold.

Convinced that more effective disfranchisement of the Negro was needed to remove him completely as a voter and as an issue in elections, Southern whites decided to write Negro disfranchisement into the constitutions of their states. This would make it possible for whites to divide on the basis of issues, would reduce corruption by eliminating the temptation of rival white candidates to purchase Negro votes, would eliminate the disproportionate influence of white politicians in "corrupt" black counties, and would prevent the rise of Negroes as social and economic competitors with the whites. The time was at hand, therefore, to disfranchise the Negro by "legal, constitutional" means, without seeming to violate the Fifteenth Amendment to the Federal Constitution.

In 1890 it was Mississippi that took the initiative by calling a convention to do what various segments of the state's population had been discussing since 1877. Oddly enough, some of the most liberal elements in the state, such as the Farmers Alliance, favored the convention, while many conservatives opposed it on the grounds that racial peace had been achieved and well enough should be let alone! Regardless of motives of those who supported the calling of the convention, it is clear that the majority of the delegates who assembled were primarily interested in devising some scheme of insuring white supremacy.

At the Mississippi convention the delegates from white counties were suspicious of most disfranchisement proposals. They were fearful that the proposed measures would operate against many of their white constituents. Finally, the leaders from the black counties were able to enlist their support for measures designed merely to eliminate the Negro voter. Thus, the Constitution was amended to grant the franchise only to those who met the state residence requirements of two years, who were free from criminal records, who had paid the poll tax of two dollars per year, and who could read or understand any section of the state constitution. While the "understanding clause" was, on the face of it, applicable to whites and blacks alike and could be used to disfranchise one group or the other, it was clear that in practice it was intended to enfranchise illiterate whites. Negroes were to be disfranchised by the literacy clause. The intentions of the framers were made clear by President S. S. Calhoon on the closing day of the convention. Even the United States Supreme Court, although feeling helpless—or disinclined—to do anything about it, took cognizance of the framers' intentions when it said that the provisions "swept the horizons of expediency to find a way around the Negro amendments to the Federal Constitution."

Southerners in other states viewed the developments in Mississippi with admiration and wondered if they could do as well. In the same year Tennessee took one feeble step by instituting a poll tax requirement, the example for which was actually set by Florida in 1889, while Arkansas followed suit in 1893. Meanwhile, Virginia and Georgia tightened their election laws in 1893 and 1894. In some instances they were administered so as to eliminate potential Negro voters from the polls.

South Carolina was the only other state that took the drastic step of constitutional disfranchisement of the Negro before the collapse of Populism. In September 1895, the "people of South Carolina assembled in convention for the third time since the Civil War to make a fundamental law." They had lived under the "Radical" Reconstruction Constitution for twenty-seven years, and in an unguarded moment some would admit that it was an excellent document. But Negroes had participated in its construction and, worse still, under it some Negroes continued to enjoy the franchise, despite the numerous election laws the state had enacted to obstruct them. In order to write a fundamental law that would disfranchise all Negroes and, at the same time, permit every white person however ignorant or poor, to vote, Ben Tillman left his seat in the United States Senate to serve as chairman of the convention's suffrage committee. By cajoling, persuading, and threatening Tillman steered through the convention a provision designed to achieve these ends.

Like the Mississippi provision, the South Carolina constitution set up a residence requirement of two years, required the payment of a poll tax, and excluded persons, who were invariably Negroes, convicted of a specified list of crimes. Up to January 1, 1898, any man who fulfilled these requirements and who could read or understand the constitution was to be a voter for life. After that date, any person who fulfilled the requirements or who paid taxes on $300 worth of property could become a voter. Once again, in order to circumvent the Fifteenth Amendment, registration and election officials were to be left free to discriminate against prospective Negro voters and show partiality for whites.

The hesitation that other Southern states had in coming to grips with the question of the Negro voter seemed to disappear as they became deeply involved with radical agrarianism in the mid-nineties. While they were afraid to call constitutional conventions as long as Populism was at high tide, lest the mischievous radicals do more harm than good, they became determined to do so at the first opportunity. Gradually, however, the corner was turned. White Populists began to buy the conservative argument that the elimination of the Negro from voting was a healthy step toward strengthening the two-party system and opening the door for constructive reform. Thus, reaction conspired with reform to accelerate the disfranchisement of the Negro toward the end of the century.

There were always those who feared that the literacy and understanding tests would, in the hands of scrupulous registrars, operate to disfranchise some whites and, thus, go beyond the real intentions of the disfranchising conventions. Some, moreover, hoped that the disfranchisement measures would remove some of the more undesirable whites as well as all the Negroes from the lists of eligible voters. It was Louisiana that sought to guard against such a deplorable eventuality. When that state revised its constitution in 1898 it followed the pattern set by Mississippi and [South Carolina] as far as residence, literacy, and understanding of the constitution were concerned. It went one step further, however, by granting the franchise to any one who, lacking the educational and property qualifications, was eligible to vote on January 1, 1867, or who was the son or grandson of a person eligible to vote on that date. The right to register under the "grandfather clause" had to be exercised by September 1, 1898. Louisiana thereby embraced a measure that Tillman's South Carolina had rejected because of doubtful constitutionality. In 1910 the young state of Oklahoma was to follow this lead and precipitate the controversy that led to the outlawing of the grandfather clause.

Thus, before the beginning of the twentieth century the basic techniques by which Negroes were to be "legally" disfranchised had been developed. In subsequent years no significant modifications were made to the methods that had been introduced by Mississippi, South Carolina, and Louisiana. The states that changed the suffrage provisions of their constitutions in the early years of the new century were content merely to refine the methods of the pioneers. But they left no doubt that they were as determined as their predecessors to destroy every vestige of political power in the hands of the

Negroes. And they seemed even less fearful of running afoul of the Fifteenth Amendment. In North Carolina the bitter campaigns of 1898 and 1900 were fought on a pledge to remove Negroes from politics. In the latter year the victors fulfilled their promise by introducing into the constitution a reading and writing qualification for voting and a temporary grand- father clause to accommodate illiterate whites.

In 1901 the Alabama convention did a good deal of "refining of" the suffrage provisions of its constitution. It experienced difficulty in developing a "scheme pure and simple" which would "let every white man vote and prevent any Negro from voting." Too many Negroes were prompt in paying their taxes for the whites to rely solely on a poll tax. Too many Negroes could establish the identity of their white ancestors to rely solely on the grandfather clause. The fact that one-half of the Negro electorate could read and write cast doubt on the effi- cacy of a literacy test. The confused delegates finally set up literacy, poll tax and property tests as the principal require- ments and placed their real hopes in the hands of election registrars who were given wide discretionary powers.

The Virginia convention, extending from the early summer of 1901 into the winter of 1902, was protracted largely because of the many disagreements regarding the most effective way to disfranchise Negroes. There seemed to be no controversy over the main purpose of the convention. It was aptly put by Carter Glass when he said, "Discrimination! Why that is precisely what we propose; that, exactly, is what this convention was elected for—to discriminate to the very extremity of permis- sible action under the limitations of the Federal Constitution, with a view to the elimination of every Negro voter who can be gotten rid of, legally, without materially impairing the nu- merical strength of the white electorate." None disagreed with the aims of Glass, but there was great difficulty in arriving at a satisfactory formula by which these aims were to be realized. After much heated debate the delegates finally agreed on lit- eracy, property, and poll tax tests and a proposal to enfran- chise any man or the son of any man who had seen service in the Confederate or United States forces or in the state militia.

For a time it appeared as though Georgia would not join the movement to disfranchise the Negro legally. Some Georgians doubted that the white public would support a disfranchising scheme, believing that the long-established poll tax, combined with time-honored "informal" methods, had all but completed the disfranchisement of Negroes. But it was the use and manipulation of the Negro electorate that finally inspired reformers to advocate the legal disfranchisement of Negroes. Led by Tom Watson, the agrarians who had formerly supported universal suffrage began a vigorous campaign for disfranchisement by 1906. They were fearful that the conservatives would enlist Negro voters in their fight against legislation designed to control railroads, corporations, and other "enemies" of the people. Consequently, the agrarians campaigned and won in 1906 on a platform that demanded the disfranchisement of the Negro. Two years later a new constitution went into effect that contained the conventional educational and property tests.

By 1910 the white supremacists could rest much more comfortably than they did in 1890. Every former Confederate state had strengthened its stand against Negro voting by "legally" disfranchising Negroes. There seemed to be nothing that anyone could do about it. The one Negro delegate in the Mississippi convention and the six in the South Carolina gathering were helpless. There were no Negroes in the conventions of the other states. Outsiders, such as Booker Washington, had no more effect in their requests for moderation and justice than the friends of Negro suffrage who sat in the conventions. And, except in the case of Alabama, the new constitutions were not submitted to the people of the several states. In the very manner in which they ignored the pleas of interested victims and in which they brushed aside the apprehensions of the "legitimate" electorate, the revisionists displayed their grim determination to drive the Negro from politics.

It is, of course, difficult to measure the success of the new machinery in achieving white supremacy at the Southern polls. In every Southern state the number of Negroes who could qualify to vote under the new constitutions sharply declined. One cannot be certain, however, that "legal" disfranchisement accomplished the neat trick of driving the Negro from the Southern polling places. As V. O. Key has observed, "Law often merely records not what is to be but what is, and ensures that what is will continue to be." Certainly the confusion created by the agrarian unrest, the suppression of the Populist revolt, and the persistence of Negro voting stimulated the fight against Negro voting. Legal disfranchisement crystallized and gave formal expression to this fight. But all these developments were occurring at the same time that another technique, extra-legal and presumably not in violation of the Fifteenth Amendment, was developing. This was the white primary. In the long run it was, perhaps, to be more effective than the legal machinery in keeping Negroes from voting. Whatever the effective techniques were, it was "legal" disfranchisement that gave the entire trend respectability and maintained in the South the fiction that it was not running over the Federal constitution but living under it.

3

The Negro
on the Plantation

HORTENSE POWDERMAKER

"After freedom" there was still the cotton to be planted, cultivated, and picked. There were still the plantations. And there was a set of mores so strongly entrenched that not even a war could dislodge them. The Negro was still the worker. The white man, much poorer than before, still made the decisions. Landlords who had sufficient wealth after the Civil War to continue as planters, translated the responsibility for slaves to

SOURCE: Hortense Powdermaker, *After Freedom: A Cultural Study in the Deep South* (New York: The Viking Press, Inc., 1939), pp. 80–92 (footnotes omitted). Copyright 1939, renewed © 1967 by Hortense Powdermaker. Reprinted by permission of the publisher.

responsibility for tenants. Sometimes a man's tenants were the same Negroes who had formerly been his slaves. Many slaves merely transferred their dependence from master to landlord. Money still played only a small part in their dealings. Nevertheless, the Negro was free. He had acquired the right to move, even though he has not always been able to exercise that right.

The organization of plantation work continues today along traditional lines. The majority of landlords are white and the majority of workers colored. In 1930 the farm operators by tenure and by color in the county were as follows:

	White and Colored	Colored	Percent Colored
Number of Full Owners	467	181	39
Number of Part Owners	43	13	30
Number of Managers	49	1	2
Number of Tenants	14,135	11,449	81
Cash Tenants	1,416	1,044	74
Other Tenants	12,719	10,405	82

According to these figures, eighty-one percent of the tenants were colored; that is, eighty-one percent of those who did the actual labor. None of the large plantations in the community hires Poor Whites, who are considered "treacherous" and "independent." They either work on small farms or rent plots for themselves. Their bitterness about the preference for Negro labor has been commented upon. At the time this study was made, no Negro was unable to find an opening as a tenant if he wished one. He might be unable to find one that he liked, or where he felt he would have a chance of breaking even; but the demand for labor was in excess of the supply. A tenant might give up farming because of discouragement, but none of them stopped for lack of a job. One fear of the Whites has always been that their labor supply would be taken from them. In the boom years there was intense feeling against northern agents who came in to entice Negro workers up north, and every effort was made to oppose them. Even during the lean years in the early thirties local Whites were troubled lest the opportunity to receive government relief should discourage Negroes from becoming tenants.

The plantation executives are the owner, manager, and overseer. Sometimes three persons occupy these posts, sometimes their functions are taken over by one or two. The executives control finances, select seeds, supervise in detail the planting, cultivating, and picking of the crops, and rule on all questions that arise. The work is usually done by tenants except during the picking season, when a small number of day workers are sometimes employed. The system operates largely through credit. The owners borrow from banks, merchants, and cotton factors. The tenants in turn receive their living expenses as an advance from the owners, against the value of the crop.

Another aspect of the plantation tradition which persists is that the entire family of a tenant is considered an economic unit, and its size determines the size of the holding he cultivates. A man and wife together work from fifteen to twenty acres. If they have three children, the acreage is twenty-five or thirty. Children five or six years old come to the fields with them and play about where they can be watched. A child of ten or twelve is a worker, and is counted as half a hand. A sixteen-year-old boy or girl is a full hand. Today, as in the past, children are an economic asset. There is practically no vocal public sentiment against child labor. On the contrary, it is so officially countenanced that the public schools as a matter of course expect children of tenants to attend only when they are not required in the fields.

The tenants are divided into two main classes, sharecroppers and renters. Of these the sharecroppers, listed in the table as "other tenants," are vastly in the majority. The sharecropper has no capital and is "furnished" by the landlord. This means that he is supplied with seed, animals, implements, and an advance in cash or credit to cover his living expenses. During 1932, the amount allowed was usually reckoned at fifty cents an acre for each work month. A family of five would thus get $12.50 a month for working twenty-five acres. Before the depression, during the period of high cotton prices, the rate was often as high as one dollar an acre.

The furnishings are rarely in cash, particularly since the depression. Sometimes the planters issue books of coupons, usable only at the plantation store. Another common system is for the tenants to get their supplies on a charge account at a plantation store. Prices at the plantation store usually average from ten to twenty-five percent higher than in town, and occasional items far exceed this figure. In a few very exceptional cases the tenant is furnished with cash which he can spend anywhere. Such an arrangement is highly prized.

The house goes with the furnishings. This too harks back to the plantation of slavery days, especially since the majority of tenants live in cabins no different from those of their slave grandfathers. By any modern standards of hygiene the living quarters on most of the plantations would be considered uninhabitable. Yet the tenants and their large families do live in them, crowding into two-room frame shacks with no sanitary conveniences of any kind. The front room is taken up with beds, the number depending on the family. Not more than three usually sleep in one bed. Sometimes there will also be a bed in the back room, where the cooking is done. Cabins with more than two rooms are as a rule equally lacking in sanitary facilities. About twenty percent of the plantations have good housing for tenants. Some landlords complain that, when a tenant is given a well-screened cottage, he tears out the screens and damages the house. Occasionally the complaint is offered as an excuse for not giving better cabins. At times it is the result of experience. Sabotage may be due to the ignorance of a tenant who is unused to any sort of convenience and either is bothered by it or does not know how to treat it. Sometimes it happens also that tenants deliberately injure the house in order to take revenge on the landlord for some grievance.

A tenant is entitled to live in his cabin the year round, but the other furnishings are given to him only during the cotton season. If he has had a good year he may choose to remain on the plantation during the winter also. One who has had a bad year, and is too discouraged to make any move, may also stay and get advances from the landlord, thus increasing his indebtedness. A few may find employment, such as cutting or hauling wood, but very little of this is available. Some of the women raise chickens or obtain occasional work cooking, washing, ironing. Many agricultural workers, however, migrate to the town for the winter. Here they may live with relatives, or rent living quarters for the off season and try to find work in town to see them through until planting begins again. Some make a point of going in so that their children can attend the town schools, which are often better than those in the country.

In return for furnishings and house, the sharecropper gives to the landlord half the cotton raised by him and his family. The other half is his share, but almost invariably the landlord sells it for him. At the end of the season, some time in December, there is a settlement. A few landowners give their tenants an itemized list of supplies bought or cash advanced, and a receipt for the cotton sold, with the difference in cash. This procedure is most unusual, however. As a rule the tenant is given no sales receipt for his cotton, nor any itemized statement of his furnishings and advances, but is merely told that he has come out even, that some small amount is due him, or that he is in debt to the landlord.

The following few cases are typical:

A middle-class family manages to "get along" with a moderate degree of comfort, by working in town during the seven months of the year when it does not work on the plantation. The man is a carpenter but does not always find employment. His wife has more regular work as a cook. Both participate in the social life of the town.

During the season, they are one of five families sharecropping on a plantation of 170 acres. They have a plot of 18 acres, 13 of which are in cotton, 4 in corn, and one in garden produce. The landlord provides seed for cotton, corn, and sorghum, but the tenants provide their own garden seed. They thought the government was to give them this and were disappointed at having to buy it. They own two pigs and a number of chickens, and the landlord furnishes all the work animals and implements. There is no store on the plantation. For five months, from March to July, they are allowed $7.50 a month for groceries at a store in town, and they are given receipts for the $37.50 thus spent. The expenses come to about $10 a month, most of this being spent for meat, coffee, sugar, flour, and rice. Fruits and vegetables from the garden are canned.

They begin work at "sun-up," about 6:30 or 7 in the morning, and continue until a little before sunset, about 6:30 P.M., with an hour off at noon. On Saturday the men work until noon, but the women do not work in the fields that day.

In 1932 they made seven bales of cotton, half of which went to the landlord. He sold their share and when the settlement was made in November they were given $36. There was no statement about the sale and they feel sure that if they had asked for one they would have been "cussed out." They have been at the plantation two years and are staying for the third because they do not see a better place to go.

A couple and their two sons have had long and varied experiences as sharecroppers; as time went on, the experiences grew more discouraging. One year they made nine bales on halves, but they "never got nothing for it." They left that place and went to another, where they made ten bales, but they got nothing for that either. The husband "was always one to talk up" and ask for what he thought was his due, and he asked for a suit of clothes. He and the landlord had words about this and the family moved off without getting any settlement at all. The husband became discouraged and refused to farm any more but did public work on the roads. His wife and the sons continued making crops.

One year they had a good landlord and cleared $400. She bought a house out of that money. Another year she cleared $490. This was her record. Now she is not strong enough to work in the fields, and her husband is dead. She still has the house, however, and works "cleaning up" in the home of an elderly white widower.

A woman who is not well enough to do much in the fields herself, keeps house for her three unmarried sons. They have 16 acres in cotton and 7 in corn and are working on half-shares for both. They receive $12 a month for furnishings, for six months beginning with March, and they can spend the money anywhere. The landlord sells their share of cotton and they are given no receipt for the sale and no statement. For the last few years they have received no money at all. Last year they plowed under, as they were instructed to do, but they received no share of what the landlord got for this.

Unless the landlord or manager presents a statement of purchases from the plantation store and receipts from the cotton, the tenant rarely asks for it. If he is illiterate, it would not do

him much good. He may know how to read and figure, and still
not be shrewd enough to want a statement. He may want it
and know it would be impossible to get, or simply be afraid
to ask for it.

One reason for preferring Negro to white labor on plantations is the inability of the Negro to make or enforce demands
for a just statement, or for any statement at all. He may hope
for protection, justice, honesty, from his landlord, but he cannot demand them. There is no force to back up a demand,
neither the law, the vote, nor public opinion. Even a request,
if voiced too insistently, may lead to trouble. The landlord
may become offended or angry, in which case there are ways
open to him for retaliation and for forcing submission. This
leaves the landlord-tenant relation a strictly individual affair.
There are landowners who carry over the tradition of paternal
concern for their tenants; there are also some who grant a fair
deal in a less paternalistic spirit. Many a prosperous Negro
today is glad to acknowledge that he owes his independence
to a white landlord. But no Southerner, white or black, would
maintain that "good" landlords are in the majority. And even
the most fair and most just of the Whites are prone to accept
the dishonest landlord as part of the system. How a man treats
his tenants is not felt to be a matter of public concern, but is
as much his private affair as what brand of toothpaste he uses.

It can be roughly estimated that not more than twenty-five
or thirty percent of the sharecroppers get an honest settlement
at the end of their five months of labor. For the year 1932,
approximately seventeen or eighteen percent of the tenants
received some profit, averaging from $30 to $150. The remainder either broke even or were left in debt to the landlord.
Obviously there is no statistical method of checking on such an
estimate; it rests on the observation of the investigator and has
been checked by members of the community, white and colored, whose range of observation has been more extended.

If a tenant feels that he is being cheated, about the only
thing he can do is to move to another plantation. As the majority of them do feel so, there is an annual migration. During
December and January the roads are filled with wagons piled
high with household goods, the families perched on top. They

are hoping to find something better, but they seldom do. Two years on one plantation is considered a good average, although there are some landlords who through fair treatment are able to hold their tenants for a lifetime.

The advantage of mobility is not always available. If a sharecropper is in debt he cannot leave without the landlord's consent. Sometimes even if he has a clear receipt after the settlement is made, he is not allowed to go. The landlord may threaten to "clean him up" if he tries; that is, to take his corn, hogs, and anything else he has. If he agrees to stay, the landlord will leave him alone.

> One landlord, on hearing that a good tenant who had no debt was planning to move, came to the man's cabin and took all his belongings, the bits of old furniture, the painted vase on the mantel, the large picture of his father and mother. He also took the chickens and the corn. The tenant stood by and saw his house looted. At last, in order to retain his few possessions, he agreed to stay on the plantation.
>
> Another case of the debt threat involved a very exceptional tenant, who had earned $200 from outside work. In addition to this, after his cotton had been sold and his bill at the plantation store subtracted from his share of the cotton receipts, he had $65 to his credit. This he might have received, if just before the settlement time he had not mentioned his plan of moving to a neighboring plantation. When the landlord, who knew about his outside earnings, heard of the contemplated move, he came and told the tenant that he owed $200. The tenant protested that he owed nothing and that in reality the landlord owed him $65. But the landlord was adamant, and said that if the tenant moved he would take the $200 from him. The man stayed.

Public sentiment is committed to the prevailing system and a common ideology supports it. The belief is general among white people that the Negro is congenitally lazy and must be kept in debt in order to be made to work. That this belief may be a convenient rationalization does not prevent it from being a strong force in helping the landlord hold his labor. That the debt may be fictitious makes it no less binding on the Negro, who is without legal or social defense. Appeal to the local courts is worse than useless. Federal courts have ruled that peonage is a crime, but appeal to them is difficult and costly. Sometimes a tenant who has been told over a long period of time that he is in debt will become so desperate that he will steal away in the night. His only recourse is to avoid the worst plantations.

> On one occasion a "good landlord" sold his place to a man notorious for his unjust and brutal treatment of tenants. When the news of the sale was made known, every tenant moved off the plantation.

When he cannot get away, or if he does move and finds himself no better off, the tenant is left helpless. He feels that he has been cheated, but there is no avenue of protest. The resentments which pile up inside him seldom have any direct outlet. Now and then a sharecropper may cripple a mule or make an animal sick; or he may "tie up" farm implements, do damage to his house, harm his employer's property in any possible way. This sort of thing is the only feasible revenge, but it seldom occurs and never does anything except harm. The landlord now feels justified in treating his tenants worse than before. It is the usual vicious circle, with each side working against the other and also hurting itself. It is interesting to note that most of the plantations which became completely insolvent during the depression were among those known to the Negroes as the "bad places." As they put it, "the unfair bosses don't hold on good."

It also frequently happens that the more just and kindly landlords prosper. The others then say of these that they can afford to be more lenient because they are getting along better. The tenants incline to feel that they get along better because they are more lenient, that better conditions make for better work and longer tenancy.

> On a place that is good, but not one of the best, the manager estimates that the labor turnover is from ten to fifteen percent. This plantation covers 5000 acres, of which 3500 are under cultivation. The rest is woodland and pasture. Of the cultivated acres, about two-thirds are in cotton and the others in corn, hay, peas, beans, etc. There are 135 tenant families

and ninety percent of them are sharecroppers. A man and wife cultivate 17 acres; a family with three children have 25. Two-thirds of each plot is in cotton, one-fourth in corn, and the remainder in garden truck.

The tenants' houses are above the average, larger than the usual cabins, whitewashed, and on the whole in good condition. There is on the plantation a well-built school of four rooms, put up several years ago by the landlord. It is conducted by three teachers and has an enrollment of 154 children in six grades, with an average attendance of 118. The school year lasts four months, beginning after the picking season is over. The owner himself has a large and handsome house on the plantation. His manager and storekeeper both live on the place and are always there, while he spends a great deal of his time in town.

The tenants on this plantation receive their furnishings in the form of coupon books, which must be used at the plantation store. A family of two gets $10 in coupons each month, and a family of two adults and three children gets $16 a month for four or five months. The prices at the plantation store are admittedly higher than in the town stores. The sharecropper is supplied with animals, seed, and implements, and gives half of the cotton and half of the corn to the landlord. The renter gives one-third of his cotton and corn, and supplies his own stock and implements. He gets the same amount for groceries and in the same manner as the sharecropper. For both of them the amount spent in furnishings is deducted from their share of the crop. Day workers get fifty cents a day.

The landlord sells the sharecroppers' share of the cotton and corn as well as his own. At the end of the season he gives his tenants a piece of paper on which is written how much the cotton and corn were sold for, how much the tenant is in debt for furnishings, and what the balance is either way. The actual receipt for the sale of cotton is not presented. In 1932 six hundred bales of cotton were produced on this place. That was considered half a normal crop.

By far the majority of the tenants are sharecroppers. A small number, however, are cash tenants or renters. In 1930 twenty-three percent of the colored tenants in the county were renters. The renter furnishes himself. He owns his tools and implements, buys and selects his own seed, and as a rule his other supplies also. In 1932 and 1933 the rents ranged from five to six dollars an acre. Some renters do not pay in cash but give one-quarter of their cotton and one-third of their corn. A number of these are probably included in the table under "other tenants." All renters are entitled to sell their own produce.

In order to become a renter a tenant must necessarily be on a higher economic level than the sharecroppers. His position has obvious advantages. Once he has attained the status of cash tenant owning his tools and implements, selecting his own seed, free to buy where he will, and above all free to sell his own crop, he may look hopefully toward independence. Renting is frequently a stage between sharecropping and owning land. On the other hand, a renter risks more than a sharecropper, and if he has bad luck he may lose as a cash tenant anything he has gained under the other arrangement.

A woman in her fifties says that during thirty-six years of farming she and her husband have cleared money six times. One year they rented, and cleared $300. The other five they sharecropped, and the amounts they made were: $175, $75, $80, $75, $50.

A couple who have both rented and sharecropped think they did better sharecropping, but that this was just a matter of luck. [The years] 1917 and 1918, when they were "cropping," were good years. In 1917 they worked for a Negro landlord and cleared $1000 and in 1918, $860. In 1919 they bought a pair of mules for $75, a plow, and feed, and they rented 50 acres. This time they made a short crop, had heavy doctor bills, and lost out. Since then they have been renting on a small scale. Last year they rented five acres, three of which they planted in corn and two in peas, sorghum, and sweet potatoes—no cotton at all, since they couldn't make anything on it. They provided their own seed, implements, and animals, the landlord supplying only the land and an unfurnished cabin. They made 40 bushels of corn, one-third of which was given to the landlord as rent. The remainder they kept for hogs and for bread. The hogs they raise to sell and to use for their own winter meat. This year they rent a two-room cabin on a plantation close to town, and pay $2 a month rent. They work out the rent on the place, plowing, chopping, cleaning up ditches, at the rate of fifty cents a day. They have a cow and chickens and also a pig, and get about $50 a year selling milk and eggs.

Some landlords prefer renters as tenants, feeling that they are more responsible, since they have a larger stake in the enterprise. Others prefer the sharecroppers, who are more open to exploitation.

One landlord who definitely prefers renters is a farmer from Iowa, who runs his plantation much as he would a midwestern farm. To most of his southern neighbors this man and his ways are incomprehensible. He and his wife rarely go to town or mingle with others, but remain on the plantation, where they live in a very simple and unpretentious house. He is his own manager and every day, dressed in overalls, is busy supervising activities. The plantation store is run by a Negro and the landlord no longer has any control over it. Originally he lent the storekeeper $500, but this has been paid back and now the Negro owns and manages his own store.

The place has about 1500 acres and 80 tenant families, approximately 400 workers. Most of the tenants are renters, but about twelve are sharecroppers. Until recently the landlord rented only for cash, and in 1919 he received $25 an acre. Since the depression he has been unable to get cash rent and he now takes a quarter of the cotton and a third of the corn as rent. He supplies seed and $8 a month in cash for a couple, during the five-month season. The money is usually spent at the plantation store.

The renter furnishes his own mule and equipment. If he does not owe anything to the landlord he can sell his own share of the crop. If he is in debt for furnishings or anything else, the landlord sells the crop and gives him the market price minus the debt. The landlord keeps his accounts punctiliously, and any tenant can get an exact statement from him at any time.

Tenants are very carefully selected. When a man applies, he is asked for references among people already on the plantation, and these are questioned about his character. The landlord refuses anyone who has a reputation as a fighter, and he will not keep a husband who beats his wife. When he first took over the plantation he gave orders that nobody could carry a gun. All those he found on tenants he threw into the lake. He himself never carries a weapon, which is unique in this section.

Another unique feature is that during the slack season for cotton other activities are pursued. A river runs through the plantation, and fishing is done on a large scale—the catch varies from one to 400 pounds a day during the season. This is sold for five cents a pound, to tenants and outsiders. Seed corn is also marketed, and the plantation peach orchard is famed for its excellent fruit.

4

Southern Paternalism
toward Negroes
after Emancipation

GUION GRIFFIS JOHNSON

By the turn of the twentieth century racial adjustment in the South had become fixed in a biracial social and economic order. The paternalistic concepts of slavery had become neatly placed within the framework of emancipation.

In 1896 the United States Supreme Court had placed its blessing upon segregation in *Plessy v. Ferguson* and had established the separate-but-equal doctrine which was to endure for more than half a century. The opinion in this case declared

SOURCE: *Journal of Southern History,* XXIII (November 1957), 483–509 (footnotes omitted). Copyright 1957 by the Southern Historical Association. Reprinted by permission of the Managing Editor.

that segregation laws were valid exercises of the police powers of the state and that they did not imply racial inferiority. As to the plaintiff's argument "that the enforced separation of the two races stamps the colored race with a badge of inferiority," the court held: "If this be so, it is not by reason of anything found in the acts, but solely because the colored race chooses to put that construction upon it."

As stated by Bishop Charles Betts Galloway at the Conference for Education in the South held in Birmingham in 1904, the position of Southern whites was as follows:

> First.—In the South there will never be any social mingling of the races. Whether it be prejudice or pride of race, there is a middle wall of partition which will not be broken down.
>
> Second.—They will worship in separate churches and be educated in separate schools. This is desired alike by both races, and is for the good of each.
>
> Third.—The political power of this section will remain in present hands. Here, as elsewhere, intelligence and wealth will and should control the administration of governmental affairs.
>
> Fourth.—The great body of the negroes are here to stay. Their coerced colonization would be a crime, and their deportation a physical impossibility. And the white people are less anxious for them to go than the negroes are to leave. They are natives and not intruders.

This hard core of paternalistic thought had emerged by the time the Southern states had begun to feel safe from the threat of federal intervention. The correlative rights and duties of the strong and weak, reminiscent of ante-bellum arguments based on Filmer and Burke were now applied to the white and black races. The superior white race, with its roots deep in the experiences of law and government, had the obligation of teaching the inferior Negro race, with its history of "four thousand years of barbarism," the precious knowledge of citizenship. The weaker race had corresponding obligations: implicit obedience, deference, loyalty, and hard work. John Adams, John C. Calhoun, Thomas Carlyle, and all the pro-slavery advocates of the late ante-bellum period added to the thinking of the South as it outlined what was soon to become "race orthodoxy."

It was held that segregation actually protected the Negro's best interests. It was his duty, therefore, to conform to it and thereby best serve the general welfare. Discrimination was the very basis of good government because it was the only means by which equality among equals might be obtained and good government itself preserved. Government existed for the best people—the intelligent, educated and wealthy. In a society where all are equally free and share alike in political privileges, there are some more fit for the exercise of good government than others. The more fit constituted the men of the upper classes who had time for leisure and study. Wherever there was any large proportion of the uneducated, laboring class present, the possibilities of republicanism were hampered; but in a community, such as the South, where the menial labor was performed by a particular race, such as the Negro, devoted only to labor and excluded from political participation, the tendency was toward the elevation of the remainder of society. Conferring suffrage upon the freedmen was tantamount, therefore, to conferring social equality.

Since the slaves had been freed, it was the duty of the strong white race to prepare them, if possible, for ultimate political participation through education. The debates on how this education was to be financed and what kind of education was best suited to the Negro were to be some of the most bitter which followed the Civil War. The position which a Southern white man took on Negro education was often a mark either of race orthodoxy or heresy and certainly determined his category of thinking on paternalism. No American writer after 1865 who has tried seriously to analyze the race problem has failed to find some comfort in the hope of education. The extent of his hope has usually depended upon his concept of the theory of progress.

The theory of progress was itself undergoing a vast change at the very time that racial equalitarianism was being incorporated into the Federal Constitution. It soon came to be held that if particular races of men seemed less advanced than others, it was because they had not progressed as far on the scale of evolution. Thus, the progression theory was capable of proving the incapacity of the Negro for immediate citizenship. Auguste Comte's theory of progress in the philosophical school, Thomas Malthus' concepts in economic theory, and Charles Darwin's implications of inborn instincts furnished Southerners with convenient hypotheses with which to modify their old paternalism.

At least five categories of paternalistic value premises emerged after emancipation. These categories have been set up on a hypothetical scale ranging from concepts most favorable to the personal welfare of the individual Negro to those least benevolent. On a scale ranging from one to ten, one might be called extreme negrophilism and ten might be extreme negrophobia. The five paternalistic concepts would probably fall between points two and eight. They might be labeled for convenience in referring to the categories: (1) modified equalitarianism, (2) benevolent paternalism, (3) separate but equal, (4) separate and permanently unequal, (5) permanently unequal under paternal supervision. These categories of white attitudes from which were evolved procedures for dealing with the Negro had no inherent relationship to the long-range, ultimate good of the Negro. Stated briefly, these attitudes were based upon the following assumptions:

1. Modified equalitarianism: The Negro is a retarded race which only needs education and the sympathetic treatment of the white race to rise eventually to the level of the superior race.

2. Benevolent paternalism: The Negro is a retarded race which performs the menial work of the South and, therefore, deserves the most benevolent considerations of the superior white race.

3. Separate but equal: The Negro is an inferior race which can be greatly improved by education but must be separated from the superior white race for the best interests of both.

4. Separate and permanently unequal: The Negro is a permanently inferior race which can be somewhat improved by education. He must be forever segregated but permitted to rise in his own society within the limits of his capacities.

5. Permanently unequal under paternal supervision: The Negro is a permanently inferior race on which it is a waste of money to attempt education but Negroes can fill the need for

unskilled labor when supervised by whites and should be protected as long as they keep their place.

MODIFIED EQUALITARIANISM

The paternalistic thinkers most favorable to the general welfare of the individual Negro believed in the power of education to lift him out of his retardation. The chief difference between the strong and the weak was the matter of education and opportunity. Like Thomas Jefferson, the equalitarians thought that the only way for American republicanism to be preserved was through an enlightened citizenry. War had emancipated the slave, and the organic law both of the federal Constitution and of the states had now declared him to be a citizen entitled to the ballot and to education. This group of Southern thinkers would get on with the business of making an intelligent citizen of the freedman. A North Carolina legislative resolution of 1877 concluded:

> . . . we recognize the full purport and intent of that amendment to the constitution of the United States which confers the rights of suffrage and citizenship upon the people of color, and of that part of the constitution of North Carolina conferring equal educational privileges upon both races: . . . we are disposed and determined to carry out in good faith these as all other constitutional provisions.

At the time this resolution was adopted, forces were already at work which were to defeat an equalitarian program. There were, however, a few in the South who secretly agreed with Northern advocates when they referred to the Negro as a "lamp blacked white man," needing only educational and economic opportunities to prove his capacities to be equal to those of whites. This was a varied group which came from the old planter aristocracy, sons of planters educated in the leading Northern schools where they had come under the influence of exponents of the theory of progress, those motivated by Christian ethics who had thought slavery a moral wrong, and upward moving groups from the lower middle class who had not forgotten the doctrines of the American Revolution.

Lewis H. Blair, born of Virginia planter aristocracy, argued in 1889 like Edmund Ruffin of ante-bellum Virginia that the Negro was as good a worker as the white man when properly directed. Blair declared that the prosperity of the South was dependent upon the elevation of the Negro. One by one he answered all the objections of Southern whites to admitting the Negro to full and equal participation in the main stream of society. Basic to his thinking was the assumption that the Negro had all the potentialities of the white man. The Negro, he said, had been forced into a caste status from which he must be rescued if the South was ever to become prosperous and share in the wealth of the world. Blair wrote:

> Before we can make men of depraved and degraded human beings, be they negro, semite, or even Caucasian, and therefore efficient producers of wealth, there are three principal things to be done. They must be inspired with self-respect, their hope must be stimulated and their intelligence must be cultivated, and especially so with the negro, for his self-respect is feeble, his hope faint, and his intelligence slight; he must economically, morally, and socially be born again, and self-respect, hope and intelligence are the trinity that will work out his elevation, and they are also the rule of three to work out our own regeneration.

The Negro should be welcomed back to the polls and the churches and be educated in mixed schools. Blair had more to say on the subject of mixed schools:

> The necessity for the abandonment of separate schools is dual—physical and moral. The physical necessity is this: With our sparse population separate schools cannot supply a clientage numerous enough to secure good teachers, upon whom the efficiency of the public schools is absolutely dependent. . . .
>
> The moral necessity is this: Separate schools are a public proclamation to all African or mixed blood that they are an inferior caste, fundamentally inferior and totally unfit to mingle on terms of equality with the superior caste. . . . Hence it follows that separate schools brand the stigma of degradation upon one-half of the population, irrespective of character and culture, and crushes their hope and self-respect, without which they can never become useful and valuable

citizens . . . when we make our implement of elevation, namely our public schools, simply a branding iron for stamping the letter "D," degraded, upon the foreheads of millions of black fellow-citizens, we deliberately tear up by the roots all our other efforts for their amelioration.

Blair's was not a lone voice raised in behalf of an oppressed race. Bishop T. U. Dudley of the Protestant Episcopal Church was taking much the same position in Kentucky, basing his arguments upon the Golden Rule and the concept of the brotherhood of man and the fatherhood of God. Agrarian leaders, making their bid for power against the Bourbons, also held out hope to the Negro, but not for long. As they came to terms with their Bourbon opponents and worked out an agreement for disfranchisement of the Negro, some of them became the Negro's most vitriolic enemy.

The new Southern equalitarianism which has been growing within the last two decades of the twentieth century is made up for the most part of the educated young, born in the new century. Two, three, and four generations removed from slavery, they have been able to free themselves from the bitterness and emotionalism which uprooted the system and to look objectively upon the findings of science, for, as Blair had said in 1889, "the clearer one sees and the more enlightened he is, the freer he is from prejudice." This neoequalitarian group is rapidly leaving the ranks of the paternalists by denying the basic assumptions of Negro retardation and placing less and less stress on the responsibilities of the whites to the blacks and more and more responsibility on Negroes for themselves.

BENEVOLENT PATERNALISM

The benevolent paternalists sprang from the planter aristocracy of the slavery regime. Long before the close of the ante-bellum period they had come to an attitude of *noblesse oblige*. They argued that the Negro was a backward, perhaps even a child-like, race of men who had cheerfully adapted themselves to slavery. Slavery had Christianized them and lifted them out of barbarism. They had cleared the land and cultivated the fields of the South, and the white man owed the Negro an ever-lasting debt of gratitude.

The Negro, however, was still a backward race, and because of this condition needed the protection of whites. It was always the responsibility of the strong, so ran the benevolent paternalist's argument, to bear the burden of the weak. The strong race by virtue of its superior intelligence, culture, and wealth was the natural protector of the Negro. The white man must not only protect good Negroes from the trickery of bad ones, but the white race as a whole must protect the black race as a whole from the machinations of bad white men such as federal agents or Northern missionaries who preached social equality, or even from bad Southern white men who took advantage of the Negro's weakness.

Because slavery at its best in the South was a patriarchal system and the entire master's family looked upon their particular set of slaves as their black family, the benevolent paternalists tended to identify themselves with the Negroes after emancipation as they had before. Just as a father always knows what is best for his child, so did the white man know what was best for the Negro. With a clairvoyance given only to Southern white paternalists, the white man also knew what the Negro thought, what he wanted, and what he needed. This assumption came to be a basic attitude of the whites as a whole toward the Negroes as a whole.

It was obviously unnecessary for the Negro to vote, to participate in government, or to be consulted in advance about matters concerning his own welfare. From this position it was easy for even the most benevolent of paternalists to argue that the Negro had not been wronged by the segregation acts of the 1880s and 1890s, by the grandfather clauses, or by the "permanent taint" acts of the twentieth century.

The question of social distance did not trouble the benevolent paternalists. During slavery this social class of whites had frequent personal contact with Negroes, and they did not fear contamination by the emancipated Negro. As Lewis H. Blair of Richmond wrote in 1889:

> Most of us above thirty years of age had our mammy, and
> generally she was the first to receive us from the doctor's

hands and was the first to proclaim, with heart bursting with pride, the arrival of a fine baby. Up to the age of ten we saw as much, perhaps more, of the mammy than of the mother, and we loved her quite as well. . . .

And when we became youths and played with negro boys, went fishing and hunting with them, gathered berries and nuts together, climbed the same trees; . . . and when we became older, young men and maidens, and had colored body-servants and colored maids, who were constantly at our elbow, and who knew all our love affairs, &c., became we then demoralized? No; and why? For the simple reason that we were higher, and the higher are rarely, if ever, demoralized by the lower.

For this reason spokesmen for the old planter class could in all calmness take the position, at a time when a Tom Watson or a Ben Tillman was demanding complete segregation, that the Negro should worship in the same churches, ride in the same conveyances, and attend the same schools as whites. Bishop Dudley, for example, urged his church to retain its Negro members and actively seek to bring back those who had wandered away. Pride of race, he declared,

is but a pretext to excuse the conduct which, in our heart of hearts, we know to proceed from the old root of bitterness— the feeling of caste which demands that the liberated slave shall be forever a menial.

I charge the Christian white men of the South to mark that the effect of this separation, on which we have insisted, has helped to drive these people into a corresponding exclusiveness, and is constantly diminishing the influence of our Christian thinkers upon their belief and their practice.

The bitterness of the times to which Bishop Dudley referred, together with the impact of Victorian romanticism, tended to blunt the personal attachment of the white paternalist for the Negro. It came now to be said that the second generation of Negroes from slavery were not the equal of their parents and, therefore, were not as deserving of the consideration due the former slave. The writings of Thomas Nelson Page reflect the new attitude of the sons and grandsons of the planter aristocracy. The rising generation of Negroes, he wrote in 1904, "are not as good workers, or as good citizens, as the generation which preceded them, and use the education so given them, where they use it at all, in ways which are not beneficial to themselves and are injurious to the whites." Other writers of the romantic school usually attributed any "bad conduct" of the Negro during freedom to the errors taught by Northern missionaries or agents of the Freedmen's Bureau, excused him, and held out the hope to Southern whites that patience and time would ultimately bring back the good relations of "yester year." W. M. Cox of Mississippi, quoted at an education conference in 1904, illustrates the tolerant spirit of the rapidly diminishing group of benevolent paternalists:

> When I consider all the circumstances of the case, the negro's weakness, his utter lack of preparation for freedom and citizenship, and the multitudinous temptations to disorder and wrongdoing which have assailed him, the wonder to me is, not that he has done so ill, but that he has done so well. No other race in the world would have borne itself with so much patience, docility and submissiveness. It is true that many grave crimes have been committed by negroes, and these have sorely taxed the patience of the white people of the South. I do not blink at their enormity, and I know that they must be sternly repressed and terribly avenged. But I insist that the entire race is not chargeable with these exceptionable crimes, and that the overwhelming majority of the race are peaceable, inoffensive and submissive to whatever the superior race sees fit to put upon them. Their crimes are not the fruit of the little learning their schools afford them. They are the results of brutish instincts and propensities which they have not been taught to regulate and restrain.

Cox has stated here the conceptual framework of what may be called the "classical position" of upper-class Southerners. Novelists, autobiographers, and Southern historians have revealed these assumptions in their writings, either as stated or hidden value premises, until the rise of the school of objectivity and the impact of cynicism following World War I dictated a reevaluation of the situation.

A continuing process of reevaluation of benevolent paternalism had constantly been under way. A planter who lost heavily during the Civil War and had difficulty making a new start easily shed his attitude of *noblesse oblige* and applied instead hard, Malthusian principles to his black labor force. As agricultural depressions and money panics came and economic crisis followed economic crisis, only those of generations of social prestige and wealth were able to cling to their "refined sentimentalities." This group of paternalists, smallest in all periods of American history, has been most subject to loss of followers and has had most difficulty in finding new recruits. Today there is but a handful left, mostly the grandparents and great-grandparents of the children of 1957.

SEPARATE AND EQUAL

An offshoot from the benevolent paternalists claimed that the Negro was a retarded race which could be elevated considerably by the right kind of education. The kind of education needed was industrial. Thomas Nelson Page, whose early writings labeled him as a benevolent paternalist, came through the bitter agrarian-Bourbon political battles of the nineties less friendly to the Negro than before. In 1904 he concluded that the Negro race, "under certain conditions of intellectual environment, of careful training, and of sympathetic encouragement from the stronger races," might "individually attain a fair, and in uncommon instances a considerable degree, of mental development." Negroes needed a different kind of education than did whites. That was one reason it would be impossible to educate them in any but separate schools. ". . . The Negro must be taught the great elementary truths of morality and duty," Page wrote. The more than "$110,000,000 contributed out of the property of the Southern whites," which the South had spent on the education of the Negro up to 1904, was "a complete failure," he declared.

He was but repeating the controversy which had been waging against the classical schools set up by Northern philanthropy during the early days of Reconstruction. The George Peabody Fund, the John F. Slater Fund, the Jeanes Fund, and later the Julius Rosenwald Fund were all attacked not only on the grounds of Northern interference with the Negro but also because it was said that the agents of these funds were giving the Negro the kind of education that "made him unfit for work." The fallacious teachings of equality fostered by these agents and the Northern white faculties of the private Negro colleges in the South had "deluded" the Negro into exchanging his skill as a craftsman, learned during slavery, for "book learning" which was of no possible use to him.

In this time of tension a Virginia-born and educated Negro, Booker T. Washington, came forward as the advocate of industrial education for Negroes. As described by a United States Bureau of Education survey of Negro education in 1916, Washington "had so happy a gift of conciliation as to win the friendship and admiration of the southern white people whenever the opportunity could be found, and to gain from them a moral support that was worth more than money to his work." Booker T. Washington himself described the situation thus:

> For nearly twenty years after the war, except in a few instances, the value of the industrial training given by the plantations was overlooked. Negro men and women were educated in literature, in mathematics and in the sciences, with little thought of what had been taking place during the preceding 250 years, except, perhaps, as something to be escaped, to be got as far away from as possible. As a generation began to pass, those who had been trained as mechanics in slavery began to disappear by death. . . . Many were trained in Latin, but few as engineers and blacksmiths. . . . For this reason they had no interest in farming and did not return to it. And yet 85 percent of the Negro population of the Southern states lives and for a considerable time will continue to live in the country districts.

Booker T. Washington became the Negro spokesman for racial peace, a man whom the white paternalists trusted and with whom they were willing to deal; a man also whom the "New Negroes," those educated and themselves several generations from slavery, began to regard as one who had led his race into a new kind of economic and intellectual bondage.

When Washington urged the Negro to "put down his bucket where he was" and become a good manual laborer, he spoke

the language of the mass of Southern white men, for the majority of white men had always thought the black race was destined by the will of God to be "hewers of wood and drawers
of water." This ante-bellum assumption had been reinforced
by the implications of the theory of racial instincts which appeared in Charles Darwin's concept of evolution. "Race pride,"
"race instincts," "instinctive brutish behavior" were scientific
terms easily available to justify subjugation of black citizens.
This concept became the new cornerstone of degradation. It
was the irrefutable justification of segregation. Charles Francis
Adams, addressing a Richmond, Virginia, audience in 1908,
pointed out the vast change in American thinking on the Negro
since 1865. The change had come about because of "a different
conception of the facts" which had been produced by Darwin's
profound works. The Negro was no longer "God's image carved
in ebony, only partially developed under unfavorable fortuitous circumstances," but a race lower on the scale of evolution,
"of widely different interests, attainments and ideals."

This assumption took for granted the physical and cultural
inferiority of the Negro. The Biblical concept of brotherhood
and equality now became, in the light of evolution, the concept
of brotherhood and inequality. "It points to heights of human
attainment where further development is possible only along
spiritual lines, by the exercise of altruism and brotherhood,
and so says, 'be patient and helpful,'" wrote a Northern theo-
logian. Bishop Atticus Haygood of the Southern Methodist
Church, who in the early years of Reconstruction had wanted
the Southern white man to keep a friendly, neighborly contact
with the freedmen, came now to justify segregation as something demanded by race instincts, which if frustrated might
result in violence:

> This [race] instinct will never be satisfied till it realizes itself
> in complete separation. Whether we of the white race approve
> matters little. . . . We may, all of us, as well adjust our plans
> to the determined and inevitable movements of this instinct
> —that does not reason, but that moves steadily and resistlessly
> to accomplish its ends. It is a very grave question to be con-
> sidered by all who have responsibility in this matter: Whether
> over-repression of race-instincts may not mar their normal

evolution—may not introduce elements unfriendly to helpful growth—may not result in explosions? I have seen a heavy stone wall overturned by a root that was once a tiny white fiber. Instinct is like the life-force that expresses itself in life or death.

Here was a convenient theory, based, it was believed, solidly upon objective science which relieved both the North and the South of the burden of applying Christian ethics to the lower caste. It was possible to interpret the Golden Rule in terms of segregation and to say that the Negro race was entirely responsible for separation. To abolish segregation would, therefore, be flouting both "natural law" and God's will.

Edwin A. Alderman, at that time president of Tulane University, explained to the American Economic Association in an address in 1903 the position of those in the South who were willing to give the Negro an opportunity to rise within the framework of separate but equal accommodations. He said:

> . . . the best Southern people not only do not hate the negro, but come nearer to having affection for him than any other people. They are too wise not to realize that posterity will judge them according to the wisdom they use in this great concern. They are too just not to know that there is but one thing to do with a human being, and that thing is to give him a chance, and that it is a solemn duty of the white man to see that the negro gets his chance in everything save "social equality" and political control.
>
> . . . This does not mean that the lower should be prevented from rising, but that it should not be permitted to break down the higher.
>
> . . . Social equality or political control would mean deterioration of the advanced group, and the South is serving the Nation when it says it shall not be so.

SEPARATE AND PERMANENTLY UNEQUAL

The segregationists of the paternalistic school were divided in their thinking as to just how far behind the Negro race was and how long, if ever, it would take it to catch up with the white race. Debates raged, North and South, in the Americas and in Europe, on whether it was possible for a retarded race to skip some of the steps toward advancement. Or, it was asked, must a backward race repeat the historical experience of the superior race in order to progress to a higher level and thus be forever behind? The Southern position on white supremacy seemed to imply permanent inferiority, but whenever the question was presented to Negro audiences, the colored man was usually given to understand that his race might eventually by hard work and self-denial win civil and economic equality—but never social equality.

The two categories of Southern paternalistic thinking most unfavorable to the Negro assumed the permanent inferiority of the race. Those who thought in this fashion constituted, perhaps, the majority of Southern whites. They were composed of the lower middle and the upper lower white classes. They were the ones who had fewest contacts with Negroes on any basis except economic competition. New planters in the deep South, a few from the old planter class, the new rich, foremen both in agriculture and industry, carpenters and bricklayers, others from the semiskilled trades made up the large group of white Southerners who thought the Negro permanently inferior.

Edgar Gardner Murphy, an Episcopal clergyman of Montgomery, Alabama, expressing the views of this group, wrote that the Negro was "a backward and essentially unassimilable people" whom the "consciousness of kind," a phrase which he had borrowed from the Columbia University sociologist Franklin H. Giddings, would forever set apart from the whites. Yet it was possible for the Negro "to enter a larger heritage than is open to any like number of his race in any quarter of the world," because of his contact with Southern whites. Murphy said further:

> . . . the negro question is not primarily a question of the negro among negroes, but a question of the negro surrounded by another and a stronger people. The negro is in a white environment; the white man is largely the market for his labor and the opportunity for his progress, as well as the social and political model of his imitative spirit. Where we find the negro in relation to the trained and educated representatives of the stronger race we find few of the evidences of racial friction.

But the Negro had no sense of race pride or integrity, and when thrown in contact with whites readily mixed with them. To those in the North who would point out that the "natural antipathy toward the Negro" should prevent such crossing of the color line, Murphy would reply with shame: ". . . the racial integrity of the Caucasian is threatened, most seriously and not by the negro but by the degraded white man." For this reason segregation must be maintained by stringent laws to lessen in every way the possible contacts of degraded whites with the backward race. The Negro must forever be kept in his place for his own protection, and in this way the debauched white man must be restrained. Murphy explained further:

> Thus understood, I think the educated opinion of the South has no war with the progress of the negro. It has feared the consequences of that progress only when they have seemed to encroach upon the life of the stronger race. It is willing that the negro, within his own social world, shall become as great, as true, as really free, as nobly gifted as he has capacity to be. It has fixed its barriers—in no enmity of temper but in the interest of itself and its civilization; and not without regard to the ultimate welfare of the negro.

The majority of Southern whites were convinced that the progress of the Negro within the confines of his own race would be limited, because the colored man was an African, "the least endowed of all the races of mankind." Despite more than 250 years of slavery, during which the white man had patiently tried to teach the Negro the ways of civilization, he was still basically an African, and, since the restraints of slavery had been removed, he was becoming "more and more like the African original."

PERMANENTLY UNEQUAL
UNDER PATERNAL SUPERVISION

It was but a step from such an argument as this to the conclusion that only under a system of paternal compulsion could the Negro be tolerated in Southern society. The propensity of the Negro to "take a social ell when extended a political inch" was sufficient indication that he must be kept strictly within his own race. Every instance of his "getting out of place" must be terribly avenged, but all "good Negroes" who knew their place and kept it should be protected.

Thomas Carlyle's *The Nigger Question*, written after emancipation in the West Indies, had widely popularized the concept of retrogression and furnished those who would exploit Negro labor with a convenient justification. The anonymous author of "The Negro and the Negrophilists," published in the *Blackwood's Edinburgh Magazine* of May 1866, stated the argument for retrogression. With Negroes, it was held, "liberty and the grave speedily become one and the same blessing." Economic laws, "typhus and smallpox, aggravated by filth and famine, make short work of the black man, and relieve overburdened charity of a task, which charity may have the will, but has not the means or the power, to perform."

The census of 1870 left still open the question of the high death rate of the Negro when in freedom, for, having been taken in a time of general unrest, it was conceded that the returns were inaccurate and inconclusive. When, however, the census of 1880 showed a large increase of Negroes, in some areas a doubling of the population in a decade, the news aroused consternation and produced a quick revision of concepts. While many abandoned the theory of the extermination of the Negroes through natural causes, they did not give up the theory of retrogression. The fact of a rapidly increasing Negro population made the predictions of the theory seem even more alarming, for an essential premise was the deterioration of the Negro when removed from the direct supervision of the dominant race.

Philip Alexander Bruce, with ancestry in the old planter aristocracy of Virginia, was one of the first Southerners to make a serious study of the problem from this point of view. His conclusion was that ultimately, and at no distant date, the Negro would "revert to the African original." Such a condition was complicated by the high fertility rate of Negroes. "The probability is that," he wrote, "in a few generations, formal and legal marriages will be much less frequent than they now are, and the promiscuous intercourse between the sexes will grow more open and unreserved." The "unlimited increase" of blacks "virtually means that a period will come when there will be a sharp contest between blacks and whites for the possession of a large part of the Southern States." The whites might kill off the blacks or they might migrate in disgust and leave the blacks in barbaric enjoyment of the South. The only real solution, he thought, was in immediate and complete deportation. But since the Negro was useful to the Southern states as an agricultural laborer, a stopgap remedy might be found. Education fostered either by the public school system, with emphasis on industrial education, or by the white evangelical denominations, sponsored by Northern philanthropy, might elevate the blacks, but he predicted that "in the course of the next ten decades American institutions would be subjected to a severer strain than they have yet endured."

In accordance with Malthusian concepts, Bruce believed that a barbaric race might be elevated to a higher cultural level only when supervised by a civilized race under a paternal system of compulsion. Whenever he found whites to be in a considerable majority, he discovered retrogression to be going on at a slower rate. He assumed, however, that the Negro's personality traits would forever prevent the black man's becoming an acceptable part of American society. He enumerated these traits as being "intellectual blindness, moral obtuseness, and a thoughtless indulgence of every appetite." For these reasons, the compulsion by which the white man must direct the black should be stern, constant, and kindly, but never indulgent.

Alfred Holt Stone, planter in the Yazoo-Mississippi Delta, whose magazine articles on the status of the Southern Negro were written in the early years of the twentieth century, based his philosophy on the theories of the permanency of type and the need for compulsion. He declared that the status of the Negro had been fixed several thousand years ago.

> ... The Negro is one of the oldest races of which we have any knowledge, and ... its very failure to develop itself in its own habitat, while the Caucasian, Mongolian, and others have gone forward, is in itself proof of inferiority ... if we blot out the achievement of the American Negro who has passed

through slavery, what has the race left to boast of? And if but we go one step farther, and from the achievement of the "American Negro" obliterate all that the American mulatto has accomplished, what ground indeed would be left to those whose sentiment and sympathy have apparently rendered them so forgetful of scientific truth?

From this pseudoscientific approach, Stone justified the prevailing opinion that the South would tolerate the Negro so long as his services were cheap and he was willing to keep his place.

Stone belonged to the school of paternalists who were most hostile to the Negro—the Simon Legrees of freedom—but who were usually kind to their own house servants and labor foremen. A Eugene Talmadge of Georgia would exploit the issues of "black domination" and the "bestiality" of the Negro to arouse the fears of the lower class whites so that he might manipulate them to his political advantage, but he would also help send his cook's son to college. Convinced of the permanent inferiority of the Negro as a race, these most dangerously aggressive of Southern paternalists, few in number but politically powerful, would use the fear of ignorant whites as a weapon of control over the lower classes of both races.

THE EROSION OF PATERNALISM

After 1914 Southern paternalism began to erode rapidly. The effect of two world wars, with their accompanying philosophies of the mission of the United States in behalf of democracy and individual freedom, had an impact upon the plight of the Negro. Although any time of crisis has been an occasion for the uneasy dominant group to maltreat the Negro, the long-range effect of both wars has been to improve the Negro's status.

The first world war started the movement of the rural Negro out of the South to the city, and the second war greatly accelerated the pace, until today not a single state among the seventeen segregation states now has a Negro population of more than 50 percent, although there are still counties in the so-called black belt with a majority of Negroes. It had been argued during the debates over the extension of slavery that it would lessen the tensions of the whites to spread the Negro population more evenly. After the Civil War, Carl Schurz had wanted the freedmen drained off into New England and the Middle West because he thought the degradation of the Negro was partly dependent upon the ratio of blacks to whites. The greater ease with which the border states with their smaller population of Negroes have begun desegregation in the public schools would indicate that the spread theory has some merit.

The prosperity of the war years has also had its effect on paternalistic attitudes. As the Negro has come within the benefits of minimum wage laws and has grown more prosperous, his white employers have rapidly lost their attitudes of economic paternalism. The Negro's eagerness to get an education and the large numbers now attending college are producing a greater mass sophistication which, while angering Southern whites who feel most threatened economically by Negroes, nevertheless increases the respect of whites for the capacity of the Negro.

The question of the Negro's capacity has itself been under scrutiny, and new answers have come forth. In 1906 William Graham Sumner, an economist and sociologist of Yale University, published his *Folkways*, which was to have a profound effect upon social thought. Using the classical economic theory of John Stuart Mill, he developed the concept of the mores. "It is not possible," he wrote, "to change them by any artifice or device, to a great extent or suddenly, in any essential element: it is possible only to modify them by slow and long-continued effort if the ritual is changed by minute variations." It was not possible, he contended, for long-established mores to be uprooted by social revolution or legislation. It was, therefore, not blind, racial instincts which caused prejudice against the Negro, but the mores. He said: "In our Southern states, before the Civil War, whites and blacks had formed habits of action and feelings towards each other." Since emancipation these traditional and customary ways had reasserted themselves. Change would come at snail's pace, but come it would.

About the same time a fellow sociologist at Columbia University, Franklin H. Giddings, was also developing a new concept, the consciousness of kind, useful in explaining Southern behavior toward the Negro, but far less effective than the concept of racial instincts in proving the permanent inferiority of the Negro. A decade later, Georgia-born and Northern-educated William F. Ogburn presented the concept of cultural lag which might be used to explain the retardation of the Negro.

Professor Ogburn's fellow sociologist at the University of Chicago, Robert E. Park, who had spent nine years at Tuskegee Institute, was also developing theories on race relations which were to have a profound effect on American thought. "Race consciousness, like the racial reserves, antipathies, and tabus," he wrote, ". . . is invariably, as far as observation goes, an acquired trait, quite as much as the taste for olives or the mania for collecting stamps." Race prejudice, therefore, was a phenomenon of status. The white man in America had assigned a low status to the Negro because of his degradation in slavery. Every change in status involves a change in social organization. Disrupture of social organization made the white man afraid and uneasy. Conflict was the natural result, and conflict would continue until some sort of accommodation of the contending forces had been achieved. "The Negro is rising in America," Professor Park said, "and the measure of the antagonism he encounters is, in some very real sense, the measure of his progress."

Anthropologists and psychologists contributed their share to the destruction of the assumption of permanent inferiority. Franz Boas, Columbia University anthropologist, published in 1911 an epoch-making volume, *The Mind of Primitive Man*, which pointed up the ability of man to develop a system of human behavior suitable to the environment in which he found himself. This assumption dealt a body blow to the classical theory of superior and inferior races. From this time on, scholars have held that the only significant test to be applied to groups is how well their behavior patterns and value systems serve them in their environment and how flexible they are in meeting change.

The term "race" came now to be examined more minutely and to be discarded by some as a useless concept. It was pointed out that there is no such thing as a pure race, and that all the so-called races of mankind are the results of intermixtures. Melville J. Herskovits, anthropologist of Northwestern University, came forward with new studies on African culture, pointing out that, when America understands and appreciates the values of African culture, Negroes will be properly recognized as a group of people with a long and honorable past flowing far back into the stream of history. Otto Klineberg, Columbia University psychologist, was also saying that it is impossible to attribute certain mental traits to large groups of people or to claim permanent retardation for some and permanent superiority for others on the basis of skin color or other physical features.

In 1950 eight world-famous social scientists signed a declaration which has become the currently accepted thesis of scholars in this decade: "The prospect of a continuing inferior status is essentially unacceptable to any group of people. For this and other reasons, neither colonial exploitation nor oppression of minorities within a nation is in the long run compatible with world peace. As social scientists we know of no evidence that any ethnic group is inherently inferior."

Psychiatrists now describe the "peculiar traits of the Negro" not as the behavior of an inferior type of people but as "marks of oppression." Dr. Abram Kardiner and Dr. Lionel Ovesey, in presenting their psychosocial study of the American Negro in 1951, described the work as having been "conceived and written on the premise that group characteristics are adaptive in nature and therefore not inborn, but acquired. . . . Hence, the book does not describe Negro racial characteristics; it describes the personality he acquired while being obliged to adapt to extremely difficult social conditions."

A year earlier, the concluding point of the UNESCO "Statement on Race," made on July 18, 1950, had declared:

21. Lastly, biological studies lend support to the ethic of universal brotherhood; for man is born with drives toward cooperation, and unless those drives are satisfied man and nations alike fall ill. Man is born a social being who can reach his fullest development only through interaction with his fellows. The denial at any point of this social bond between man and man brings with it disintegration. In this sense, every man is his brother's keeper. For every man is a piece of the continent, a part of the main, because he is involved in mankind.

Within this frame of reference, the United States Supreme Court delivered its decision of May 17, 1954:

> Segregation of white and colored children in public schools has a detrimental effect upon the colored children. The impact is greater when it has the sanction of the law; for the policy of separating the races is usually interpreted as denoting the inferiority of the Negro group. A sense of inferiority affects the motivation of a child to learn. Segregation with the sanction of law, therefore, has a tendency to retard the educational and mental development of Negro children and to deprive them of some of the benefits they would receive in a racially integrated school system.
>
> Whatever may have been the extent of psychological knowledge at the time of Plessy v. Ferguson, this finding is amply supported by modern authority. Any language in Plessy v. Ferguson contrary to this finding is rejected.

The legal walls supporting segregation had been crumbling gradually since about 1935. In that year the University of Maryland Law School had been opened to Negroes by a federal district court decision (*Pearson v. Murray*) based upon the doctrine of separate-but-equal. The argument had been that the equal protection clause of the Fourteenth Amendment had been violated because Maryland had a law school for whites but none for Negroes. In case after case coming before the court within the next thirteen years Jim Crow laws and racism were steadily undermined.

In 1943, for example, in the case of *Hirabayashi v. United States*, the court used strong language against race as a criterion of civil liberties, saying: "Distinctions between citizens solely because of their ancestry are by their very nature odious to a free people whose institutions are founded upon the doctrine of equality." It was no surprise to students who had been following the unfolding of the new concepts of individual liberties that the Sweatt Case against the University of Texas in 1946 and the McLaurin Case against the University of Oklahoma in 1948 carried the interpretation of the Fourteenth Amendment to a point from which segregation in elementary schools could be attacked. This attack came in the decision of the School Segregation Cases in 1954. In rapid succession there followed other decisions denying the right of a state, within certain limits, to segregate on the basis of race in public recreation areas and public transportation facilities.

The majority of Southern white men, however, have been unaware of the Supreme Court's gradual departure from the old doctrines of *Plessy v. Ferguson.* The decision in the School Segregation Cases threw the South into a virtual state of shock, and each succeeding reversal of the old doctrine has deepened the emotional reaction. The ante-bellum arguments in behalf of slavery and the adaptation after emancipation of these arguments in defense of a biracial social structure have been dusted off and proclaimed from the governor's chair, the pulpit, the press, and the college lecture room. It has been said that if the South had been apprised over the years that this change was in process and had been told that the change must soon be faced in its totality, Southern whites would have been prepared for the school desegregation decision and could have accepted the situation with greater emotional maturity. Others have pointed out that the expanding concept of the free individual has never been accepted in the South and only partly in other regions of the United States, and that no educational process for change could have softened the South's reaction.

Whatever the basic considerations, all media of communication in the South point to a recrudescence of paternalistic attitudes toward the Negro, albeit a somewhat angry and bitter recrudescence. Southern whites, especially those in the deep South and those with membership in the some eighty-four organizations which have been formed to preserve the public schools from desegregation, are confident that they know what the Negro thinks, what he wants, what he needs, and what is best for him. The argument against mixing in the schools stresses again the concept of superior and inferior races and the obligation of the superior to give the inferior equal but separate facilities so that the Negro may have the opportunity to rise within his own social system. In this way, God's plan will be carried out, for He separated the races and it is a violation of His will for blacks and whites to be mixed in educational facilities.

Instead of the Freedmen's Bureau and Northern missionaries, the scapegoats are now the National Association for the Advancement of Colored People and the Communists. In February 1956, for example, the Alabama Senate passed a resolution unanimously calling for investigation of Communist activity in connection with the NAACP, and United States Senator James O. Eastland of Mississippi declared: "The court has responded to a radical pro-Communist political movement in this country."

About this time, Dr. W. C. George, professor of histology in the Medical School of the University of North Carolina and president of the prosegregation North Carolina Patriots, Inc., declared in a public meeting in Raleigh that, while he has great affection for his Negro friends, he feels constrained to point out that: (1) the Negro is a permanently inferior race, (2) desegregation in the public schools will lead to amalgamation, (3) amalgamation will cause the deterioration of the white race, and (4) the deterioration of the white race will destroy American civilization. About a week later, an open letter in the Greensboro (N.C.) *Daily News* repeated the refrain which may be found almost any day in the Southern press: "I shall fight for liberal treatment, broader opportunities and better education of the Negro; but I shall oppose with all my might all attempts to establish conditions conducive to the elimination of the white and Negro races—in short, integration of our public schools."

Almost a year earlier, the president-elect of the United States Chamber of Commerce, Boyd Campbell of Jackson, Mississippi, addressing the Southern Association of Chamber of Commerce Executives, called for an enlightened leadership in the South to deal with the problems of racial desegregation in the schools. "Once Southern leaders admit that the Supreme Court's ruling won't be reversed, we can get along with our work," Campbell said. He predicted that desegregation will come slowly because, he thought, "educational integration must be followed closely by social and cultural integration."

In 1956 Paul Green, North Carolina's Pulitzer Prize-winning playwright, rephrased this thought at a conference on world affairs in Chapel Hill. The Southerner's role in world affairs, he said, was to complete the task started almost a hundred years ago of incorporating the colored citizen into the body politic. Economic forces which were at work industrializing the South were surely spelling an end to the old paternalism toward the Negro. The moral and spiritual strength of the Southern people must now be applied to usher in the new day in the New South.

Weeks later, a religious body of great prestige, the Protestant Episcopal Church, announced guiding principles to help rid it of racial barriers throughout the country: "Any attitude or act in the House of God which sets brethren of different races apart from one another is sinful."

In the political and legal struggles of the post-Civil War South, leaders constantly pointed out that the Reconstruction Amendments were sleeping thunder which might be hurled against the "domestic tranquillity" of the South at any moment by a Congress or a Supreme Court favorable to the Negro. It was held then that the Fourteenth and Fifteenth Amendments negated the major assumption of Negro inferiority and that the preservation of this assumption was basic to the preservation of a segregated social order. As the years wore on after 1865, the paternalistic rationale of biracialism began to crumble.

In the third decade of the twentieth century a philanthropic foundation, created out of the wealth accumulated in America by a penniless Scottish immigrant, Andrew Carnegie, concluded that it was time to make an appraisal of the Negro in America. A Swedish economist, Gunnar Myrdal, was brought to this country for that purpose, and the substance of his findings and those of the large staff of American scholars, both white and Negro, whom he gathered about him was that America is faced with a dilemma. Within the framework of an equalitarian constitution, America by law and custom denies equality to more than 15,000,000 citizens because of race.

Processes had already long been under way to solve this dilemma. The year the Myrdal study was published, 1944, the Supreme Court delivered a death blow to the white-primary system. The concept of inferiority, nevertheless, still prevails in the minds of both white and colored citizens. The second emancipation, as most Negro writers like to call the Supreme Court decision in the School Segregation Cases, may now begin to nibble away at the value premises of this assumption just as the forces at work in society after 1865 finally undermined the paternalistic rationale of segregation.

FOR FURTHER READING

Books marked with an asterisk are available in paperback. Dates are those of the paperback editions.

The most comprehensive text on black history is *John Hope Franklin, *From Slavery to Freedom* (New York, 1969). Shorter and more interpretive but excellent is *August Meier and Elliott Rudwick, *From Plantation to Ghetto* (New York, 1968); and a popular survey is *Lerone Bennett, Jr., *Before the Mayflower* (Baltimore, 1966). An introduction to the study of black history is *Erwin Salk, *A Layman's Guide to Negro History* (Chicago, 1966). A collection of essays covering the entire sweep of black Americans' history is *Melvin Drimmer, *Black History* (New York, 1969). A classic study is E. Franklin Frazier, *The Negro in the United States* (New York, 1957).

Racism is treated in *Thomas Gossett, *Race: The History of an Idea* (New York, 1965). Rayford Logan also discusses this subject in *The Betrayal of the Negro* (New York, 1965). Southern white attitudes can be found in *Claude H. Nolen, *The Negro's Image in the South* (Lexington, Ky., 1968). I. A. Newby, *In Jim Crow's Defense* (Baton Rouge, 1965) is useful, as is the article by Guion Johnson, "The Ideology of White Supremacy, 1876–1910," in Fletcher Green (ed.), *Essays in Southern History* (Chapel Hill, 1949). Segregation and racism in the Protestant churches are discussed in David M. Reimers, *White Protestantism and the Negro* (New York, 1965).

The best study of the disfranchisement movement is *Paul Lewinson, *Race, Class and Party* (New York, 1965). Among the best state studies of southern blacks are: *Vernon Wharton, *The Negro in Mississippi 1865–1890* (New York, 1965); *George Tindall, *South Carolina Negroes, 1877–1901* (Baton Rouge, 1966); and Charles Wynes, *Race Relations in Virginia, 1870–1902* (Charlottesville, 1961). A brilliant study of the public education movement and racism is *Louis Harlan, *Separate and Unequal* (New York, 1968). *Ray Stannard Baker, *Following the Color Line* (New York, 1964) contains information on both the North and South written by a man who lived in the early twentieth century. Some interesting essays are found in *Charles Wynes (ed.), *The Negro in the South since 1865* (New York, 1968); and C. Vann Woodward, *The Origins of the New South, 1877–1913* (Baton Rouge, 1951) is essential for an understanding of the South.

Although written about life in the 1920s and 1930s, extremely valuable for an understanding of sharecropping and black life in the early twentieth century are: *Arthur Raper, *Preface to Peasantry* (New York, 1968); *Charles Johnson, *Growing Up in the Black Belt* (New York, 1967) and *In the Shadow of the Plantation* (Chicago, 1934); *John Dollard, *Caste and Class in a Southern Town* (New York, 1949); and *Allison Davis and John Dollard, *Children of Bondage* (New York, 1964).

Some developments in the North can be discovered in *Gilbert Osofsky, *Harlem: The Making of a Ghetto* (New York, 1966); *Allan Spear, *Black Chicago* (Chicago, 1969); *Sterling D. Spero and Abram L. Harris, *The Black Worker* (New York, 1968); and *W. E. B. Du Bois, *The Philadelphia Negro* (New York, 1967).

THE
BLACK RESPONSE

If Frederick Douglass was the dominant black leader of the middle part of the nineteenth century, Booker T. Washington was the most powerful at the turn of the century. Washington's philosophy of accommodation and compromise, with its emphasis upon industrial education and economic development, found a ready white audience. Washington seemed to many whites to accept the segregation of blacks and their elimination from politics and to offer a different approach to the nagging issue of racial conflict from that proposed during Radical Reconstruction.

The origin and nature of Washington's philosophy are discussed in August Meier's essay. The author also points out that Washington was sometimes vague and was himself a paradox. Washington, for example, while urging blacks to forget politics and concentrate on economic development, was advising Presidents on political appointments. The man who accepted social segregation in the South dined with the President of the United States.

A number of black leaders found Washington's policies unacceptable and regarded the founder of Tuskegee Institute as a hindrance to the advancement of the black community. Some of these leaders followed the line of Douglass and urged political activism through the Republican party. Others worked through various organizations such as the Afro-American League and tried to exert pressure on both political parties and Congress. They supported measures to enforce the Fourteenth and Fifteenth Amendments in the South. Among the Radical opponents of Washington were militants such as Monroe Trotter, fiery editor of the *Boston Guardian*, but the most important voice of opposition was that of W. E. B. Du Bois, the brilliant scholar, polemicist, and editor of *The Crisis*. Du Bois, who was born in the North and educated at Fisk, Harvard, and Berlin, eventually became so critical of Washington that a break between the two leaders was unavoidable.

Du Bois was dissatisfied with Washington's approach to education for blacks. Du Bois believed that industrial education, with its emphasis on thrift, work, property ownership, and skill, was necessary, but he also wanted higher education for the Negro elite, the "talented tenth." He was fearful that an excessive emphasis on industrial education would mean a permanent second-class status for black Americans and leave them unprepared and uneducated for the tasks of the twentieth century. Du Bois also objected to Washington's tendency to accept the disfranchisement of blacks and the loss of political power. Finally he attacked Washington for his apparent acceptance of Jim Crow, the loss of basic civil rights. Du Bois acknowledged that Washington had protested against lynching, disfranchisement, and Jim Crow, but he insisted that the impression left by the Tuskegee educator was that the South was justified in its attitude toward its black citizens by their degradation. At bottom the outspoken Du Bois condemned Washington because "his doctrine has tended to make the whites, North and South, shift the burden of the Negro problem to the Negro's shoulders and stand aside as critical and rather pessimistic spectators; when in fact the burden belongs to the nation, and the hands of none of us are clean if we bend not our energies to righting these great wrongs. The South ought to be led, by candid and honest criticism, to assert her better self and do her full duty to the race she has cruelly wronged and is still wronging. The North—her co-partner in guilt—cannot salve her conscience by plastering it with gold."

Du Bois and his black followers founded the Niagara Movement, but it had little success. However, following the horrifying 1908 race riot in Springfield, Illinois, a group of white liberals joined with the remnants of the Movement to found the National Association for the Advancement of Colored People.

Although the NAACP was largely white-financed and white-run in its early years, its dominant figure was Du Bois, who edited its journal, *The Crisis*. The program of the NAACP reflected Du Bois's views and those of the Niagara Movement. It called for an end to disfranchisement, repeal of Jim Crow laws and all discriminatory laws, an end to lynching, and full civil rights for blacks. In short, the NAACP insisted upon first-class citizenship for black Americans.

Realization of the NAACP's program was extraordinarily difficult in the face of white racism, especially in the early years of the twentieth century. The Association concentrated on countering racist propaganda; it attempted, for example, to halt the showing of the film *Birth of a Nation*. It sponsored conferences and publications challenging racist arguments and promoted the achievements and contributions of black Americans. It tried to get the federal government to take action to halt lynching and to modify some federal policies of segregation and discrimination. Above all, the Association assaulted racism in the courts and began its long legal campaign to uphold the Fourteenth and Fifteenth Amendments.

Other black leaders formed groups to deal with social problems during the Progressive era, but the most important one
besides the NAACP was the National Urban League. Like the
NAACP, the Urban League was interracial, but unlike the
Association the League did not actively involve itself politically and in court fights. The Urban League concentrated its
efforts on improving the conditions of rural migrants who had
moved to the cities by finding them better housing and jobs
and by helping them obtain an education. Basically the League
represented a social work approach to the problems of black
urbanites and was conservative in its political outlook and
program.

To some black Americans, neither the Washington philosophy of accommodation with its long-range hope of equality,
nor the Urban League, nor the NAACP, nor political parties
offered hope. To these leaders only some form of separatism
was the answer, because they believed that blacks would never
find justice in a white-controlled society. Separatism, a form
of black nationalism, was not new to the black community.
Before the War of 1812 Paul Cuffe, a black merchant from
Massachusetts, had urged blacks to return to Africa; at his own
expense Cuffe took a group back to the west coast of Africa.
In the 1850s Martin Delany and several black leaders had
urged emigration to Africa or South America. On the eve of
the Civil War, even Frederick Douglass flirted with emigration
as a solution to the crisis of those years. In the post-Civil War
decades schemes for emigration, separate towns, and states
were occasionally put forth. At times employing the technical
language of sociology, William Bittle and Gilbert Geis discuss
some of these movements and the attempt of Alfred Sam to
take one group back to Africa. Though most of these projects
failed, they represented a long tradition which would achieve
a larger following in the Garvey movement of the 1920s.

Given the intensification of white racism at the turn of the
century, the acceptance of Booker T. Washington in the white
community is understandable. Of course, hard-core racists
found even Washington objectionable, especially when he sat
down to dine with President Roosevelt. The white founders
of the NAACP also found Washington objectionable, but for

different reasons. They shared Du Bois's belief that his program represented capitulation to racism. They were especially concerned that Washington's emphasis on industrial education was a tacit admission of black inferiority. These white Radicals believed that a new spirit of abolition was required to halt the growing discrimination, segregation, and violence that plagued both northern and southern blacks.

But the white Radicals were in a minority, for most whites preferred the soothing words of Washington. When politicians and Presidents wanted advice about racial issues, especially in the South, they consulted Tuskegee. When white philanthropists sought assistance about how to aid the black community and especially black schools, they turned to Washington. White leaders generally hailed the Tuskegee educator as a great American and hoped that he spoke for the masses of black Americans.

Washington was clearly aware of his audience. His "Atlanta Compromise" address was aimed at placating whites, while being vague at certain points so that blacks could also accept it. His autobiography *Up from Slavery,* which became an immediate best seller, was a rags-to-riches story in the grand American tradition. Here was a man born a slave who had been received at the Court of St. James and at the White House. It was written to appeal to whites and was a success in attracting white money to his causes and institution. Moreover, Washington was a skilled public relations man and ran an efficient organization to extend his influence. His critics called it the "Tuskegee Machine." These activities got results. Washington more than any other black man appealed to white America in the early twentieth century.

The extent of Booker T. Washington's following in the black community is difficult to determine. As the essays indicate, a number of leaders, from the militant Monroe Trotter to the moderates like Kelly Miller and T. Thomas Fortune, did not wholly accept Washington. Washington probably enjoyed his greatest following among black leaders around the turn of the century, and opposition grew steadily until his death in 1915. Even Du Bois flirted with Washington's views at one time, and in its early years the NAACP tried to make peace with

Tuskegee. Certainly Washington used the "Tuskegee Machine" to enhance his position among blacks. He used his contacts with the black press skillfully and on occasion subsidized it. His entree to the white community, and hence access to white money, gave him an advantage, as black colleges depended upon white support. If black educators wanted funds they could not afford to be too militant.

Washington's emphasis upon economic development appealed to a growing black middle class whose existence depended upon a growing segregated community. Washington urged the development of black-owned businesses and organized the National Negro Business League to foster black capitalism. The Washington philosophy also appealed to many educators and ministers because of its emphasis on morality, self-help, character building, piety, and thrift. The black colleges' heavy emphasis on morality and religion was Washingtonian in tone.

But the more highly educated blacks criticized Washington more and more. Apart from the usual arguments against Washington's program, it was not succeeding. The assumption that white society would accept blacks as they acquired skills and property and became productive was proving false. Middle-class blacks were scorned as much as the poor. White society seemed to offer them only more segregation and discrimination, not increased opportunity, acceptance, and political rights. Appeals to the "best whites" did not halt lynching. The black colleges with their meager funds and their industrial-education orientation showed few signs of being able to produce graduates trained to deal with the emerging industrial and urban society with its rapid technological changes. The skills that Washington urged and the exhortations to stay on the land were unreal to the sharecropper who found it nearly impossible to rise to the position of an independent landowner. Even Washington himself, shortly before his death, had some doubts about his assumptions, though his general optimism still prevailed.

Later defenders of Washington insisted that at his time alternatives for black Americans were limited. Yet Washington himself was in part responsible for this state of affairs, for he gave whites the feeling that compromise was acceptable, and he was somewhat intolerant of black dissent. It may be true that he was merely the spokesman for an age and that blacks had few options, but that is only another way of saying that for black America the age of Washington was grim.

5

Booker T. Washington:
An Interpretation

AUGUST MEIER

Booker T. Washington had assiduously cultivated a good press and from time to time had received the attention accorded leaders who were, as the phrase went, "succeeding." Yet it was with relative suddenness that he emerged at the Atlanta Exposition in September 1895 as a figure of national reputation and the acknowledged leader of Negroes in America.

To Washington the solution of the race problem lay essen-

SOURCE: August Meier, *Negro Thought in America, 1880–1915* (Ann Arbor: The University of Michigan Press, 1963), pp. 100–118 (footnotes omitted). Copyright © 1963 by The University of Michigan Press. Reprinted by permission of the publisher.

tially in an application of the gospel of wealth, and he opened and closed his address that memorable afternoon with references to material prosperity. He urged Negroes to stay in the South, since when it came to business, pure and simple, it was in the South that the Negro was given a man's chance. Whites were urged to lend a helping hand in the uplifting of the Negroes in order to further the prosperity and well-being of their region. Coupled with this appeal to the self-interest of the white South was a conciliatory phraseology and a criticism of Negroes. Washington deprecated politics and the Reconstruction experience. He criticized Negroes for forgetting that the masses of the race were to live by the production of their hands and for permitting their grievances to overshadow their opportunities. He grew lyrical in reciting the loyalty and fidelity of Negroes—"the most patient, faithful, law-abiding and unresentful people that the world had seen." He denied any interest in social equality when he said: "In all things that are purely social we can be as separate as the five fingers, yet one as the hand in all things essential to mutual progress." In conclusion he asked for justice and an elimination of sectional differences and racial animosities, which, combined with material prosperity would usher in a new era for "our beloved South."

Washington's emphasis upon economic prosperity was the hallmark of the age. The pledges of loyalty to the South and the identification of Negro uplift with the cause of the New South satisfied the "better class" of Southern whites and Northern investors; the generalities about justice to the Negro, of interracial cooperation in things essential to mutual progress, coupled with a denial of interest in social equality, encompassed a wide range of views that could be satisfied by ambiguous phraseology. Washington's generalized references to justice and progress and uplift soothed the pallid consciences of the dominant groups in the nation and at the same time allowed the white South to assume that justice could be achieved without granting Negroes political and civil rights. Yet a careful reading of the address indicates that it could also be interpreted as including ultimate goals more advanced than white Southerners could possibly support. Negroes must begin at the bottom, but surely Washington believed that eventually they would arrive at the top. Most Negroes interpreted social equality as meaning simply intimate social relationships which they did not desire, though most whites interpreted it as meaning the abolition of segregation. Even though Washington said that "it is important and right that all privileges of the law be ours; but it is vastly more important that we be prepared for the exercise of these privileges," and that "the opportunity to earn a dollar in a factory just now is worth infinitely more than the opportunity to spend a dollar in an opera house," his Negro supporters emphasized the future implications of his remarks, and his statement that "no race that has anything to contribute to the markets of the world is long in any degree ostracized." Unlike Negroes, the dominant whites were impressed by his conciliatory phraseology, confused his means for his ends, and were satisfied with the immediate program that he enunciated.

Washington captured his audience and assured his ascendancy primarily because his ideas accorded with the climate of opinion at the time. His association with industrial education, his emphasis upon the economic, and his conciliatory approach were undoubtedly important reasons why he was selected to speak on this prominent occasion. As Charles S. Johnson has suggested, Washington was effectively manipulating the symbols and myths dear to the majority of Americans. It cannot be overemphasized that Washington's philosophy represents in large measure the basic tendencies of Negro thought in the period under consideration. Armstrong at Hampton had expressed the identical program as a ground of compromise between the white North, the white South, and the Negro. Indeed, it is clear that the chief source of Washington's philosophy was his experience at Hampton Institute, for he unmistakably bore the stamp of its founder.

How much the youthful Washington was shaped by his Hampton experience it is hard to say. He later recounted his strenuous efforts to obtain an education while working in the salt and coal mines at Malden, West Virginia, his lessons of cleanliness, thoroughness, and honesty as the servant of the wife of Yankee General Lewis Ruffner, and his bold trip, largely on foot, of five hundred miles from his home to Hampton. These were all evidences of the self-reliant personality that was his. Consequently, Yankee, Puritan, industrious Hampton and this ambitious and industrious youth of sixteen, who presented himself at its doors in the fall of 1872, clicked from the first. "At Hampton," he wrote later, "I found the opportunities . . . to learn thrift, economy and push. I was surrounded by an atmosphere of business, Christian influences, and the spirit of self-help, that seemed to have awakened every faculty in me."

Armstrong was undoubtedly the most influential person in Washington's life, and his viewpoint contained the major ingredients of Washington's philosophy. Yet Washington was not fully committed to the Hampton idea when he left the school in 1875. He taught for two years in his home town in West Virginia, attended briefly the liberal arts Wayman Seminary in Washington, toyed with the idea of a political career, and started the study of law. Like the majority of his future students he at no time seriously considered practicing a trade for a livelihood. All questions were settled, however, when he was asked to return to Hampton to teach in 1879. Then, in 1881 Washington set forth to establish his own school at Tuskegee, Alabama, on the meager appropriations that resulted—paradoxically enough—from a political deal on the part of an ex-Confederate colonel who solicited Negro votes by promising to introduce a bill for a Negro industrial school in the legislature. From then until 1895 Washington was engaged in building the school—a story of trial and success in the best Hampton tradition.

In discussing Washington's ideology it will be necessary to examine both his overtly expressed philosophy of accommodation and his covertly conducted attack on racial discrimination. His conciliatory approach was an important factor in his achieving eminence, and his continued ascendancy in Negro affairs, due as it was to the support of dominant white elements, depended upon his playing this tactful role to the fullest extent. Yet his very prominence brought him into situations that led to secret activities that directly contradicted the ideology he officially espoused.

 . . . Washington's expressed ideology remained remarkably consistent throughout his public life. There appear to have been no significant changes in his publicly stated outlook except for a somewhat more accommodating attitude after 1895 than before, and except for a growing emphasis upon racial solidarity and economic chauvinism after the turn of the century. Through the years he was conciliatory in manner toward the white South, emphasized the ordinary economic and moral virtues, claimed that he regarded political and civil rights as secondary and ultimate rather than as primary and immediate aims, held up Negro moral and economic progress to public view, even while criticizing the weaknesses of Negroes and insisting that they should shoulder much of the blame for their status and the primary responsibility for their own advancement, and optimistically insisted that race relations were improving.

The central theme in Washington's philosophy was that through thrift, industry, and Christian character Negroes would eventually attain their constitutional rights. To Washington it seemed but proper that Negroes would have to measure up to American standards of morality and material prosperity if they were to succeed in the Social Darwinist race of life. Just as the individual who succeeds can do something that the world wants done well, so with a race. Things would be on a different footing if it became common to associate the possession of wealth with a black skin. "It is not within the province of human nature that the man who is intelligent and virtuous, and owns and cultivates the best farm in his county, shall very long be denied the proper respect and consideration."

Consequently Negroes, he felt, must learn trades in order to compete with whites. He blamed Negroes for neglecting skills acquired under slavery, for the loss of what had been practically a monopoly of the skilled labor in the South at the close of the Civil War. He feared that unless industrial schools filled the breach, the next twenty years would witness the economic demise of the Negro. He was often critical of higher education. He never tired of retelling the anecdotes about the rosewood piano in the tumble-down cabin, or about the young man he found sitting in an unkempt cabin, studying from a French grammar. He denied that he intended to minimize the value of higher education, and his own children in fact enjoyed its advantages, but practical education, he believed, should come first in the rise of a people toward civilization. Occasionally, he praised higher education, but he often cited cases of college graduates who were accomplishing nothing, and once at least he referred to "the college bacillus."

Fundamentally, Washington did not think in terms of a subordinate place in the American economy for Negroes. Though his language was ambiguous, he thought in terms of developing a substantial propertied class of landowners and businessmen. There was, as he often put it, a great need for "captains of industry." He felt a deep sympathy with the wealthy, and he preferred to talk most of all to audiences of businessmen who, he found, were quick to grasp what he was saying. In all this he was thoroughly in accord with the New South philosophy. He praised Robert C. Ogden of Wanamaker's (a trustee of Tuskegee and Hampton and chairman of the General Education Board) and H. H. Rogers, the Standard Oil and railroad magnate, as men whose interest in uplifting the Negro was partly motivated by their desire to develop one of the neglected resources of the South.

Part of Washington's outlook toward capital and the New South was his antagonistic attitude toward labor unions. He recollected that before the days of strikes in the West Virginia coal mines where he had worked, he had known miners with considerable sums in the bank, "but as soon as the professional labor agitators got control, the savings of even the more thrifty ones began disappearing." To some extent, he felt, the loss of the Negro's hold on the skilled trades was due to the unions. He boasted that Negro labor was, if fairly treated, "the best free labor in the world," not given to striking. Later, writing in the *Atlantic Monthly* in 1913, Washington, though still basically hostile, appeared somewhat more favorable toward unions. He admitted that there were cases in which labor unions had used their influence on behalf of Negroes even in the South, and he knew of instances in which Negroes had taken a leading part in the work of their unions. Nevertheless, he felt that unions would cease to discriminate only to the extent that they feared Negro strikebreakers.

Exceedingly important in Washington's outlook was an emphasis on agriculture and rural landownership that has ordinarily been overlooked. He constantly deprecated migration to cities where, he said, the Negro was at his worst and insisted that Negroes should stay on the farmlands of the South. Since all peoples who had gained wealth and recognition had come up from the soil, agriculture should be the chief occupation of Negroes, who should be encouraged to own and cultivate the soil. While he called Negroes the best labor for Southern farms, he optimistically looked forward to an independent yeomanry, respected in their communities.

Also associated with Washington's middle-class and Social Darwinist philosophy were the ideas of the value of struggle in achieving success, of self-help, and of "taking advantage of disadvantages." As he put it, "No race of people ever got upon its feet without severe and constant struggle, often in the face of the greatest disappointment." He turned misfortune into good fortune, and middle-class rationalization of the strenuous life into an accommodating rationalization of the Negro's status. Paradoxical as it might seem, the difficulties facing the Negro had on the whole helped him more than they had hindered him, for under pressure the Negro had put forth more energy which, constructively channeled, had been of untold value.

While whites had some responsibility, the most important part in the Negro's progress was to be played by the Negro himself; the race's future recognition lay within its own hands. On the negative side this emphasis on self-help involved a tendency to blame Negroes for their condition. Washington constantly criticized them for seeking higher rather than practical education, for their loss of places in the skilled trades, for their lack of morality and economic virtues, and for their tendency toward agitation and complaint. But in its positive aspects this emphasis involved race pride and solidarity. Negroes should be proud of their history and their great men. For a race to grow strong and powerful it must honor its heroes. Negroes should not expect any great success until they learned to imitate the Jews, who through unity and faith in themselves were becoming more and more influential. He showed considerable pride in the all-Negro communities. At times he espoused a high degree of racial solidarity and economic nationalism. On one occasion he declared: "We are a nation within a nation." While

Negroes should be the last to draw the color line, at the same time they should see to it that "in every wise and legitimate way our people are taught to patronise racial enterprises."

If emphasis upon racial pride and self-help through economic and moral development formed one side of Washington's thinking, another was his insistence that interracial harmony and white good will were prerequisite to the Negro's advancement. In appealing to whites Washington spoke in both moral and practical terms. Southern whites should aid Negroes out of economic self-interest and should act justly since to do less would corrupt their moral fiber. Washington constantly reiterated his love for the South, his faith in the Southern white man's sense of justice, his belief that the South afforded Negroes more economic opportunity than the North. In 1912, answering the question "Is the Negro Having a Fair Chance?" he did go so far as to admit the existence of the standard grievances, but declared that nowhere were there ten million black people who had greater opportunities or were making greater progress than the Negroes of the South; nowhere had any race "had the assistance, the direction, and the sympathy of another race in all its efforts to rise to such an extent as the Negro in the United States." Washington devoted one whole book, *The Man Farthest Down* (1912), to the thesis that American Negroes were better off than the depressed classes in Europe. In general, Washington appealed to the highest sentiments and motives of the whites and brushed lightly over their prejudices and injustices in an attempt to create the favorable sentiment without which Negro progress was doomed. He frequently referred to the friendship Southern whites exhibited toward Negroes and constantly cited examples of harmonious relations between the races. At a time when Mississippi was notorious for "whitecapping" (the attacking of business establishments owned by prosperous Negroes who were then run out of town), he opined that "there, more than anywhere else, the colored people seem to have discovered that, in gaining habits of thrift and industry, in getting property, and in making themselves useful, there is a door of hope open for them which the South has no disposition to close." He was incurably optimistic in his utterance—as he said, "We owe it not only to ourselves, but to our children, to look always upon the bright side of life."

Washington constantly deprecated protest and agitation. Leading virtuous, respectable lives and acquiring wealth would advance the race more than any number of books and speeches. Speaking at the Afro-American Council in July 1903 he urged patience and optimism:

> In the long run it is the race or individual that exercises the most patience, forbearance, and self-control in the midst of trying conditions that wins . . . the respect of the world. . . . We have a right in a conservative and sensible manner to enter our complaints, but we shall make a fatal error if we yield to the temptation of believing that mere opposition to our wrongs . . . will take the place of progressive, constructive action. . . . Let us not forget to lay the greatest stress upon the opportunities open to us, especially here in the South, for constructive growth in labor, in business and education. . . . An inch of progress is worth more than a yard of complaint.

While Washington never changed his basic ideology, before 1895 he tended to be more frank, though always tactful, regarding the Negro's goals. In 1894, for example, he admitted that conventions and organizations whose aims were to redress certain grievances were "right and proper," though they should not be the chief reliance of the race, and went on to declare that if his approach did not in time bring every political and civil right then everything, even the teaching of Christ, was false. As conditions grew worse Washington became more rather than less conciliatory. The outstanding exception to his general policy was his address at the Jubilee celebration held in Chicago after the Spanish-American War, where with President McKinley in the audience, he made one of his famous *faux pas*. Reviewing the valorous deeds of Negroes in the military history of the United States, especially in the recent war, he contended that a race that was thus willing to die for its country should be given the highest opportunity to live for its country. Americans had won every conflict in which they had been engaged, "except the effort to conquer ourselves in the blotting out of racial prejudice. . . . Until we thus conquer our-

selves I make no empty statement when I say that we shall
have a cancer gnawing at the heart of this republic that shall
some day prove to be as dangerous as an attack from an army
without or within." This statement aroused considerable ire
in the Southern press, and Washington characteristically qualified his remarks. He explained that he seldom referred to prejudice because it was something to be lived down rather than
talked down, but since that meeting symbolized the end of
sectional feelings he had thought it an appropriate time to ask
for "the blotting out of racial prejudice as far as possible in
'business and civil relations.'"

On the three major issues of segregation, lynching, and the
franchise, the Tuskegeean expressed himself with characteristic
circumspection. Prior to the Atlanta address he had made it
clear that he opposed segregation in transportation. Speaking
in 1884 he had said that "the Governor of Alabama would probably count it no disgrace to ride in the same railroad coach
with a colored man." As late as 1894 he urged Negroes to follow the example of Atlanta citizens who had boycotted the
newly segregated streetcars and predicted that such economic
pressures would make it respectable for both races to ride in
the same railway coach as well. But after 1895 he held that
separate but equal facilities would be satisfactory. As he once
put it: "All . . . parts of the world have their own peculiar customs and prejudices. For that reason it is a part of common-
sense to respect them." And he did respect the customs of other
parts of the world. He accepted President Roosevelt's dinner
invitation in 1901 after careful consideration. He was on intimate terms with distinguished philanthropists and was entertained in circles in the North and abroad that few white Southerners could have entered. Yet he declared that the objection
to the Jim Crow car was "not the separation, but the inadequacy of the accommodations." Again, speaking in 1914 on
the matter of municipal segregation ordinances, Washington
stirred up a hornet's nest of criticism by remarking: "Let us,
in the future, spend less time talking about the part of the city
that we cannot live in, and more time in making the part of
the city that we can live in beautiful and attractive." Yet in a

posthumously published account of "My Views of Segregation Laws" Washington—or his ghostwriter—tactfully gave his reasons for condemning them, and in a most unusual concluding statement openly declared that segregation was "ill-advised" because it was unjust and all thoughtful Negroes resented injustice. There was no case of segregation, he said, that had not widened the breach between the two races. That Negroes did not constantly express their embitterment, he added, was not proof that they did not feel it.

Even on lynching Washington expressed himself rarely, but when he did his statements received considerable attention. He generally emphasized the harm lynching did to the whites —to their moral fiber, to economic conditions, and to the reputation of the South—and at the same time counseled Negroes to cultivate industry and cease the idleness that led to crime. Yet he could be forthright in his condemnation of mob violence. "Within the last fortnight," he said in a statement issued to the press in 1904,

> three members of my race have been burned at the stake; one
> of them was a woman. No one . . . was charged with any
> crime even remotely connected with the abuse of a white
> woman. . . . Two of them occurred on Sunday afternoon in
> sight of a Christian church. . . . The custom of burning human
> beings has become so common as scarcely to excite interest.
> . . . There is no shadow of excuse for departure from legal
> methods in the cases of individuals accused of murder.

Ordinarily, Washington did not discuss politics, but there were occasions when he did admit that "I do not favor the Negro's giving up anything which is fundamental and which has been guaranteed to him by the Constitution. . . . It is not best for him to relinquish his rights; nor would his doing so be best for the Southern white man." He was critical of Reconstruction, when Negroes had started at the top instead of the bottom, in the senate instead of at the plow, and had been the unwitting instruments of corrupt carpet-bagger politicians. "In a word, too much stress had been placed upon the mere matter of voting and holding political office rather than upon the preparation for the highest citizenship." Washington's solution

to the question of political rights was suffrage restriction applied to both races—a notion that had been growing in popularity since about 1890. "The permanent cure for our present
evils will come through a property and educational test for
voting that shall apply honestly and fairly to both races." In a
letter to the Louisiana Constitutional Convention of 1898 he
outlined his views. He was, he said, no politician, but had
always advised Negroes to acquire property, intelligence, and
character as the basis of good citizenship, rather than to en-
gage in political agitation. He agreed that franchise restrictions were necessary to rid the South of ignorant and corrupt
government, but suggested that no state could pass a law that
would permit an ignorant white man to vote and disfranchise
ignorant Negroes "without dwarfing for all time the morals of
the white man in the South." In 1899, in referring to the disfranchisement bill before the Georgia legislature, he had force-
fully declared that its object was to disfranchise the Negroes.
Yet three years later he became notorious for his defense of
the disfranchisement constitutions: "Every revised constitution
throughout the Southern States has put a premium upon intelligence, ownership of property, thrift and character," he wrote
in a general letter to the press. But his hope that these qualifications would be equitably applied remained unfulfilled, and
after 1905 Washington no longer rationalized about the disfranchisement constitutions, as he had done, but simply held
that the acquisition of character, wealth, and education would
break down racial discrimination.

All in all, in viewing Washington's philosophy, one is most
impressed by his accommodating approach. By carefully selected ambiguities in language, by mentioning political and
civil rights but seldom and then only in tactful and vague
terms, he effectively masked the ultimate implications of his
philosophy. For this reason his philosophy must be viewed as
an accommodating one in the context of Southern race relations. In the context of the Negro thinking of the period, perhaps the most significant thing in his philosophy was his
emphasis upon self-help and racial solidarity.

In certain quarters Washington did not like to be considered
an extreme accommodator. Writing to Francis J. Garrison of

the New York Evening *Post* in 1899 he said that he hesitated
to appear on the same platform with W. H. Councill, who "has
the reputation of simply toadying to the Southern white
people." In a letter to the noted author and lawyer, Charles W.
Chesnutt, he denied that he was interested only in education
and property, and he enclosed two recent statements he had
made on the franchise and lynching. True, he spoke only when
he thought it would be effective, rather than agitating all the
time, but "I cannot understand what you or others want me
to do that I have left undone." He conceded that agitation had
its place; justice he believed would be attained both through
education and agitation. "You will assist in bringing it about
in your way and those of us who are laboring in the South
will do something to bring it about in our way."

Although overtly Washington minimized the importance of
the franchise and civil rights, covertly he was deeply involved
in political affairs and in efforts to prevent disfranchisement
and other forms of discrimination.

For example, he lobbied against the Hardwick disfranchisement bill in Georgia in 1899. While his public ambiguities permitted Southern whites to think that he accepted disfranchisement if they chose to, through the same ambiguities and by
private communications Washington tried to keep Negroes
thinking otherwise. In 1903 when the Atlanta editor Clark
Howell implied that Washington opposed Negro officeholding,
he did not openly contradict him, but asked T. Thomas Fortune to editorialize in the *Age* that Howell had no grounds for
placing Washington in such a position, for it was "well understood that he, while from the first deprecating the Negro's making political agitation and office-holding the most prominent
and fundamental part of his career, has not gone any farther."
Again, while Washington opposed proposals to enforce the
representation provisions of the fourteenth amendment (because he felt that the South would accept reduction in representation and thus stamp disfranchisement with the seal of
constitutionality), he was secretly engaged in attacking the
disfranchisement constitutions by court action. As early as 1900

he was asking certain philanthropists for money to fight the electoral provisions of the Louisiana constitution. Subsequently, he worked secretly through the financial secretary of the Afro-American Council's legal bureau, personally spending a great deal of money and energy fighting the Louisiana test case. At the time of the Alabama Constitutional Convention in 1901 he used his influence with important whites in an attempt to prevent discriminatory provisions that would apply to Negroes only. He was later deeply involved in testing the Alabama disfranchisement laws in the federal courts in 1903 and 1904. So circumspect was he in this instance that his secretary, Emmett J. Scott, and the New York lawyer Wilford Smith corresponded about the cases under pseudonyms and represented the sums involved in code. Washington was also interested in efforts to prevent or undermine disfranchisement in other states. For example, in Maryland, where disfranchisement later failed, he had a Catholic lawyer, F. L. McGhee of St. Paul, approach the Catholic hierarchy in an attempt to secure its opposition to disfranchisement and urged the Episcopal divine George Freeman Bragg of Baltimore to use his influence among important whites. Washington contributed money generously to the test cases and other efforts, though, except in the border states, they were unsuccessful. In 1903 and 1904 he personally "spent at least four thousand dollars in cash, out of my own pocket . . . in advancing the rights of the black man."

Washington's political involvement went even deeper. Although he always discreetly denied any interest in politics, he was engaged in patronage distribution under Roosevelt and Taft, in fighting the lily-white Republicans, and in getting out the Negro vote for the Republicans at national elections. He might say that he disliked the atmosphere at Washington because it was impossible to build up a race whose leaders were spending most of their time and energy in trying to get into or stay in office, but under Roosevelt he became the arbiter of Negro appointments to federal office. Roosevelt started consulting Washington almost as soon as he took office, and later claimed that Washington had approved of his policy of appointing fewer but better-qualified Negroes. Numerous politicians old and new were soon writing to Tuskegee for favors, and in a few cases Roosevelt consulted Washington in regard to white candidates. Ex-Congressman George H. White unsuccessfully appealed to Washington after the White House indicated that "a letter from you would greatly strengthen my chances." Scott reported that the President's assertion to one office seeker that he would consider him only with Washington's endorsement, had "scared these old fellows as they never have been scared before." Washington had at his disposal a number of collectorships of ports and internal revenue, receiverships of public monies in the land office, and several diplomatic posts, as well as the positions of auditor of the Navy, register of the Treasury and recorder of the deeds. As Roosevelt wrote to a friend in 1903, his Negro appointees "were all recommended to me by Booker T. Washington." Furthermore, Roosevelt sought Washington's advice on presidential speeches and messages to Congress and consulted him on most matters concerning the Negro. Every four years also Washington took charge of the Negro end of the Republican presidential campaign.

If Washington reaped the rewards of politics, he also experienced its vicissitudes. From the start he was fighting a desperate but losing battle against the lily-white Republicans. His correspondence teems with material on the struggle, especially in Louisiana and Alabama, and in other states as well. As he wrote to Walter L. Cohen of the New Orleans land office on October 5, 1905: "What I have attempted in Louisiana I have attempted to do in nearly every one of the Southern States, as you and others are in a position to know, and but for my action, as feeble as it was, the colored people would have been completely overthrown and the Lily Whites would have been in complete control in nearly every Southern State." Later, troubles came thick and fast after Taft's inauguration. The new president appointed fewer Negroes to office and did not consult Washington as much as Roosevelt had done. Not until 1911, after desperate efforts at convincing the administration of the need for some decent plums in order to retain the Negro vote, was it finally arranged to make a few significant appointments, most notably that of W. H. Lewis as assistant attorney general—the highest position held by a Negro in the federal government up to that time.

In areas other than politics Washington also played an active behind-the-scenes role. On the Seth Carter (Texas) and Dan Rogers (Alabama) cases involving discrimination in the matter of representation on juries, Washington worked closely with the lawyer Wilford Smith and contributed liberally to their financing. He was interested in preventing Negro tenants who had accidentally or in ignorance violated their contracts from being sentenced to the chain gang. He was concerned in the Alonzo Bailey Peonage Case, and when the Supreme Court declared peonage illegal, confided to friends that he and his associates had been working at the case for over two years, securing the free services of some of the best lawyers in Montgomery and the assistance of other leading white people. Yet Washington characteristically interceded to reduce the sentence of the convicted man, who was soon released.

Of special interest are Washington's efforts against railroad segregation. At Washington's suggestion Giles B. Jackson of Richmond undertook the legal fight against the Jim Crow Law in Virginia in 1901. When Tennessee in 1903 in effect prohibited Pullman accommodations for Negroes by requiring that such facilities be entirely separate, he stepped into the breach. He worked closely with Napier in Nashville and enlisted the aid of Atlanta leaders like W. E. B. Du Bois. This group, however, did not succeed in discussing the matter with Pullman Company president Robert Todd Lincoln, in spite of the intercession of another railroad leader, William H. Baldwin, president of the Long Island Railroad, an important figure in the Pennsylvania and Southern systems, and Washington's closest white friend. And, though Washington wanted to start a suit, the Nashville people failed to act. Again, in 1906, employing the Howard University Professor Kelly Miller and the Boston lawyer Archibald W. Grimké as intermediaries, Washington discreetly supplied funds to pay ex-Senator Henry W. Blair of New Hampshire to lobby against the Warner-Foraker Amendment to the Hepburn Railway Act. This amendment, by requiring equality of accommodations in interstate travel, would have impliedly condoned segregation throughout the country, under the separate-but-equal doctrine. The amendment was defeated, but whether due to Blair's lobbying or to the protests of Negro organizations is hard to say.

Thus, in spite of his accommodating tone and his verbal emphasis upon economy as the solution to the race problem, Washington was surreptitiously engaged in undermining the American race system by a direct attack upon disfranchisement and segregation, and in spite of his strictures against political activity he was a powerful politician in his own right.

Comparable to Washington's influence in politics was his position with the philanthropists. He wielded an enormous influence in appropriations made by Carnegie, Rosenwald, the General Education Board, and the Phelps-Stokes and Jeanes Funds. Negro schools that received Carnegie libraries received them at Washington's suggestion, and even applied for them upon his advice. Contributors sought his advice on the worthiness of schools; college administrators asked his advice on personnel. His weight was especially appreciated by the liberal arts colleges. Washington accepted a place on the boards of trustees of Howard University in 1907 and of Fisk University in 1909. In the case of Fisk he proved exceedingly helpful in attracting philanthropic contributions. So complete was Washington's control over educational philanthropy that John Hope, president of Atlanta Baptist College, and a member of the anti-Bookerite Niagara Movement, found the doors of the foundations entirely closed to him. Only through the intercession of his friend Robert Russua Moton, a member of the Hampton circle and Washington's successor at Tuskegee, was Hope able to obtain Washington's necessary endorsement of his school to philanthropists such as Carnegie.

Washington's popularity with leading whites and his power in philanthropic and political circles enhanced his prestige and power within the Negro community. His influence was felt in multifarious ways beyond his control over philanthropy and political appointments. His power over the Negro press was considerable and in large measure stifled criticism of his policies. His influence extended into the Negro churches, and his friendship and assistance were eagerly sought by those seeking positions in the church. Between 1902 and 1904 and perhaps longer, Washington controlled the avowedly protest Afro-American Council, the leading Negro rights organization prior to 1905. Whether or not Washington was a "benevolent despot," as one recent biographer has asserted, is an open question, but that he wielded enormous power over the Negro community is undeniable.

It was this quasi-dictatorial power as much as anything else that alienated W. E. B. Du Bois from Washington and his program. Once Washington had achieved eminence he grew extremely sensitive to adverse criticism from Negroes. From the first some had opposed his viewpoint, and while many rushed to his support after he became the puissant adviser to Theodore Roosevelt, somehow "the opposition" (as Washington often referred to his critics) grew apace. Objections were raised to the arbitrary power of the "Tuskegee machine," as Du Bois called it, and to Washington's soft-pedaling of political and civil rights. From 1903 on Washington found himself increasingly under attack. He used every means at his disposal to combat his critics—his influence with the press, placing spies in the opposition movements, depriving their members of church and political positions. The high point of the attack on Washington, the formation of the National Association for the Advancement of Colored People in 1909–10, came at the very time when his political power was slipping, and after 1913 he had no political influence at all, while the NAACP was becoming stronger. By the time he died Washington had lost much of his power.

Washington's struggle against the various protest groups is interesting in that they had the same ultimate goal as he did, and came out frankly for the very things for which he was working surreptitiously. Yet Washington appears to have regarded them as more dangerous to the welfare of the race than "friends" like Carnegie, Taft, and Roosevelt, who were not genuine equalitarians and who thought Negroes should not emphasize politics and civil rights. Washington sincerely believed that his program would be the most effective in the long run, but he did not object too much to militance and agitation in the newspapers that supported him. His attacks upon "the opposition" suggest that something more than tactics or ideologies was at stake. It appears that Washington feared the effect of his critics on his personal power and prestige. He did not object to protest too much as long as it was not aimed at him and his policies. As he wrote R. C. Ogden, "wise, conservative agitation looking toward securing the rights of colored people on the part of the people of the North is not hurtful."

It would appear to this author that a large part of Washington's motivation was his desire for power. To a large extent he had to be satisfied with the substance rather than the symbols of power. His desire for power and prestige, however, does not necessarily indicate insincerity or hypocrisy. It is usually hard to distinguish where altruism ends and self-interest begins. So thoroughly and inextricably bound together in Washington's mind were his program for racial elevation and his own personal career, that he genuinely thought that he and only he was in the best position to advance the interests of the race.

Thus, although Washington held to full citizenship rights and integration as his objective, he masked this goal beneath an approach that satisfied influential elements that were either indifferent or hostile to its fulfillment. He was not the first to combine a constructive, even militant emphasis upon self-help, racial cooperation and economic development with a conciliatory, ingratiating, and accommodating approach to the white South. But his name is the one most indissolubly linked with this combination. He was, as one of his followers put it, attempting to bring the wooden horse within the walls of Troy.

Washington apparently really believed that in the face of an economic and moral development that assimilated Negroes to American middle-class standards, prejudice would diminish and the barriers of discrimination would crumble. He emphasized duties rather than rights; the Negro's faults rather than his grievances; his opportunities rather than his difficulties. He stressed means rather than ends. He was optimistic rather than pessimistic. He stressed economics above politics, industrial above liberal education, self-help above dependence on the national government. He taught that rural life was superior to urban life. He professed a deep love for the South and a profound faith in the goodness of the Southern whites—at least of the "better class." He appealed more to the self-interest of the whites—their economic and moral good—than to their sense of justice.

The ambiguities in Washington's philosophy were vital to his success. Negroes who supported him looked to his tactfully, usually vaguely worded expressions on ultimate goals. Conservative Southerners were attracted by his seeming acceptance of disfranchisement and segregation, and by his flattery. Industrialists and philanthropists appreciated his petit bourgeois outlook. Washington's skillful manipulation of popular symbols and myths like the gospel of wealth and the doctrines of Social Darwinism enhanced his effectiveness. Terms like "social equality," "civil relations," "constitutional rights," "Christian character,' "industrial education," and "justice" were capable of a wide variety of interpretations. The Supreme Court, for example, did not appear to think that the fourteenth and fifteenth amendments prohibited segregation and the use of various subterfuges that effected disfranchisement. Washington shrewdly used these ambiguities, and they were an important source both of his popularity and of the acrimonious discussion over his policy that occupied Negroes for many years.

Washington did not appeal to all groups. Extremists among white Southerners liked him no more than did the Negro "radicals." Men such as Governor Vardaman of Mississippi and the author Thomas Dixon, who feared any Negro advancement, opposed the Tuskegeean's program of elevation and uplift. Washington basically appealed to conservative, propertied elements both North and South. His stress upon the economic rather than the political was parallel to the New South philosophy of emphasizing industry rather than politics as a way of advancing the South in the councils of the nation. Yet he also capitalized on the myth of the small farmer, and the romantic agrarian traditions of the South. His call for a justly applied property and educational test that would disfranchise ignorant and poor Negroes and whites alike, and enfranchise the propertied, taxpaying, conservative Negroes, met the approval of important elements in the Black Belt plantation and urban areas of the South, who had no more love for "poor whites" than Washington did. Again, Washington espoused a Social Darwinism of competition between individuals and races, of uplifting backward races, that was congenial to his age. He conveniently put Negro equality off into a hazy future that did not disturb the "practical" and prejudiced men of his generation. At the same time, by blaming Negroes for their condition, by calling them a backward race, by asserting that an era of justice would ultimately be ushered in, by flattering the whites for what little they had done for Negroes, he palliated any pangs of conscience that the whites might have had.

His program also appealed to a substantial group of Negroes —to those Negroes who were coming to count for most—in large part to a rising middle class. In fact, stress upon economics as an indirect route to the solution of the race problem, interest in industrial education, the appeal to race pride and solidarity, and denial of any interest in social equality were all ideas that had become dominant in the Negro community. The older upper-class Negroes in certain Northern centers, who had their economic and sometimes their social roots in the white communities, were less sympathetic to Washington. But to self-made middle-class Negroes, and to lower middle-class Negroes on the make, to the leaders and supporters of Negro fraternal enterprises, to businessmen who depended on the Negro community for their livelihood, Washington's message seemed common sense. Interestingly enough, this group, especially in the North, did not always express Washington's conciliatory tone, but assumed that Washington was using it to placate the white South.

To what extent Washington directly influenced Negro thought is difficult to evaluate. Washington was acceptable to Negroes partly because of the prestige and power he held among whites, and partly because his views—except for his concilatory phraseology—were dominant in the Negro community throughout the country, and his accommodating approach was general throughout the South. Then, too, his Negro supporters read a great deal into his generalizations about eventual justice and constitutional rights. The fact that

Negroes tended to see in his words what they already believed would appear to minimize his direct influence. Yet his prestige, the teachers sent out by Tuskegee and her daughter schools, and the widespread publicity generated by the National Negro Business League of which Washington was the founder and president, undoubtedly had a significant impact on Negro thought, reinforcing tendencies already in the foreground.

6

The National
Afro-American League,
1887-1908

EMMA LOU THORNBROUGH

Today, almost a century after the abolition of slavery in the United States, the fight to secure equal civil and political rights for Negroes continues. For half a century the most conspicuous part in the fight has been played by the National Association for the Advancement of Colored People, but it was not the first organization with this objective. In the latter part of the nineteenth century there were several unsuccessful and almost forgotten attempts at permanent organizations to

SOURCE: *Journal of Southern History*, XXVII (November 1961), 494–512 (footnotes omitted). Copyright © 1961 by the Southern Historical Association. Reprinted by permission of the Managing Editor.

fight against racial discrimination. Of these the most important was the National Afro-American League, which was later revived as the National Afro-American Council. So completely has this organization been forgotten that the best general history of the Negro in the United States does not even mention it, but speaks of the Niagara Movement, founded in 1905, as "the first organized attempt to raise the Negro protest against the great reaction after the Reconstruction."

The dominant figure in the Afro-American League was T. Thomas Fortune, editor of the New York *Age,* who was regarded by his contemporaries as the most able Negro journalist of his day. Although he made his reputation in the North, Fortune knew from personal experience what it was to be a Negro in the South during the Reconstruction and post-Reconstruction era. Born a slave in 1856, he saw the Ku Klux Klan in action as a boy in Marianna, Florida, the scene of some of its worst outrages. With little formal education, but with practical knowledge of the printer's trade, Fortune came to New York in 1879. Soon after his arrival he became part owner and editor of his own newspaper, the *Globe,* which later became the *Freeman,* and finally the *Age.* The reputation of the *Age* as the best Negro paper of its day rested principally on the editorial page, which was an expression of Fortune's views and personality. His editorials, sometimes bitter, sometimes sardonically humorous, in their denunciation of all forms of racial discrimination, attracted comment in the white press in both the North and the South.

In 1887, just ten years after the end of Reconstruction, Fortune called upon Negroes to form an organization to fight for the rights denied them. The legal status of Negroes was not yet as degraded as it was to become in a few years, but the guarantees of the Fourteenth and Fifteenth amendments were already being widely ignored in the South, and in the North there was generally acquiescence in this state of affairs. In an editorial in the *Freeman* of May 28, 1887, Fortune said,

> We think that it has been thoroughly demonstrated that the white papers of this country have determined to leave the colored man to fight his own battles. . . . There is no dodging

the issue; we have got to take hold of this problem ourselves, and make so much noise that all the world shall know the wrongs we suffer and our determination to right these wrongs.

He called for the organization of the National Afro-American League and listed six principal grievances which the organization should combat. First on the list he put the suppression of voting rights in the South, which, he said, had the effect of denying Negroes a voice in the government in the very states in which they were most numerous. Second he attacked "the universal and lamentable reign of lynch and mob law," which was all the more outrageous because it existed in states where the lawmaking and law enforcing machinery were in the hands of the persons who resorted to these lawless methods. The third grievance was the inequities in the distribution of funds between white and colored schools. The fourth was "the odious and demoralizing penitentiary system of the South, with its chain gangs, convict leases, and indiscriminate mixing of males and females." Fifth was the "tyranny" practiced by Southern railroads, which denied equal rights to colored passengers and permitted white passengers to subject them to indignities. Sixth, and last, was the denial of accommodations to Negroes in such places as hotels and theaters.

Except for the last, all of the grievances were either peculiar to the Southern states or were more aggravated in that region than in the North. Because the most serious injustices were found in the South and because the bulk of the Negro population lived there, Fortune felt that the stronghold of the organization should be in the South, while in the North its principal function would be to arouse public opinion and to exert political pressure. He recognized the peculiar difficulties to be faced in setting up such an organization where freedom of speech and assembly on the part of Negroes were curtailed. He admitted that Southern members might be subjected to personal danger. He even intimated that the use of force might be necessary under some circumstances when he said,

> We propose to accomplish our purpose by the peaceful methods of agitation, through the ballot and the courts, but if others use the weapons of violence to combat our peaceful arguments it is not for us to run away from violence.

Later, realizing that his advocacy of violence would probably prove fatal to the cause he was trying to promote, Fortune retreated. In an article explaining the constitution which he proposed for the League, he explained that the purpose should be "to secure the ends desired through peaceable and lawful means" and that members who engaged in acts of violence might be expelled.

A large part of the Negro press in both the North and the South as well as a few prominent individuals at once gave enthusiastic support to the League idea. From Tuskegee Institute in Alabama, youthful and still relatively unknown Booker T. Washington wrote, "Push the battle to the gate. Let there be no hold-up until a League shall be found in every village." But other Southern Negroes warned of the dangers and practical difficulties involved in attempting such a movement in the South. A Negro member of the Florida legislature, T. V. Gibbs, explained his reasons for doubting the success of the proposed League. First of all, he said, in the places where the need for such an organization was most acute, colored people would be too ignorant and too dependent to maintain it. Because of his economic dependency a Negro was unable to stand on an equal footing with the "land own-ing, contract making, figuring white man." He summed up the situation by saying, "The whites have money, arms, educa-tion, and courts and the machinery of government—the colored people have none of them." He admitted that from a Northern standpoint his position would probably seem "weak and pusillanimous," but, he insisted, "facts are facts, and he is not a wise man who does not heed their deductions."

A few white journals in the South took notice of Fortune's proposal. The Charleston, South Carolina, *News and Courier* warned,

> The colored people it is certain, have nothing whatever to gain by organization in the race or color line. This merely strengthens racial divisions . . . and strengthens the very groups who are strongest in their opposition to the very rights which Negroes are demanding.

The Atlanta *Constitution* declared, "There is no conceivable direction in which an organization can do the Negro race any good, and it might do great harm." In the North, in *Harper's Weekly*, George William Curtis gave qualified approval to the League idea, but pointed out that lawsuits, which would have to be the chief weapon of the organization, would require money. Failure to raise the necessary funds would do further harm to the reputation of Negroes by furnishing evidence of their alleged lack of practical ability.

Fortune's plan was to organize local and state leagues before attempting to effect a national organization. In the months following his initial proposal, local leagues of varying size and strength were formed—in New England, Pennsylvania, New York, Illinois, Minnesota, and even in distant San Francisco. In the South organizations were attempted in Virginia, Texas, North Carolina, Tennessee, and Georgia. In January 1890, one hundred forty-one delegates from twenty-three states assembled in Chicago to form a permanent national organization. As might have been expected, the largest numbers were from states in the Chicago area, but somehow seven persons from Georgia managed to attend, and South Carolina, North Carolina, Texas, Tennessee, and Virginia were also represented. It was an all-Negro meeting. No effort had been made to invite interested white persons. A few whites, among them the novelist Albion W. Tourgée, sent messages of good will, but even such expressions were viewed with suspicion by some of the delegates, who were convinced that white men interested themselves in the affairs of Negroes only to dominate them.

Fortune as temporary chairman of the convention made a long, earnest, and carefully prepared address in which he reviewed earlier examples of man's long fight against tyranny and oppression and called upon his listeners to continue the struggle in behalf of members of their race in America. He cried,

> We have been patient so long that many believe that we are incapable of resenting insult, outrage and wrong; we have so long accepted uncomplainingly all the injustice and cowardice and insolence heaped upon us, that many imagine that we are compelled to submit and have not the manhood necessary to resent such conduct.

He ended on a solemn note:

> As the agitation which culminated in the abolition of African slavery in this country covered a period of fifty years, so may we expect that before the rights conferred upon us by the war amendments are fully conceded, a full century will have passed away. We have undertaken no child's play. We have undertaken a serious work which will tax and exhaust the best intelligence of the race for the next century.

The convention adopted a constitution along the lines which Fortune recommended. It declared that the objects of the League should be attained "by the creation of a healthy public opinion through the medium of the press and the pulpit, public meetings and addresses, and by appealing to the courts of law for redress of all denial of legal rights." One article stated that the League was a nonpartisan body and provided that any officer of the League who was elected or appointed to a political post must resign his League office. Fortune insisted that the organization must refrain from identifying itself in any way with partisan politics in order to prevent it from being used as a mere adjunct of the Republican party as most earlier Negro organizations had been. His insistence upon this point undoubtedly was the reason that few prominent Negro politicians supported the League and one of the reasons why the League did not attract a greater following.

In electing a president the convention passed over Fortune, probably because some of the delegates feared that he was too militant and because they considered him a political maverick, and chose instead a Southern Negro, Joseph C. Price, president of Livingston College in North Carolina. William A. Pledger of Georgia became vice-president, and Fortune secretary.

The proceedings of the convention received some attention in the Northern press, not all of it favorable. Among the Chicago papers the *Tribune* spoke disparagingly of Fortune's address as an "oily harangue" and characterized him as "a tricky New York coon" who was playing the part of "a Democratic decoy duck." A St. Louis paper insisted that the convention did not represent "the decent Negroes of the South."

It considered the Southern Negro a useful member of society, but a Northern Negro, like Fortune, who called himself an "Afro-American," it considered a "ridiculous blatherskite." The *Nation* accused the convention of seeking "class legislation" and expressed the opinion that such gatherings as the one in Chicago only strengthened the growing resentment against Negroes. On the other hand the New York *Sun*, speaking of the League, said, "The attempt may not succeed, but the object is entirely legitimate and respectable. The colored citizens are only exercising their rights as citizens to organize, agitate, cooperate."

In spite of the fact that the Chicago meeting appeared to be a success, the League lacked vitality and failed to attract mass support. At a second national meeting held in Knoxville in 1891, only a handful of delegates showed up. Those who came paid their own expenses because the local leagues lacked funds. Fortune was elected president of the languishing organization, but he was unable to carry out any part of the program he had envisaged when he first proposed the League. He had pinned his hopes upon a test case to attract attention and win support for the League, but all of his efforts in this direction were frustrated. Serious consideration was given to instituting a case after a member of the Afro-American League who was traveling by railroad in Tennessee was compelled to leave a Pullman car and ride in the Jim Crow coach. But plans for the suit were dropped because the League treasury was empty, and, as Fortune pointed out, it was "tomfoolery" for a group without funds to try to sue a railroad.

In August 1893 Fortune announced that the League was defunct because of lack of funds, lack of mass support, and lack of support from race leaders. He declared himself thoroughly discouraged and disillusioned and expressed the opinion that the attempt to organize the League had been premature. But as the condition of Southern Negroes continued to worsen, as lynchings increased and the disfranchisement movement gained strength, there were calls for a revival of the League. At a meeting in Rochester, New York, in September 1898, it was agreed to reconstitute the organization and to adopt a statement of objectives almost identical with the original platform

of the League. The revised organization, which took the . . .
name of National Afro-American Council, included in its membership most of the prominent Negroes of the day and received
much more attention in the white press than had the League,
but its achievements were few, and, like the League, it failed
to win a following among the Negro masses.

During this second phase three men were dominant. The
ostensible leaders were Fortune and Alexander Walters, a
bishop of the African Methodist Episcopal Zion Church, who
had been active in the Afro-American League in New York
City, and who took the initiative in calling the meeting in
Rochester. Between them the two men held the presidency and
the chairmanship of the executive committee during almost the
entire history of the Council. In the background loomed the
enigmatic figure of Booker T. Washington, who since 1895
had been acclaimed by the white press as a kind of official
leader and spokesman for the entire Negro population. Washington held no office in the Council and only occasionally
attended meetings, but his influence was great and pervasive.
The fact that the Council was identified with him was the
reason some Negroes supported it and accounted in part for
the publicity which the Council received. On the other hand
there were Negroes who held aloof and attacked the Council
because of hostility to Washington.

To most of his contemporaries Washington was the symbol
of the conservative, compromising, conciliatory approach to
race problems. In his published writings and utterances he
gave priority to economic progress and self-help as means for
improving the status of Negroes. He deprecated emphasis
upon political activity and made statements which could be
interpreted as indicating acquiescence in disfranchisement.
Behind the scenes he worked secretly against segregation, disfranchisement, and the Lily White movement, and was himself to become a powerful figure in the administration of
Theodore Roosevelt. These particular activities were so carefully concealed that only a few persons were aware of them,
and Washington was constantly under attack by Negro intellectuals who accused him of a willingness to betray his race
and a willingness to accept second-class citizenship for South-

ern Negroes. Washington himself sedulously sought to silence
or discredit his critics and to preserve a façade of racial
solidarity and unanimous support for his leadership. The
history of the Afro-American Council, which Washington
sought to dominate, was inextricably linked with the fight
over Washington as race leader. Almost every convention of
the Council became a battleground between supporters and
opponents of the Tuskegee Wizard with the result that other
issues tended to be obscured or confused.

Throughout the history of the Council, Washington and
Fortune, who had become friends soon after Washington went
to Tuskegee, were on terms of intimacy. In spite of marked
differences in temperament and personality there was a strong
bond of mutual admiration and affection between the two men,
and for years Fortune was one of Washington's closest con-
fidants. Although Fortune was by nature militant and impatient with compromise, he felt that he and Washington
were in agreement as to ultimate objectives and admitted that
residence in the South imposed peculiar restraints upon
Washington. In later years the friendship of the two was
punctuated by violent quarrels behind the scenes, but publicly
they continued to cooperate and Fortune continued to defend
Washington against his critics. Because of his support of Washington, Fortune, who a few years earlier had been the symbol
of aggressive, militant race leadership, came increasingly
under attack by Negro intellectuals and the anti-Washington
press which labeled him as Washington's subservient tool.
Washington's relations with Bishop Walters were never as
close as they were with Fortune. At times Walters appeared
to waver and to move in the direction of the anti-Washington
group, but for the most part he cooperated with the Tuskegeean
and helped to promote the appearance of racial solidarity under
Washington's leadership.

Washington's critics were openly active at the second
national convention of the Afro-American Council, which met
in Chicago in August 1899. One whole session was consumed in
debating resolutions condemning him, none of which was
adopted. W. E. B. Du Bois of Atlanta University, later to
become one of Washington's leading opponents, took an

active part in the convention but was careful to dissociate himself from the anti-Washington group. He told newspaper reporters that attacks upon Washington did not represent the true spirit of the convention and that he personally would be "very sorry if it went out into the world that this convention had said anything detrimental to one of the greatest men of our race."

In 1900 Washington was accused of attempting to undercut the Afro-American Council by calling a meeting in Boston to organize the National Negro Business League just prior to the date on which the Council convention was to meet in Indianapolis. The Chicago *Conservator,* one of his staunchest critics, declared that Washington, "instead of going to Indianapolis and helping Prof. Du Bois and the Council," had called an "opposition meeting" which would be injurious to the Council. It concluded, "It looks like Mr. Washington is determined to help no movement he does not inaugurate."

Whatever Washington's misgivings about the Council may have been in 1900, two years later his influence there was clearly in the ascendancy. At the convention in St. Paul in 1902, the first he attended, a slate of officers friendly to him was elected, with Fortune made president. In a letter to Washington, his private secretary gloated over the discomfiture of Du Bois and Ida Wells Barnett at their inability to control the convention. He exulted,

> It is not hard for you to understand that we control the Council *now.* . . . It was wonderful to see how completely your personality dominated everything at St. Paul.

Negro newspapers opposed to Washington were less pleased. The Boston *Guardian,* organ of Washington's most vitriolic critic, Harvard graduate Monroe Trotter, declared that Fortune would be president in name only—that the real power would be wielded by Washington.

> It is well known [the *Guardian* asserted], that Fortune is only a "me too" to whatever Washington aspires to do.
> These two men have long since formed themselves into one twain in their dealings with the Negro race, Fortune furnishing whatever brain the combination needs, and Washington the boodle.

At the 1903 convention in Louisville where Fortune was reelected, Trotter made a bitter attack upon Washington from the floor but was shouted down when he tried to introduce a series of resolutions against the Tuskegeean. Meanwhile Du Bois, whom Trotter had criticized after the 1902 convention for not challenging Washington, had by now openly aligned himself with Washington's critics.

While leaders fought among themselves for control of the Afro-American Council, the rank and file of the Negro population remained indifferent. The Council was having little more success than the earlier League in attracting members. Few of the local councils were active or had any real vitality, and none of them gave more than nominal financial support to the national organization. Early in 1904 Fortune went on a lecture tour in New York State and the Middle West for the purpose of organizing local councils and raising funds. He returned thoroughly discouraged, having spent on his personal expenses fifty dollars more than he was able to raise for the Council. Soon afterwards he resigned from the presidency of the Council, partly because of his discouragement over the apathy of the masses, partly as the result of one of his bitter periodic quarrels with Washington. In his letter of resignation he declared that race leaders had done what they could, "with small response from the masses of the race, to stem the fearful tide of civil and political and material degradation of the race to a condition of pariahs in the citizenship of the Republic." Of himself he said,

> I have grown old and impoverished in the lone struggle, and I must now take heed to my age and precarious health and devote my time and energies to repairing my personal fortunes in the interest of my immediate family.

Torn as it was by internal dissension and, more important, lacking adequate financial support, the Council made little progress in carrying forward the fight for racial equality. Every convention adopted resolutions embodying very much the same list of grievances against which Fortune had complained when he first called for the organization of the Afro-American League. At the top of the list was usually the denial of voting rights to Negroes. For example, the address to the nation adopted at the first convention of the Council in 1898 called attention to the persistent attempts to eliminate the Negro from politics in the South and declared,

> We are not to be eliminated. Suffrage is a federal guarantee and not a privilege to be conferred or withheld by the States. We contend for the principle of manhood suffrage as the most effective safeguard of citizenship.

But members of the Council disagreed among themselves as to the best method of implementing this declaration. One group insisted that the most effective way of forcing Southern states to permit Negroes to vote was to enforce the clause in the Fourteenth Amendment which provided for reduction of representation in the House of Representatives and in the Electoral College for states which limited the voting rights of citizens over twenty-one. Fortune was strongly opposed to this approach. He insisted that for the Council to endorse reduction of representation would give the impression that they acquiesced in disfranchisement and would give color to the idea that a state could legally disfranchise part of its citizens. Both Walters and Washington were won over to Fortune's position, and Washington in turn persuaded President Theodore Roosevelt not to recommend reduction of Southern representation. But Washington and Fortune were not always in complete agreement as to the position which the Council should take with regard to suffrage. Washington at various times indicated that he was not opposed to literacy and property requirements for voting if applied in the same way to both blacks and whites and not used merely for the purpose of disfranchising Negroes while permitting the illiterate and propertyless whites to vote. Doubtless as the results of Washington's influence the address adopted in 1898, mentioned above, while endorsing the principle of manhood suffrage, stated that the Council was not opposed to "legitimate restrictions of the suffrage," provided they applied to citizens of all states. In an editorial in the *Age* just before the Louisville convention of the Council in 1903, Fortune asserted that he and Washington differed on the suffrage question and

denied that he had ever been in agreement with accepting
educational or property requirements. He declared that the
right of voting was fundamental to citizenship and that it
should be protected by the federal government and that control of federal elections should be taken away from the states.
He prepared an address for delivery in Louisville in which he
said that all the wrongs which Negroes suffered grew out of
the abridgment of voting rights. The text of the speech appeared in the Louisville newspapers, but apparently it was not
actually delivered. Washington's critics insisted that the
speech had been suppressed at his orders. On the floor of the
convention Washington once more reiterated that he had no
objection to the disfranchisement of the ignorant Negro,
"provided the same class of the other race is similarly dealt
with," but he admitted that the purpose of suffrage measures
recently adopted in the South was primarily to disfranchise
Negroes.

In spite of the restraining influence which he seems to have
exercised in the matter of Fortune's speech and other public
pronouncements made in the name of the Council, behind the
scenes Washington lent his support to efforts to initiate test
cases against disfranchisement. As early as January 1899, he
and Fortune were discussing the possibility of a test of the
Louisiana suffrage law of 1898. It was decided that the Afro-
American Council of New Orleans should institute a case
with the sympathy and support of the national organization.
The services of a group of Negro lawyers were enlisted to
prepare a case. Part of the money for the lawyers' fees was
furnished by the Council, part of it from Washington's personal
funds, and the remainder by white philanthropists to whom
Washington appealed. Much time and a considerable sum of
money were expended, but the case never actually material-
ized. Fortune laid the blame for the failure upon the New
Orleans attorneys.

The Council took partial credit for bringing to trial a case
testing the Alabama voter registration law. The case grew out
of the refusal of the registrars of Montgomery County to enroll
Negro voters. One of the Negroes sought a court order to
compel the officers to register him. When the lower court

refused to issue the order, its decision was appealed and reached the United States Supreme Court in 1903. Wilford Smith, who had the distinction of being the only Negro lawyer who had won a case before that court, was employed to prepare the case. The Supreme Court upheld the refusal of the lower court to grant the order. Justice Oliver Wendell Holmes, who wrote the opinion, argued that the wrong complained of was political in nature and hence the remedy for it must be sought through legislation and not through the courts. In the light of this decision Wilford Smith expressed doubt as to whether it would even be possible to bring a case resulting in a decision which would cause the Fifteenth Amendment to be enforced in a practical way. He was convinced that the most effective way of insuring voting rights would be a federal registration law.

After Fortune's resignation as president in 1904 the Afro-American Council languished, but it was revived in 1905 by a call from Bishop Walters. The call for a revived Council came just after W. E. B. Du Bois and a group of anti-Washington intellectuals launched the Niagara Movement as a militant organization to fight for racial equality. The platform of the new group, including demands for suffrage and civil rights and economic betterment for Negroes, Fortune accused Du Bois of stealing from the declaration of principles which he had framed for the Afro-American League in 1890. Washington, alarmed by the challenge to his leadership which the Niagara Movement represented, sought to undermine the new organization by planting spies in its ranks, influencing the Negro press against it, and by persuading white philanthropists not to support it.

Newspapers opposed to Washington interpreted the move to revive the Afro-American Council solely as an effort to counteract the Niagara Movement and declared that the Council was dead. But in spite of its allegedly moribund condition the Council held the largest and most ambitious convention in its history in New York City in 1906. Booker T. Washington, who privately expressed the hope that the convention would adopt a conservative platform, was much in evidence. He gave a characteristic speech in which he condemned inflammatory statements by northern Negroes and stressed racial harmony, but the general tone of the convention was militant and uncompromising. An innovation was the participation of several white speakers. Among them was Oswald Garrison Villard, later to issue the call resulting in the formation of the National Association for the Advancement of Colored People, who spoke at Washington's invitation. Another was John E. Milholland, president of the Constitutional League, who was to become vice-president of the NAACP. In spite of previous failures plans were laid to raise funds to continue the fight in the courts against disfranchisement.

The ambitious plans discussed in New York failed to materialize. The Council continued to exist but was little more than a name. In the months following the New York meeting Washington apparently lost interest in the Council. He and Walters, who continued to serve as Council president, did not quarrel openly, but it was evident that Washington's influence over Walters and the Council had waned. Walters made some efforts at *rapprochement* with the Niagara group. There were newspaper reports that some of the Niagara men were present at the convention of the Afro-American Council in Baltimore in June 1907, and that most of the delegates to the convention "denounced Booker T. Washington as a Judas to his race." By 1908 Bishop Walters had joined the Niagara Movement, and in the political campaign of that year made common cause with Washington's arch enemy, Monroe Trotter, in an unsuccessful effort to swing the Negro vote away from Taft, whom Washington supported. But by this time it was evident that the Niagara Movement had little prospect of becoming an effective force. Du Bois himself admitted that there was less enthusiasm for the movement than there had been at the time of its founding.

In 1909 a group of white persons took the initiative in the formation of the National Association for the Advancement of Colored People. Among the six Negroes who joined in signing the call for the new organization were Bishop Walters, as president of the National Afro-American Council, and Du Bois from the Niagara Movement. At the national conference on the Negro which met in New York City in 1909 and took the preliminary steps in the establishment of the NAACP, resolutions reminiscent of the statements formed by Fortune in 1887 and 1890 were adopted. They demanded:

(1) That the Constitution be strictly enforced and the civil rights guaranteed under the Fourteenth Amendment be secured impartially to all.

(2) That there be equal educational opportunities for all . . . , and that public school expenditure be the same for the Negro and the white child.

(3) That in accordance with the Fifteenth Amendment the right of the Negro to the ballot on the same terms as other citizens be recognized in every part of the country.

Booker T. Washington's name was conspicuously absent from the list of Negroes who participated in the formation of the NAACP. In fact, he tried to undermine the new group. Nor did Fortune have any part in its formation. In 1907 he had suffered a nervous collapse, which was followed by years of mental and physical illness, and he became an almost forgotten figure. But the program of the NAACP, both in its objectives and methods, was essentially the program which Fortune had conceived for the Afro-American League twenty years earlier.

7

The Overture to Protest: Beginnings of the Du Bois-Washington Controversy

ELLIOTT RUDWICK

In 1899 the Georgia legislature was in a mood to consider the elimination of Negroes from politics and debated the Hardwick Bill which set literacy and property qualifications for voting. Although, before and after, Du Bois minimized the value of legislative lobbying, he and several others issued a statement opposing the bill. After sending it to the lawmakers, he took his case to a wider audience and wrote an article for the *Inde-*

SOURCE: Elliott Rudwick, *W. E. B. Du Bois: A Study in Minority Group Leadership* (Philadelphia: University of Pennsylvania Press, 1960), pp. 54–76 (footnotes omitted). Copyright © 1960 by the University of Pennsylvania Press. Reprinted by permission of the publisher.

pendent. He assured readers that his protest was presented in "calm and respectful terms." The Atlanta professor did not object to the actual qualifications; he simply asked that they be applied to both races in a fair manner. He attacked the "grandfather clause" and the part of the bill dealing with a citizen's ability to interpret the Constitution. Du Bois realized both sections would transform the colored race into political pariahs. The lawmakers did not enact the bill, but within a few years, Georgia (and other Southern states) effectively disfranchised Negroes by amendments to state constitutions.

In 1900 Du Bois led a group of Georgia Negroes in presenting another petition to the legislature; this time they hoped to prevent the passage of a law intended to reduce state appropriations for Negro education. As usual, the Du Bois protest was restrained and he argued that the welfare of the state was his primary concern. He contended that literate Negroes contributed more to the community because the public schools taught them to be thrifty and industrious; he suggested, if country schoolhouses closed, Negroes would become discontented, migrate to cities, and thus create labor shortages in rural districts. He observed (with tongue in cheek) that if Negroes were inherently deficient, the frustration of an educational challenge would force them to accept a lower level of aspiration. He also pointed out that an unfair division of the state appropriations would be an excuse for intervention by white philanthropists or the federal government, thereby possibly removing Southern whites from control over the Negro educational system.

At the turn of the century, Du Bois was also designated spokesman for a committee of Georgia Negroes who complained they could not use the new Carnegie Library in Atlanta. Receiving no satisfaction from the board of directors, Du Bois published an account of the interview in the *Independent* as a propaganda piece, depicting an educated Negro's peremptory exclusion from a social institution which was ostensibly dedicated to the pursuit of learning. Du Bois admitted that whites needed libraries, but he asserted Negroes had greater need of them. He questioned the legality of expending public funds for the exclusive benefit of the whites.

The head of the board thought a special library would be built for Negroes "in the future," probably financed by Northern philanthropists and the city of Atlanta. He added that the new white library might even come to be considered inferior to the projected Negro one, and at this point the interview was terminated "politely." Du Bois and the Negro delegation "walked home wondering."

Du Bois used his talent as an essayist to publish numerous articles in popular magazines such as the *Atlantic Monthly*, *World's Work*, and the *Independent*, and his reputation increased as a leading interpreter of the Negro problem. The pieces were often impressionistic; their author was essentially a propagandist seeking the sympathy of the whites. He attempted to persuade whites that they did not know very much about his race, and that a careful study would confirm the damage which racism had done to Negroes. He observed that slavery had made large numbers of colored people careless and dependent; poorer Negroes were taught during the Reconstruction period that crooked politics represented a small, but necessary, source of income. In the face of charges that the Negro was a criminalistic race, Du Bois replied that "the first and greatest cause of Negro crime in the South is the convict-lease system." Crime was a "symptom of wrong social conditions," and, according to the Atlanta professor, colored people could hardly place their faith in a law which permitted lynchers to go unpunished.

Du Bois pointed out that the race was being maligned, although it had proven itself capable of advancing. In one article, he noted increases in property and land acreage as indices of racial growth. For effect, he stretched the truth and attempted to create the impression of a high degree of unity among the leaders and followers within the race. He discussed the Afro-American Council, representative of the "mental attitude of the millions," and noted that the organization had recently declared the United States government was duty-bound to protect the "life, liberty and due process" of the race and to legislate against lynching. Once more, he admitted the "weaknesses" of the Negro masses and in 1901 even acknowledged "that it is possible and sometimes best that a partially undeveloped people should be ruled by the best of their stronger and better neighbors for their own good, until such time as they can start to fight the world's battles alone."

He wanted to see the reestablishment of friendship and a "community of intellectual life" between "the best elements of both races." In seeking to encourage the good will of the whites, he had ambivalently minimized the effectiveness of legislative lobbying and propaganda presentations, but he did not relax his request for Negro suffrage and federal aid to education.

Du Bois even tried to frighten the whites into remedying conditions and stated that he observed rumblings of Negro resentment which could become dangerous to the established order. Southern Negroes, forced to be a party to the "hypocritical compromise," flattered the whites but whispered their "real aspirations." Northern Negroes, beaten down by discrimination, were drifting toward "radicalism." The "pent up vigor" and the "might of powerful human souls" would erupt inexorably into a strong protest, the exact nature of which Du Bois in 1901 left to the imagination of the whites. Examining a poverty-stricken rural Georgia Negro community, Du Bois foresaw the genesis of "a cheap, dangerous socialism." In some of his essays of the period, the disheartened Negroes were pictured as the blundering or the faithless minority of the race; in others, the bitterness was described as more pervasive. In these articles the theme of radicalism was extremely overdrawn, probably for its shock effect. Du Bois also conveyed a higher level of unity within the race than the facts warranted. Taken together, these essays indicate that Du Bois, while accepting the separation of the Negro masses, was focusing more and more on the rights inherent in the "American creed."

In vain, Du Bois exhorted the Southern whites to demonstrate evidences of friendship and without success he had tried legislative lobbying. In 1901 he considered judicial review as a method of raising the status of the educated and more affluent Negroes, against whom a Georgia law had been passed denying them the privilege of using Pullman car facilities, even when travelling outside of the state. In reply to Du Bois' inquiry, the United States Interstate Commerce Commission suggested the name of a Negro lawyer to prepare the test case, and the Atlanta University professor, whose financial resources were small, sought the counsel of Booker T. Washington. The Tuskegeean was pleased Du Bois had managed the project so well, and considerably later he agreed to contribute anonymously. Washington and Du Bois attempted to arrange an interview with Robert T. Lincoln, the president of the Pullman Company, but the latter was not eager to meet with them. After years of delay, the lawsuit was finally shelved.

Du Bois involved himself in other limited social action skirmishes. In 1903 he heard that an official from the Rhodes Scholarship Foundation would visit Georgia in search of candidates, and the Negro sociologist reminded the representative that Atlanta University's faculty and students would not be invited to the scholarship conference which the white schools had scheduled. Du Bois learned that although Atlanta University might not be on the itinerary, Booker T. Washington would be consulted. The Tuskegeean was informed later that Du Bois' school had been ignored because its Mathematics Department was below caliber. According to Washington's account, he pleaded the cause of the Negro college men and had been assured the Rhodes Foundation would give them favorable consideration in the future.

The Pullman and Rhodes cases are illustrations of the cooperation between Washington and Du Bois before the complete rupture in their relationship in 1904. As early as 1900, the Tuskegeean recommended the Atlanta professor for the top administrative position of the segregated school system in the nation's capital. Du Bois attended several of the Hampton and Tuskegee annual conferences and at the time called them "great" schools. However, in 1901, he wrote another appraisal of Washington. Obviously the Atlanta professor had formed significant reservations which he was not ready to publicize as his own views. He observed that Washington's leadership was not a "popular" one, and that many "educated and thoughtful Negroes" (among them Paul Lawrence Dunbar) only mildly appreciated the Hampton-Tuskegee philosophy of industrial education. According to Du Bois, these men could not truly support the Tuskegeean because of their advocacy of the Fisk-

Atlanta program of higher education. Many placed their faith in racial "self-assertion" and suffrage, and distrusted Washington because of his close identification with Southern whites.

On the other hand, Du Bois portrayed Washington's emphasis on industrial education as an essential link with the expansion of the Southern economy. He noted that the program attracted much-needed Northern and Southern aid. Washington was presented as the product of history and as the reflection of the industrial emergence of a nation "a little shamed of having bestowed so much sentiment on Negroes and was [now] concentrating its energies on Dollars." The "successful" Tuskegeean was a man of "evident sincerity of purpose," although the demands of the new system caused him to be "a little narrow."

Relations between the two men remained cordial—at least on the surface. During the summer of 1901 Du Bois was invited to be a house guest at Washington's camp in West Virginia, but declined because of previous writing commitments. The following year, however, Du Bois—concerned about the growing "breach" between the Negro colleges and industrial schools—asked the Tuskegeean to address the Atlanta Conference on the Negro Artisan. Washington agreed, and in his speech he discussed the primacy of agriculture, the evils of urban life, and the superfluity of college education which left students unprepared for "fundamental . . . wealth producing occupations." His message undoubtedly succeeded in further widening the cleavage, although he recognized the contributions of Du Bois and the Atlanta conferences. Certainly, no one could quarrel with Washington's statement that agriculture would continue to be the race's basic industry for a long time, but his characterization of "parasite" jobs must have offended many of the Atlanta alumni: "I would much rather see a young colored man graduate from college and go out and start a truck garden, a dairy farm, or conduct a cotton plantation, and thus become a first-hand producer of wealth, rather than a parasite living upon the wealth originally produced by others, seeking uncertain and unsatisfactory livelihood in temporary and questionable positions."

About this time, Du Bois considered the possibility of an

explicit division of labor between Atlanta University (for em-
pirical research) and Hampton Institute (for practical applica-
tions). He suggested that the General Education Board, and
Booker T. Washington, be approached to support the plan,
although he was somewhat hesitant and wondered if he would
have independence and "freedom" under such an arrangement. During this same period, he was approached by Booker
T. Washington's friends, who tried to persuade him to work for
Hampton Institute and become an editor of a new Negro
periodical. In the clearest terms he demanded the right to
establish editorial policy, refusing to be controlled by the
"Tuskegee philosophy." Nothing more came of the Hampton
invitation. Other backers of Booker T. Washington told Du Bois
he could have a bright future at Tuskegee Institute, but the
school's founder seemed "suspicious" of him. Du Bois wanted
to continue his annual researches and doubted Washington's
interest in them; he also feared he might be required to serve
as a Tuskegee "ghost-writer." Both men came to distrust each
other and, in order to understand the controversy which became public in 1903, the basic beliefs of Washington should be
examined.

Booker T. Washington, according to white Southern leaders,
espoused "a perfect system of accommodation" between Negroes and whites in the "New South." He became the spokesman for those who wanted the Negro race to be a labor force
and not a political force. He separated politics and economics
and argued that, when colored people had advanced economically and produced industrious workers and successful businessmen, whites would not oppose Negro suffrage. Washington
and his followers did not seem to consider it too significant that
there were many incompetent whites who were voting and
many competent Negroes who were not. Nor did the Washingtonians appreciate that political power could also improve, to
a limited extent, economic conditions in the race. While he said
he wanted nothing less than what was promised in the Constitution, he emphasized that Negroes would receive "all privileges of the law" *after* they were "prepared." He believed the
acquisition of property would make Negroes "conservative"
voters, especially if they "consulted the whites before voting."

Actually, Washington did not condone racial disfranchisement although most whites thought he did. When the Louisiana legislature sought to disfranchise Negroes in 1898, Washington complained to the lawmakers and newspapers. After the law was passed he secretly gathered names of people in Boston who would contribute money to test the law in the courts. Yet he continued to minimize politics as a road to racial advancement. Paradoxically, he also served as presidential personnel adviser to Roosevelt and was consulted on both Negro and white appointments.

Since ballots were not as essential as jobs, the Tuskegeean dedicated himself to training Negroes for vocational opportunities. He believed Southerners, with their long history of racism, would not support Negro education unless they were convinced a docile, efficient labor supply would result. Industrial training, therefore, evolved from an environment of expediency, but under the Tuskegeean it became the absolute principle embracing nearly every virtue. Three years after he opened Tuskegee Institute in 1881, the state legislature of Alabama was so impressed it voted the school an annual appropriation. The Negro leader had discovered he gained tangible help by refusing to protest against injustice and by emphasizing harmony within the framework of the caste system. Finding so much opportunity for moral growth in "beginning at the bottom," he almost seemed overjoyed that the whites made it possible for Negroes to start with so little.

He said his people should educate themselves for those tasks which the community would permit. Since he contended that the race's main concern was with industrial-agricultural pursuits, he believed the educational system must reflect that fact. According to him, white and black proponents of higher education would benefit the Negro race if they recognized industrial education as the proper beginning. When property had been acquired, art and literature could then be cultivated. On countless occasions, the Tuskegeean denied his program was opposed to Negro higher education. However, for every statement of Washington which seemed to support liberal arts, there were many others in which he demonstrated a distrust. He made innumerable references to a young man living in a hovel, dressed in grease-splattered clothes, but busily studying a French grammar. He often spoke of the Negro boy who went to Hell in the big city after receiving the kind of education that caused him to lose interest in his father's farm. Certainly, Washington was critical of the Negro colleges. It was fashionable for writers of the period to state that higher education did not really compete with industrial education and that both contributed to each other; actually, the Tuskegeean, while seeming to grant Negro higher education its own small sphere of influence, proposed to make industrial education a universal training ground.

After his sentiments were acclaimed at the Atlanta Exposition in 1895, it was not a difficult matter to find financial aid and cooperation from Northern philanthropists (such as Andrew Carnegie), whose economic philosophy Washington had appropriated. In 1901 he helped to form the Southern Education Board; the organization was composed of prominent educators and industrialists and subsidized Negro institutions which preached the gospel of industrial education. The following year the program was expanded and the General Education Board was established. To influential whites Washington had become the only *bona fide* representative of the Negro race.

Now that the Washingtonian ideology has been reviewed, it will be compared and contrasted with the Du Boisian program at the beginning of the twentieth century. Up to that time, Du Bois differed with Washington on many things, but he was not so far from the Tuskegeean ideologically as were other men who later regarded the Atlanta professor as the firebrand apostle of the anti-Washingtonian movement. For the most part, Du Bois and Washington respected each other, although their personalities were too different to build a friendship. With the Tuskegeean he placed his emphasis upon securing the good will of the white upper class, instead of relying primarily upon legislation to raise the status of the Negroes. Nevertheless, both men sought to prevent racist legislation from being passed and both attempted to test racist laws which had been enacted.

The two leaders pointed up Negro "weaknesses" and exhorted the race to transform itself morally and become increasingly industrious and thrifty. Washington and Du Bois argued that their race, living in a milieu of separateness, had its own destiny and its own differentness. According to Du Bois, his people were essentially musical, artistic, humble, and jocular; all of these traits provided a necessary complement to American commercialism. Washington saw his people as cheerful, devoted, tractable, and humble; these attributes served to furnish an excellent labor force for the capitalist system. Du Bois on occasion was more critical of capitalism but still supported Negro entrepreneurs. The two educators favored Negro nationalism or racial self-sufficiency. Washington's system was domestic, while Du Bois' "Pan-Negroism" encompassed the United States as well as other lands, such as Africa and the West Indies.

As already shown, the major difference between the two philosophies was in connection with education. Du Bois suggested a plan centered around the Negro college, with a cultured brain trust urging the race forward; while the Tuskegeean emphasized industrial education and repudiated "abstract knowledge." It is questionable that there would have been a conflict between these ideologies if the Washingtonians had not insisted their program was so valuable it warranted universality, and if they had not annointed their chieftain as "the accepted representative man among ten million of our fellow citizens." As a result, many whites begrudged Negro colleges their meager operational budgets because of the belief that such money was squandered on the teaching of useless subjects, and should have been earmarked in the first place for industrial schools, where some good could have been accomplished. At a time when Du Bois watched his beloved Atlanta University starving, the Washingtonians were enjoying prosperity and ever-increasing influence.

Another difference which was slowly becoming apparent concerned the suffrage question. Both men advocated it for literate Negroes, although Washington stressed "preparation" for the ballot more than he propagandized for immediate voting. While evident before 1902, this split was to be sharper in the following months. Whites were soothed by Washington's gradualism, happy in the knowledge that nothing "dynamitic"

would be attempted by Negroes. Pursuant to the Washingtonian formula, slowness was actually speed because it guaranteed the race's salvation, when Negroes could "be great and
yet small, learned and yet simple, high and yet the servant of
all." While Du Bois disavowed useless complaint, he seemed
to hold Negroes less responsible for their condition than Washington did. The Great Barrington Negro protested calmly, but
he presented a picture to the whites of racial discontent and
incipient revolution. He wanted a rapprochement but his
words suggested more urgency than Washington's.

In Du Bois' 1901 article in *Dial*, he had pointed out that
there were some Negro leaders who opposed Washington's
conciliatory approach. Unmentioned among the insurgents was
William Monroe Trotter, who founded the Boston *Guardian*,
the organ which became the thorniest critic of Washingtonian
policies. The *Guardian* editor asked Booker T. Washington:

> To what end will your vaulting ambition hurl itself? Does not
> the fear of future hate and execration, does not the sacred
> rights and hopes of a suffering race, in no wise move you?
> The colored people see and understand you; they know that
> you have marked their very freedom for destruction, and yet,
> they endure you almost without murmur! O times, O evil
> days, upon which we have fallen!

In the sharpest language, Trotter termed Washington a political boss who masked his machine by pretending to be an
educator. He resented the Tuskegeean's connections with President Roosevelt, because the apostle of industrial education,
according to the editor, opposed Negro participation in politics. Trotter also criticized Washington for trusting the President (who encouraged the lily-white Republican party in the
South). On one occasion the *Guardian* editor accused Washington of being instrumental in the appointment of a lily-white
Republican to replace a white Democrat as Collector of Internal Revenue in Alabama; the journalist implied that a cash
reward was expected for that political chore.

Trotter, besides editing the *Guardian*, was the "spearhead
of sentiment" of the Boston Radicals, a group of Negroes who
had graduated from various New England colleges. By 1902

the lines of battle were becoming more sharply drawn and Trotter demanded that a man support the Washingtonians or the Radicals. He was particularly desirous of wooing Du Bois into the Radical camp, since the latter's academic achievements impressed educated Negroes. According to Kelly Miller, Trotter was sensitive to the charges of the Washingtonians that his position was visionary, and the *Guardian* editor was determined to set up an organizational structure and attract wider support for social action projects. Miller contended Trotter was aware of his own oratorical shortcomings and "began to cast about for a man of showy faculties who could stand before the people as leader of his cause. He wove a subtle net about W. E. B. Du Bois, the brilliant writer and scholar, and gradually weaned him from his erstwhile friendship for Mr. Washington, so as to exploit his prominence and splendid powers in behalf of the hostile forces."

Actually it need not be hypothesized that Trotter hatched a cunning plot to secure Du Bois' assistance or that Du Bois had become his unwitting tool. By 1902 Du Bois, while not "in absolute opposition" to Washington, had moved closer ideologically to the Boston journalist. The Atlanta professor's redefinitions essentially resulted from his increasing disenchantment with the Tuskegeean's methods and platform. Du Bois could only have responded with wrath to a typical Washingtonian statement of that year: "One thousand bushels of potatoes produced by the hands of an educated Negro are worth more in solving our problems than dozens of orations or tons of newspaper articles."

Nevertheless, he refused to be actively and publicly anti-Washingtonian, not only because he did not disagree with the Tuskegeean's Negro nationalism and self-help themes, but also because he believed that as a social scientist he should be removed from the tumult of a leadership struggle. According to Maude Trotter Stewart, her brother was very frustrated when he discovered that Du Bois was "just not strong in wanting to fight."

In September of 1902, Du Bois attacked ideas to which Booker T. Washington obviously subscribed, but the Tuskegeean was not directly named. The Atlanta professor was critical of those who discouraged a liberal arts education for Negroes. He considered the exclusive preoccupation with industrial education was futile and reaffirmed that the only effective foundation was higher education, since "progress in human affairs is more often a pull than a push, a surging forward of the exceptional man, and the lifting of his duller brethren." Because of the "dangerous" segregation patterns, educated Negroes would serve as stewards of the race, but Du Bois clearly defined their roles as temporary. Once more, in wrestling with his conflicting desires for Negro nationalism and integration, he seemed to conclude in favor of the latter: "The present social separation and acute race-sensitiveness must eventually yield to the influence of culture, as the South grows civilized."

Trotter was so delighted with Du Bois' article that he used it as the basis of an editorial in the *Guardian* which was entitled, "Two Negro Writers, But How Different." He made a stinging comparison between a selfish, unoriginal, and thoroughly unenlightened Washington; and a brilliant and resourceful Du Bois, whose contribution was "beyond all praise, with one or two exceptions it is without a doubt the very best thing that has been said by a Negro on the question of Negro education in America." Du Bois' reaction to this fulsome editorial is not known, but it would have been understandable if he were overjoyed by such a reception, especially in view of the mounting atmosphere of distrust and condemnation between him and the Washingtonians. Perhaps such red-carpeting by the Boston Radicals enabled him to make his break with Booker T. Washington more easily. Within a few months, in January of 1903, Trotter wrote a front-page article announcing Du Bois would soon speak on a program sponsored by the Boston Literary Association. The following week Trotter reported Du Bois was given an "ovation" and "the presence of this educated Negro must have won over every one present to the positive advocacy of the higher education for the race, though Prof. Du Bois said nothing of that subject."

During the spring of 1903, Du Bois published *Souls of Black Folk*, a book which James Weldon Johnson described as having "a greater effect upon and within the Negro race in America than any other single book published in this country since Uncle Tom's Cabin." There was no doubt that the chapter, "Of Mr. Booker T. Washington and Others," created an intellectual and emotional flutter for many, and Johnson credited this analysis of racial leadership with effecting "a coalescence of the more radical elements and [it] made them articulate, thereby creating a split of the race into two contending camps. . . ." Basil Mathews, one of Booker T. Washington's biographers, agreed that this essay was a crucial factor in furnishing "the anti-Washington movement, for the first time, with a coherent argument." William Ferris, a contemporary Negro observer, contended that Du Bois' volume became the "political bible" of the educated segment of the race and that Du Bois was honored as the "long-looked-for political Messiah." Actually, the evidence seems to indicate that, although the Radicals thrived on Du Bois' book, the Atlanta professor still refused to take an active leadership role in the promotion of a formal organization and continued "to occupy middle ground."

Whatever Du Bois' desires, *Souls of Black Folk* completely alienated him from the Tuskegeeans, and a perusal of the contents of the chapter, "Of Mr. Booker T. Washington and Others," will disclose the reasons quickly. Essentially, Du Bois said nothing that he had not stated before; this time, however, he *explicitly* indicted Washington. It seemed to Du Bois that Booker Washington arose primarily as a compromiser between the North and South and that his ideology "practically accepts the alleged inferiority of the Negro." Du Bois observed that within the last years, his race had become disfranchised and suffered egregious losses in civil status, as well as in the support of its institutions of higher education. While the Atlanta professor admitted these deprivations were not the direct consequences of the Tuskegeean's teachings, he did hold Washington accountable for their acceleration. He charged that the Tuskegeean had sealed an economic bargain with the South, wherein civil rights and college degrees were unimportant, at least temporarily. Du Bois argued that the race could not forge ahead without the attainment of these very objectives which had been surrendered. He did not deny the importance of pacifying the South, but he refused to pay Washington's price which he interpreted as degradation and virtual slavery. Du Bois, acknowledging the Tuskegeean had lobbied to prevent the Negroes' disfranchisement, charged the leader had also condoned the ever-tightening caste system. He proposed several "supplementary truths" to Washington's "dangerous half-truths" that Negroes bore the major responsibility for remedying their problems: slavery and race prejudice were important causes of the low status of the race; an adequate Negro educational system depended on the training of teachers by the colleges; and self-help required more effective encouragement from affluent whites. The Atlanta University professor advised disaffection from "part of the work of [the Negroes'] greatest leader."

After *Souls of Black Folk,* the *Outlook,* a white weekly friendly to Booker T. Washington, portrayed Du Bois as a whining, impractical racial renegade who was "half ashamed of being a Negro." The Tuskegeean-dominated press embarked upon a campaign to vilify and intimidate Du Bois. For example, the Washington *Colored American* vigorously urged President Bumstead of Atlanta University to silence the professor:

> If Atlanta University intends to stand for Dr. Du Bois' outgivings, if it means to seek to destroy Tuskegee Institute, so that its own work can have success, it is engaged in poor business to start with; and in the next place, the assurance can safely be given that it will avail them nothing. Tuskegee will go on. It will succeed. Booker Washington will still loom large on the horizon, notwithstanding the petty annoyances of Du Bois and his ilk. Dr. Bumstead in his Northern campaigns has pretended to acknowledge the efficacy of Tuskegee's methods and also to recognize the necessity of the two kinds of education—the very thing Booker Washington himself does. Visitors who were at Tuskegee during the late Negro Conference will readily remember a speech made there by Dr. Bumstead, in which he declared most positively that there was no friction between the two schools, and was also most loud in his protestations of friendship and interest. Let him prove himself by curbing the outgivings and ill-advised criticisms of the learned Doctor who is now in his employ; that is, if Du Bois does not really represent him and the sentiment of Atlanta University. . . .

Perhaps the fairest analysis and evaluation of Du Bois' aims appeared in an essay by J. S. Bassett in the *South Atlantic Quarterly*. (Trotter was so pleased with this piece that he gave it front-page treatment in the *Guardian*.) Unlike many others, Bassett did not view *Souls* as a frenzied, malevolent assault on Tuskegee. Since the college-trained Negroes had been all but ignored in the tumult of industrial education, Bassett held that Du Bois' defense of their interests was understandable and justifiable in any intelligent consideration of the methods to establish an interracial peace. Recognizing that Negroes did require cultured leaders as well as skilled workers, Bassett tried to allay the economic fears of the southerners by assuring them that there would always be an ample Negro labor force, because only a small minority would ever pursue higher education. Commenting on a popular racist book entitled, *The Negro a Beast or the Image of God*, he asked whether a "Beast" could have produced *Souls of Black Folk*.

In July of 1903 Du Bois took another step closer to the Boston *Guardian* when he too made it clear that the Tuskegeean was actually a political boss. He went further than he had in his critique of the preceding spring and unfairly increased Washington's responsibility for the anti-Negro attitudes of the whites: "He has so manipulated the forces of a strained political and social situation as to bring about among the factors the greatest consensus of opinion in this country since the Missouri Compromise." The last thing Washington wanted to be called was a political colossus and friendly newspapers answered this "covert sneer."

While Du Bois was willing to flail away at Washington he was still reluctant to take an active leadership role in marshalling the Radicals. He did not accompany William Monroe Trotter to the annual Afro-American Council meetings at Louisville in the summer of 1903, and the *Guardian* editor led the Radicals' unsuccessful struggle to wrestle control of the Council from the Washingtonians. At the sessions Washington was execrated as a villain who sold his soul, and a free-for-all ensued after the Council passed a resolution endorsing Theodore Roosevelt. Trotter, accurately charging Washington owned the organization, was defeated after he was unable to substitute a resolution condemning the President for not influencing Congress to help the Negroes. The Boston *Guardian* editor also damned Roosevelt for selecting white Democrats to fill political posts in the South, while sending Negro Republicans home empty-handed. The Radicals sought to generate interest for a prompt reconvening of the Council, and Booker T. Washington commissioned Emmett J. Scott, his private secretary, to persuade Negro newspaper editors to pay no attention.

The infuriated Trotter returned to Boston and on the night of July 30–31, 1903, he led a rebellion against the Tuskegeean which came to be known as the Boston Riot. It was this incident which finally brought Du Bois into active leadership of the Radicals. The Atlanta professor did not have any connection with the fateful skirmish and did not arrive in Boston (where he stayed with Trotter as a house guest) until after the disturbance. His first reaction after hearing about the uprising was a feeling of exasperation and anger—at Trotter's impetuosity. However, after making an investigation, he concluded the riot was actually precipitated by a Washington man. He fumed when the *Guardian* editor was jailed as a provocateur, and the professor wrote a letter (which the Boston *Guardian* printed) supporting the journalist. Perhaps it was this published letter which caused some "prominent and influential man" (George Foster Peabody, a backer of Booker T. Washington) to broadcast the rumor that Du Bois was linked "with Trotter and [the] conspiracy." The note certainly disturbed trustees of Atlanta University and it was discussed at a meeting of the school's executive committee. President Bumstead maintained complete confidence in Du Bois, and the group took no punitive measures against the sociologist.

Nevertheless, both the President and Chaplain of Atlanta University were anxious about the rumor. Du Bois understood their fears and dispatched a note to Peabody, disclaiming any responsibility for the riot. In frankness, he rejected Trotter's excesses but respected his honesty. He asserted his friend was "far nearer the right" than Booker Washington, who was "leading the way backward." Naturally, this second Du Bois letter

did not please Bumstead, who had hoped the Atlanta professor would have been conciliatory and simply acknowledge his
innocence in the Boston episode. He was unprepared for
Du Bois' comparison and feared the reaction of Peabody and
other Tuskegeean friends. When Atlanta University's leading
trustees examined a copy of the note, there was "quite an out-
burst of dissent from fully half of those present." Bumstead
remained loyal to his friend but seemed more conscious than
ever "of the difficulty of being honest with ourselves and at the
same time being judicious in dealing with those who do not
agree with us."

The Boston Riot itself demonstrated the plethora of emo-
tions which were evoked and the rising tide of resistance which
was evident when Booker T. Washington arrived at the African Methodist Episcopal Church for a Business League rally.
For several months the Tuskegeean had prudently declined
speaking engagements in Boston, the Radical capital, because
he wished to avoid the kind of disturbance which finally occurred. Washington's circumspection only caused Trotter to
announce belligerently that the educator would not make a
public appearance because of cowardice. The group at the
church on that night of July 30 was a large one, since the
Washingtonians, overzealous in their acceptance of the Radicals' challenge, made strenuous efforts to publicize the program
and printed a long list of their prominent supporters. Many
people came to the church because they heard "something"
was going to happen. W. H. Lewis and T. Thomas Fortune,
both Washingtonians, addressed the assemblage, and, whenever they referred to their leader, hissing sounds reverberated
throughout the room. The crowd grew restless and angry. After
the Tuskegeean was introduced, he was unable to say more
than a few words because of the furor, and finally twenty-
five policemen were called. When the Negro chieftain proceeded, he unwisely chose to unwind an old anecdote about a
mule, and the Trotter men began to fume again. Trotter arose
and asked Washington several loaded questions on education
and voting: "In view of the fact that you are understood to
be unwilling to insist upon the Negro having his every right
(both civil and political) would it not be a calamity at this

juncture to make you our leader? . . . Is the rope and the torch all the race is to get under your leadership?"

The audience by this time was completely out of control; men were yelling and hissing; simultaneously, some enterprising partisans brought forth "red pepper and stink bombs." Trotter was arrested and became a martyr—his followers conducted sympathy services in Washington, New York, and Chicago.

Booker T. Washington philosophically described the Boston Riot as inevitable and his friends sought to discredit the Radicals as emotionally unstable, offering the excesses during the affair as proof. The Boston white newspapers such as the *Herald* and the *Transcript* reported the episode and held Trotter responsible. Emmett J. Scott and Washington efficiently dispatched these comments to various Negro newspapers for reprinting. Since the clippings in the white press and in most of the Negro papers were friendly to Washington, Scott was undoubtedly correct in saying that the Radicals had lost ground. Washington went further and wrote to his friends that he was convinced Trotter and Company had "completely killed themselves" among all elements—Negro and white—in Boston. Since Du Bois' name did not appear among the culprits, it seems reasonable to conclude the Tuskegean knew that the Atlanta professor was not involved in the fracas. According to Washington's version, Trotter was removed from the church "in handcuffs, yelling like a baby." Actually, the Boston editor enjoyed his martyrdom and spurned an opportunity to avoid incarceration and accept probation. Though locked up, he continued to write for the *Guardian*.

Two weeks after the riot, Washington wrote to President Roosevelt and told him that after a calm analysis (in a "purely unselfish . . . disinterested" light) he felt only pity for the Radicals. In his supposedly unbiased opinion, the Radicals were simply jealous of his good fortune; these men were parasites who had never come up the hard way through "natural and gradual processes." Their present life was therefore "artificial" and they believed Washington should place the race in a similar "artificial" milieu. Years later, Washington recalled the night of July 30 and indicted the "intellectuals" who thought "the world owes them a living." Unbelievably, he contended that some of these educated men profited so much from protesting that they would have been unhappy if the Negro problem were solved.

It is difficult to assess how much of Washington's implacable stand toward the opposition was caused by his own jealousy of their college degrees and cultural advantages. How much of his resentment of their demands for independent thinking was due to psychological uneasiness in dealing with these intelligent men, and what proportion of his unyielding attitudes was the result of guilt feelings, caused by his frustrating silences before the white philanthropists? Did Washington's antipathy for the Radicals stem in part from the historic social distance between free Negroes and those who, like himself, experienced the slave status. Most of his opponents had forebears who were free for many decades before the Civil War. They possessed a sense of reverence, perhaps even snobbishness, about their lineage. In Du Bois' own writings about his family, for example, there was an obvious sense of pride in "our free birth."

At any rate, the Washingtonians were determined to have their full measure of revenge and they continued in their efforts to penalize all of the principals of the Boston Riot. Emmett J. Scott pursued George Washington Forbes, the cofounder of the *Guardian,* and tried to pull strings to have him dismissed from his Boston library job. Another attempt was made in 1903 to hurt the *Guardian.* Many weeks before the July 30 disturbance, William Pickens, a suspected Washingtonian, delivered an address in Boston on Haitian history, and Trotter said unkind things about him in the newspaper. In the fury after the riot, Washington's attorney visited Pickens and recommended the institution of a libel suit against Trotter. In October, Du Bois, hoping to quash the Tuskegee-financed suit, dispatched a letter to a good friend of Pickens. Although Pickens eventually withdrew the suit, the Atlanta professor knew who had instigated the legal affair.

In the wake of the Boston Riot, Trotter's imprisonment, and the legal activities against the Boston *Guardian,* Du Bois increased his emotional commitments to the Radicals. He had painfully observed the power and implacable influence of Booker T. Washington and was filled with disgust and anger. Now he was finally able to overcome his reluctance to assume command of the social movement which was dedicated to the Negroes' prompt realization of the promises in the "American creed." A few months after the riot he led the Radicals in a fruitless attempt to negotiate an honorable peace with the Tuskegeeans; in 1905 he founded the Niagara Movement, an organization which waged an all-out war upon the gradualist approach to race relations.

8

Alfred Sam and an African Return: A Case Study in Negro Despair

GILBERT GEIS AND WILLIAM BITTLE

In the pre-dawn grayness of August 21, 1914, the British merchant vessel *Liberia* cleared the port of Galveston and steamed off into the Gulf of Mexico, en route to the Gold Coast Colony, British West Africa. On board were sixty American Negroes, their jubilance somewhat restrained by their apprehensions, but intent, nonetheless, upon resettling in a location where life might be easier for them and where political and social equality would be their right. They were returning, they believed,

SOURCE: *Phylon*, XXIII (Summer 1962), 178–94 (footnotes omitted). Reprinted by permission.

to their own people and a better existence than they had found in the New World.

The leader of the group was Alfred Charles Sam, an implausible, "low, brown man" who had spent the past year recruiting emigrants from back-country cotton farms in eastern Oklahoma. Slow-speaking and with a convincingly ungrammatical accent, Sam claimed to be an Ashanti chief born in the interior of the Gold Coast and ruling, at one time, over a town in West Akim. His followers, feverish to believe him, called him "Chief."

Left behind as the *Liberia* labored slowly away from her berthing in the Bolivar Roads were some five hundred persons, part of two remnant groups of Sam's followers who could not make the African trip this first time. These people, standing on the dock and waving their farewells, tried not to show their disappointment in having been left, but resolved to return to their tent city on the outskirts of Galveston and ready themselves for the return of the *Liberia* and their eventual emancipation.

The other body of Sam's faithful were breaking camp at "South Gold Coast," a pathetic and sordid settlement at Weleetka, Oklahoma, where for eight months they had collected, awaiting news of the departure for Africa. Though Chief Sam had repeatedly warned his followers not to dispose of their lands and possessions prematurely, many had, in their anticipation of the exodus, disregarded his warning and had ultimately found themselves expatriates in the Weleetka camps, destitute for the most part, and with the fleeting symbol of the *Liberia* the only one upon which to pin their hopes.

Persons other than Sam's followers also noted with no little interest the sailing of the ship. From his diplomatic post in Washington, Sir Arthur Cecil Spring-Rice, Britain's ambassador to the United States, had continually attempted to abort the colonization project. To Spring-Rice, his own government now threatened with disastrous involvement in the European crisis, the Sam affair could not have been more trivial. Yet the possibility of a large Negro exodus from the United States to a British colony posed an embarrassing prospect for the ambassador, and he moved to stem the migration.

From the Gold Coast, too, came an expression of concern over the project. The Governor of that colony urged, on several occasions, that "every effort should be made to prevent the continuance of Sam's operations in the United States . . . for were he to succeed in inducing a number of American Negroes to attempt colonization in the Gold Coast his victims would be foredoomed to disappointment."

The warning was prophetic, but it had little deterrent effect. British and American authorities, despite their methods, often petulant in their frustration at having so little effect, were unable to deter Chief Sam or to discourage his following. The Chief had violated no statute and his scheme, unorthodox though it was and impractical as it seemed, was legally unassailable.

The exodus began, then, early on a warm August morning. The *Liberia* carried its sixty passengers to anticipated freedom in what they, in their frightened phantasies, had defined as their ancestral home.

The movement failed. When the *Liberia* finally did return to the United States two years later, she was on the end of a tow-line, and she no longer belonged to Sam and the African pioneers. There was no proud return to those men and women who had earlier been waiting; for long ago these faithful had given up hope and had filtered back to Oklahoma, physically and emotionally destitute. Of those few who had gone on the first voyage, some had died en route to the Gold Coast, while others had perished shortly after their arrival in an inhospitable land. Infinitely complicated by British colonial law, much of it enacted while the *Liberia* was still at sea, the landing on the Gold Coast was a fiasco, and the lands which the colonists had hoped to find failed ever to really materialize. Only a few of those Negroes ever returned to the United States, and fewer still found permanent homes in Africa.

Although African returns infrequently dot American history, none of those preceding the Sam exodus had been Negro conceived and Negro implemented throughout. Both before and after the Civil War, the African continent had appeared a reasonable place to send manumitted slaves. But such schemes depended less upon Negro receptiveness to an African return than upon the expediencies adopted by a nation somewhat embarrassed by its slavery, but unwilling to live with its one-time chattel on equal social and political terms. The freedman, indeed, was often the most articulate opponent of African colonization, and even the respectable backers of the American Colonization Society met with Northern Negro protests in their attempts to colonize the Republic of Liberia.

Until 1914, the American Negro had lacked not only a champion with whom he could successfully identify and in terms of whom the Negro population could be put into direct and intimate touch with Africa, but, more important, he lacked the appropriate emotional and attitudinal climate necessary for emigration.

It is to this general climate that one must turn to explicate not only the genesis of the movement, but its largely unpredicted success. For the attitudes which the Negroes involved in the exodus shared with one another provided both impelling motives and irrefutable rationales for an African return.

Despite the fact that Sam's followers were drawn from a number of states, including Kansas, Texas, Arkansas, and even Massachusetts, it was from Oklahoma that the bulk of the emigrants came. It is for this reason, then, that the present discussion will center around the Negro milieu in Oklahoma.

Eastern Oklahoma had early received a relatively large Negro component, both from migration into the area and from the residual Negroes who had earlier come as slaves with members of the Five Civilized Tribes. The component swelled in the years prior to statehood, when a number of all-Negro communities were founded in the state.

In the first days of these all-Negro towns, little difficulty was encountered with the whites. They were relieved, it seems evident, at the voluntary maintenance of residential segregation, a pattern which had functioned for so long in the Deep South. Further, land was sufficiently abundant that the Negroes posed no immediate threat to white economic success. Previous to statehood, too, elections were entirely local, each town electing officials to manage its affairs, so that a large Negro element in any part of an area could be dismissed as a political *non sequitur,* posing, after all, no danger to white political supremacy in the all-white towns.

The Negroes moved into the all-Negro communities from other states in response both to new and available land and the hope of finding economic and social equality on this ambiguous frontier. For the Negro family resettling in Oklahoma, a town like Boley (the largest and most dominant of the Negro communities) constituted an exclusively operated Negro entity, physically independent of white communities and, at least superficially, unconnected with the economic matrix of the white areas. The all-Negro town was not interpreted by the Negro as a ghetto, but rather as a racial experiment, a manifest example of Negro self-fulfillment.

The early Negro immigrants into Okfuskee County (in which Boley is located) were principally laborers. Though many of these men had come to work on the railroads with embryonic ideas of remaining, they were essentially rootless. As the area boomed, though, ever-increasing numbers of Negroes moved in with their families, and townsite promoters, some free-lancing for an easily made dollar, others designated by the railroad, established the all-Negro towns and sold land to all comers. In time, these enclaves became well enough established to attract middle-class professionals from the Deep South and the border states. These people, vocationally frustrated in their previous homes, trooped to Oklahoma in the hope of making use of their special skills and training in a context of unrestricted opportunity without the familiar prejudices of superordinate whites.

The later migrants, recruited with vigor from the South, were principally farmers, individuals who had been lured to Oklahoma by brochures and the elegant blandishments of the Negro press at Boley.

The development of the self-fulfillment ethos in the Negro towns was largely the result of the middle-class professionals, though, with grim irony, they suffered least in the disillusionment which ultimately beset the Negroes. It was especially true for the professionals that the articulation of a "great opportunity" motto was most important, since the Negro farmers were

already finding their own self-fulfillment in the sheer ownership of land.

With the constant reiteration of the self-fulfillment goal in
the press, and with the reinforcement of this goal by the pres-
tigeful and economically centripetal middle-class, the farm
population ultimately interiorized the ethic and conceived
themselves in their current occupancy of the land as evidence
of great success for their race.

Race relations in general were somewhat indefinite in this
area. Negro-white contacts were minimal, and the whites
tended even to find something a little amusing in the development of all-Negro enclaves. In addition, there was the "frontier"
context in which there was a sharp situational difference from
the plantation South. The traditionally backward economic
status of the South was relieved, and the whites could well
afford to allow the Negro a new freedom, one which [they]
could not have afforded to grant before.

In the context of this new freedom, the Negro communities
flourished and gained notably in size. Five years after the
founding of Boley, the vicinity immediately surrounding the
town had nearly five thousand Negroes in residence. The same
phenomenal growth, but to a proportionately smaller degree,
was experienced by the other Negro towns.

It was not really until the first election that the whites began
to realize slowly what Negro numerical dominance in this
almost artificially democratic environment might mean. In
1906, when the State Constitutional Convention was held, the
Boley vote numbered nearly 300. The white towns, of which
there were three immediately surrounding Boley, cast 875
votes. But these votes were split almost evenly between the
Republican and Democratic delegates, and the Boley vote,
almost a solid bloc against the Democrats, threw the election
to the Republicans. The whites did not tarry, recognizing the
Convention vote as but an insignificant rehearsal of what was
to come. When the first local election after statehood was held
in Okfuskee County, the Negroes captured the Republican
County Convention with no difficulty, named two Negroes to
the slate as county commissioners, and, to the absolute dismay
of the whites, proceeded to elect this slate at the September

election. The whites moved rapidly, and the County Election Board declared the returns from the Negro precincts invalid. Though the case underwent almost immediate litigation, a series of maneuvers pushed it through the higher courts until at last the State Supreme Court upheld the action of the Election Board. From the point of view of the Negroes, the clearly immoral act of the Election Board had now received official sanction, and the character of race relations in the county now underwent a drastic definitional change. To the Negroes, the Supreme Court decision was essentially irrelevant, since it was reached at the end of the terms of office which their duly elected commissioners would have held. The important fact had been the summary dismissal of the Negro vote, for this clearly pointed the extent to which the whites were prepared to go in their disenfranchisement of the Negroes. The evasively worded decision of the Supreme Court some two years after litigation began simply reiterated in more awesome form the white affirmation that Negro dreams of equality, to say nothing of control, were vapid.

Election after election, the Negroes were defeated. Gerrymandering, cavilling objections to the Republican slate (which remained for some time the Negro-Republican slate), and outright threats of physical violence to the person of the Negro who attempted to exercise his franchise were all employed as tactics. The very symbol of equality which the Negroes had demanded in their increasingly unfeasible empire now became an anathema. With the vote, the Negroes came into open conflict with white interests; without it, they regressed to the positions they had held in the South. Finally, in 1910, the people of Oklahoma settled the problem in another way by approving a constitutional amendment which effectively removed the Negro from the political scene on the basis of his ancestry. The disenfranchisement was complete.

Shortly after the enactment of the "grandfather clause," the whites in Okfuskee and adjoining counties, having now had the Negro defined as politically nonexistent, attempted to render him physically nonexistent as well. Little by little, through unashamed threats Negro farmers were displaced by whites, and Farmers' Commercial Clubs enlisted members who signed oaths in which they bound themselves not to employ Negro labor. The patent object of the organizations was to choke off Negro [immigration] into the county and to encourage Negro exodus from it. Though many Negroes resisted the persuadings of the Clubs (violence was constitutionally outlawed to their membership), others felt greater discomfort by their persistence. Unlike the townspeople, well insulated in their strongholds, the farmers had no place of retreat, and it was with them that the whites had the greatest vis-à-vis contact.

By 1913, a brutal lynching had taken place in the county, again punctuating the growing feeling that the Negro would not be tolerated on any but the most subordinate of grounds.

The falling price of cotton contributed additional hardships to the Negro communities, and many farmers lost their holdings altogether. Totally unable to withhold their crops for a day of higher prices, they moved quietly away to the urban centers of the state. Many left Oklahoma altogether, for it was now becoming as infamous for its race contacts as the South.

Into this fertile context in which the Okfuskee Negroes were pathetically casting about for a new solution to their problems walked Alfred Charles Sam. Full of vision of a mass exodus from what had now become a land of mockery, and with the apparent support of His Majesty's Government, Sam was a potent figure indeed.

Sam had been raised in a small town in the interior of the Gold Coast. During his youth he attended the Basel Mission Society School at Kibi, and there had come into contact with European traditions. As a young man, Sam was occupied in several rubber exporting ventures, and it was during this period that he conceived his idea of establishing an exclusively Negro trading company that would traffic in goods between the United States and his African homeland.

In 1911, he came to the United States for the first time, and formed here a corporation in terms of which he could effect his plan. Taking its name from the land of his birth, the Akim Trading Company flourished briefly, transporting tropical products to New York. In early 1913, however, and for reasons compelling to Sam, he chose to short-circuit the New York offices of the company, and independently drew up contracts with several London fruit merchants. When the Gold Coast-New York trade fell off, Sam was called for an accounting before his board of directors. In a fashion which later became typical of him, he was unable to give a clear accounting of his actions, and he was hastily impeached by an angry board and dropped entirely from the company.

Unconcerned with this setback, Sam promptly formed a new company, and unembarrassedly called it the Akim Trading Company, Ltd. He incorporated it for one million dollars, splitting the stock into forty thousand shares. In his prospectus, he not only provided for trade between the Gold Coast and the United States, but "in foreign countries as shall from time to time be found necessary and convenient." He also proposed to found a "college of agriculture and industry in all the trades of manufacturing and agriculture . . . [and to] construct hotels, restaurants, bath houses, theaters, and other places of amusement."

The real and most immediate purpose of the company, however, was to sell stock. Sam had earlier corresponded with a number of leading Negroes in Oklahoma, and had been invited to visit Okfuskee County and describe the opportunities which Africa offered. Sam arrived in the state on May 11, 1913, with a plan which was marvelously simple.

The principal business of the company was to conduct trade. But since the ships to be used (and yet to be acquired) would be large, it would be possible to transport a limited number of colonists to the Gold Coast on each voyage. These people would be established on lands for which Sam had previously arranged and would promote colonies, designed both as havens for American Negroes and as centers of instruction for Africans. Since the company would soon be engaged in a highly lucrative trade, the cost of transportation for the colonists would be small. Sam decided that the purchaser of any one share of stock would be entitled to a trip to Africa for himself and his dependents. Food for the voyage would be provided on board for a slight additional fee.

Sam's personal contacts in the state were supplemented by clubs, formed under the aegis of P. J. Liddell, a "professor" from Boley who came ultimately to be the executive secretary of the African group. The clubs were organized throughout the state, intent upon spreading the word of the African return, and selling, incidentally, Sam's stock.

Sam himself met personally with large groups of people during the remainder of the year. His appeal was extraordinary, and there was no denying its durability. With each encounter he attracted more people to the movement, and his activities soon spilled over into Kansas, Texas and Arkansas.

The more solid element of the local Negro population, its aspirations and interests firmly tied to the all-Negro communities, maintained a running fire of doubt and dire prediction about the project. One of the most outspoken opponents of the plan, W. S. Peters, a Boley attorney, though shocked by the obvious shallowness of the scheme, reported that by early September more than four hundred families in the Boley area had purchased shares in the company and were preparing to leave on a moment's notice for their new homes in Africa. Peters reported Sam's claims that in Africa "the negroes don't have to work or even wear clothes, and . . . crops grow without difficulty, and life is one long, sweet dream. . . ."

But at public meetings, where the fervor of the emigration plan and the generous doses of interjected religious interest caught everyone in their spell, Sam had little difficulty in assuaging any doubts which the pariahs might raise. He talked of trees which bore bread, and of cotton bushes as tall as trees. The doubters might protest, but Sam was routinely able to cope with them.

One night, during a meeting at Clearview, a local physician challenged Sam on a practical point.

"How many bushels of cotton do you get from one of those trees?" he asked.

"Many, many, many," said Sam and abstractly waved his hand above his head.

Sam talked of diamonds that might be found in the gullies after a hard rain, and the Negroes took this tortured truth as evidence of incredible wealth on the Gold Coast.

Peters' activities, however, soon brought Sam's schemes to the attention of the Governor. Somewhat apathetically, the chief executive contacted the Okfuskee County Attorney and arranged to have Sam arrested during one of his visits to Boley. The Chief was hauled before the Justice of the Peace of that town and accused of obtaining money under fraudulent pretenses. Apparently having earlier arranged for a complainant, the County Attorney felt confident that he could prove his charges against the movement's leader. But at the last minute the complainant turned refractory and refused to testify, and the case was dismissed.

But though the cry against Sam from the local middle class did not cease after this incident, it was silenced in part when Sam provided tangible evidence of good faith. He began negotiations with the Munson Steamship Company for an old steamer, the *Curityba,* which had carried vacationers between New York and Cuba. Though the ship was old (it had been built in 1887), and though it lacked the wireless facilities necessary for a trans-Atlantic cruise, Sam felt it was the very vessel the movement could best employ.

No sooner were negotiations opened, however, than the British government, becoming vaguely aware that Sam was somehow posing as an immigration agent for the Gold Coast Colony, ordered its diplomatic machinery to apply pressure to the Oklahoma Governor.

The British Consul in St. Louis, writing to Lee Cruce, apprised him of the Sam affair and warned that Sam was not only not an accredited colonization agent for the Gold Coast Government, but that he might even be wanted by the West African police for questioning. The Consul suggested that the affair be stopped as soon as possible.

But Governor Cruce could do very little. He wrote to the County Attorney at Okemah once again and waited impatiently for a reply. When one finally arrived, it was only to inform the Governor that men were on the job at Sam's meetings, but that it was at that time impossible to take Sam into custody, no criminal charges having been filed against him.

The movement, meanwhile, grew by leaps and bounds. Despite Sam's periodical warnings to his followers that they should maintain their farms until the affairs of the movement were better formalized, and despite his awareness that ten ships the size of the *Curityba* could not carry his now five thousand stockholders to Africa, many of the colonists, eager to be done with Oklahoma, sold their possessions and cheerily established themselves in tent-cities at Weleetka. During the late fall of 1913, the "Gold Coast Camps" were quite pleasant. Freed from the routine agricultural duties which had annually characterized their lives, they interacted socially with one another and talked about their future in Africa.

As winter came on, however, the camps became centers of despair. Food and clothing were short, and the majority of the colonists had invested all of their excess capital in the movement. Weleetka, a small town, afforded no opportunities for employment and starvation seemed to be imminent.

Sam's plan at the moment was to outfit the *Curityba*, which he had lately renamed the *Liberia*, in New York and then to sail to Galveston, where he would pick up the waiting colonists. But delays and financial insolvency had slowed the outfitting of the vessel, and the date for her departure from the East Coast changed almost weekly.

After an abnormally bleak winter at Weleetka, Sam and several of his followers left for New York, intent upon hurrying the preparation of the ship. The campers viewed this new move as one guaranteed to speed their departure and their spirits rose, if only temporarily.

Sam's New York adventures, however, proved as unfortunate as possible. The metropolitan newspapers took a dim, if facetious, view of the entire project and, spurred by vicious editorials in the New York *Age,* picked away at the movement and its leader.

The Post Office Department, brought into the arena by the Department of State (which felt the nudgings of Spring-Rice), instituted an investigation of Sam, hoping to prove that he had used the mails for fraudulent purposes and to halt the movement [by] his imprisonment. The British Ambassador, too, demanded an interview with Sam. Though none of the agencies were able to stop him, Sam spent his time in New York more in the company of harassing officials than on the dock at the Erie Basin where the *Liberia* was tied up.

Finally, desperate and furious at the obstacles being placed in his way, Sam outfitted the ship with a makeshift crew, removed the men and women who had taken up residence on it, and sent the *Liberia* off to Portland, Maine, alleging that he would receive less discriminatory treatment in that New England port.

But Portland proved hardly more hospitable than had New York. Tipped off about his coming, the Portland papers advertised the movement several days before the *Liberia* docked. Dredging their memories for information, the Portland newsmen found a certain vague similarity between Sam and an earlier messiah, and rumors were soon rampant that Sam was involved in the renascence of the Holy Ghost and Us Society.

Founded some years before by the Reverend Frank W. Sandford, a bizarre ascetic who found both life insurance and swine unclean, the Holy Ghost and Us Society had established the Kingdom Yacht Club and had set out on a world gospel mission. At home, the Shiloh Colony carried on the continental activities of the Society. Sandford's efforts were at length aborted when he was convicted of using the mails to defraud, and the Society's leader was sent promptly to the Federal Prison at Atlanta.

Although the connection between Sandford's group and the African movement was tenuous in the extreme, the Portland papers made the most of it. Sam denied the alliance but the rumors were given credibility by the fact that some of his pioneers were Holy Ghosters. The evidence is inconclusive, but there is little reason to doubt Sam's statements. Though the Holy Ghost members were more than happy to render what aid they could to Sam and the colonists, the African leader had little reason to court their active support, his own movement having previously flourished without it. Apart from sundry advices on ship outfitting, the Kingdom Yacht Club official could do little for Sam.

Portland meant more delays and more investigations for Sam. While the wireless equipment was being installed, spurred on by the reports of the Holy Ghost involvement, Collector of the Port Simmons demanded Sam's presence at a hearing and queried him once again on his activities. Though the harassments were as futile in Portland as they had been elsewhere, they unnerved the "low, brown man," and he soon rendered himself and his ship's crew incommunicado, preventing any member of his group from speaking with an outsider.

In Oklahoma, meanwhile, the "Gold Coast Camp" settlers were growing impatient. Lines of communication between Weleetka and the East Coast were poor, and the campers remained for weeks on end unapprised of Sam's activities. Finally, both unwilling and unable to wait longer for news of the ship's departure for Galveston, a large complement of the Camp's occupants boarded trains and moved off to the Gulf, hoping to find there at least a geographically greater promise of the African venture than they could find in Oklahoma.

The ship languished at length in Portland, and while the city officials at Weleetka were relieved by the dwindling camps, their counterparts in Galveston were alarmed at the influx of Negroes. One of Sam's agents, stationed in Galveston, took the pioneers to a park where they established themselves in short order. But as more and more people moved in, the city officials grew disquieted over the possibility of an outbreak of disease, and finally, after considering the condition of the camp, they ordered the Negroes to disperse and take up residence outside of the city.

At a critical moment, when the Weleetka desperation was again beginning to afflict the Galveston pioneers, news arrived that the *Liberia* had completed her outfitting and had left Portland on her way to pick up the passengers and begin the long awaited trip.

A celebration had been planned for June 19, the day on which the Negroes of Texas first heard of their emancipation from slavery. A traditional holiday for them in Texas, the occasion was to be even more resplendent now that the *Liberia* would be in port. But as the day approached, no word was heard from the ship. Early on the morning of the 18th, however, the ship hove into sight, and though its berthing was delayed while a pipeline across the channel was repaired, the principal symbol of the movement was finally beheld by the colonists and their hopes were renewed once more for an early sailing.

When the ship finally docked, Sam was ecstatic. His moment of complete triumph over the doubters was at hand, and he exploited it to the fullest. Speaking from the ship's deck, he reiterated his plans:

> This trip to Africa is mainly for the purpose of locating our colony. . . . We have no land, yet, but have been assured that we can readily secure all that we will need on the west coast of Africa from the native tribes. If we can purchase lumber and cement at reasonable prices in Galveston we will take a quantity along to build the nucleus of our colony, which will probably be a dormitory, a chapel and a store. Our people are not homeless. They are not idlers or drones. . . . When our colony is established and the people of our race see that we are successful, this boat will be crowded on every trip that she makes to Africa.

In the days that followed, Sam set up "a sort of African court, holding receptions and giving almost daily entertainments with the deck and cabin of the ship as the theater of action." Though the story is certainly apocryphal, the Texas papers reported that Sam, on certain days, would serve refreshments to the passengers. Crocodile sandwiches and tiger stew, "the carnal ingredients of the delicacies . . . having been brought across the sea," formed the major part of the diet.

In due time, and with pomp well suited to the occasion, the ship was formally christened and, again, the reality of its very steel presence gave hope to the pioneers. The situation in Weleetka, however, was growing grimmer.

It was by now apparent to all that the relatively small vessel could carry no more than sixty passengers on its first trip. Though an untold amount of stock had been sold to people whose only interest was to support the movement, several thousand had, in fact, made definite plans for sailing. At Weleetka, the townspeople were ordering the closing of the "Gold Coast Camps," and many of the colonists, utterly fatigued and despairing of ever even seeing the *Liberia,* were going back to the farms they no longer owned. Others sought refuge with relatives in the surrounding countryside.

Sam, plagued anew by financial difficulties, spent the remaining weeks before the sailing in the almost impossible task of renewing the enthusiasm for the movement which had once existed in Oklahoma. He moved from town to town, begging for assistance. But his recent revision of the land question had done his appeal little good. Pressed on all sides by documents from the Gold Coast Colony Government, Sam had finally admitted that although he had "arrangements" for land in the Gold Coast, he did not, in fact, hold title to such land.

In Galveston, his lieutenants were selecting the delegates who would sail to Africa in the first shipload and report home, eventually, to the other stockholders. The mathematical enigma of the movement was also given public announcement by the newspapers, decreasing, once more, Sam's stature and appeal.

Compared with the notoriety which had characteristically accompanied almost every move Sam had previously made, the eventual sailing of the *Liberia* was relatively quiet. On August 20, clearance was given the ship, and on the next morning, with a few early risers watching from the pier, the *Liberia* slipped away from her berthing and steamed out into the Gulf of Mexico. The cargo of the ship, in addition to its sixty passengers, consisted of cement, flour, lumber, hardware, breadstuffs, some arms, ammunition and the household effects of the pioneers.

Though the *Liberia* could hardly have chosen a more inopportune time to venture out from Galveston and attempt a perilous crossing of the Atlantic under the British flag, the first part of the trip was relatively uneventful. Cozy on their racial island, the passengers spent the weeks in teas and other social events designed to pass away their time. Though the *Liberia* was once reported sunk by a German cruiser, the passengers of the ship were singularly unaware that a war was even in progress.

But the last months of the voyage, as the ship finally approached her destination, were filled with untoward events.

There was a strange episode in which the *Liberia* met another British ship on the seas and immediately prepared to salute it. The mutual recognition of vessels according to the impersonal codes of ocean transportation was always one of the most satisfying experiences of the *Liberia's* passengers. But on this occasion the British ship hesitated in returning the *Liberia's* salute, and though the flag finally dipped almost imperceptibly, the passengers aboard the *Liberia* blew the incident up beyond all proper proportion and took it as a personal affront.

Seasickness and bad weather also took their toll on the passengers' morale during the last months, and as the weeks trailed by each again took stock of his reasons for embarking. A death at sea proved a final sobering experience, and by the time the ship reached the Cape Verde Islands, all aboard were more than eager to get ashore for a time.

The stopover had a penalty, however. Shortly before the ship was to sail, she was set upon and boarded by the members of a British man-of-war, and ultimately, in charge of a prize crew, the *Liberia* was sailed to Sierra Leone for detention and inspection.

The month and a half that she lay at Freetown proved a disaster. For although the ship was ultimately freed, food and coal had now become perilously short, and the passengers were again experiencing the agonies they had suffered at Weleetka.

Finally, on January 30, the *Liberia* moved into the harbor at Saltpond after five months at sea. The landing was the fulfillment of every hope for the passengers, and one of them, writing home, likened it to the return to Canaan of the Israelites.

Though the Gold Coast natives welcomed the Negroes with open arms and open houses, the British Colonial Government felt somewhat differently. While the ship had been at sea, the Governor had summarily caused legislation to be enacted which imposed a hundred and twenty-five dollar per capita tax on each colonist who landed in the Colony. Such a sum was to be held by the proper authorities against the return of the colonist in the event of his destitution on the Gold Coast.

Already crippled financially, this last sum was almost impossible for the colonists to raise.

But Sam finally produced the amount and the colonists were permitted ashore. Though the first weeks in Saltpond were relatively pleasant, Sam's eccentric behavior began to trouble members of the group. Their leader would disappear for long periods of time and then suddenly reappear, sullen and confused. When they pressed him on their next move, he would retreat to generalities and finally disappear into his cabin.

Revolt finally developed, and the colonists insisted that if Sam would not lead them to the lands they were to farm, they would bring criminal charges against him. Their principal grievance hinged on Sam's alleged misuse of their funds, though Sam, in a boiler-room conference, soon put any fears they might have had at ease and reassured them that if they would follow his plans to the letter, he would not only return their monies but would lead them to their lands.

Apparently contrite, the Americans began making the necessary preparations for the trek inland to Akim Swedru, the town near which Sam proposed to establish his colony.

After a grueling journey on foot through brush so dense that one colonist asserted later that "you had to stoop down and squint to see only a few feet," the troop reached Akim Swedru. The town, really only a small village, was a terrible disappointment. And because the Negroes were not accustomed to the native materials with which they had to work, they had grave difficulty in adapting them to the techniques they had brought from the New World.

Over the weeks, though some attempted desultory farming and others amused themselves with anteater hunts, the pioneers grew restless. The village chief imposed restrictions on their movements which piqued the Americans and, on several occasions, thefts took a heavy toll of their meager household effects. Soon some began to drift back to the coastal areas, where opportunities for activity and employment seemed better. But work was difficult to obtain, and several of the group had created a mild panic by succumbing to tropical disorders.

Sensing the difficulty, and having had vague communications with one of the pioneers, a friend back in Oklahoma petitioned the American State Department for relief of the now stranded victims of Sam's scheme. But the State Department, acknowledging the condition of the emigrants, remarked that it had no funds available for such repatriation.

The British, still determined to do what they could to prevent additional ingresses of American Negroes, turned their attention to the *Liberia*. The government had forbidden the sale of coal to the ship and had, thereby, effectively stranded it at a point between Saltpond and Annamabou. The colonists were permitted to move on and off the vessel at will, though many of them preferred make-shift accommodations at Saltpond.

The crew of the ship, unpaid from the beginning of the voyage, finally brought charges against Sam, and, as he fled, the government seized the vessel and sold it, reimbursing the claimants. The crew finally made their way home as distressed seamen, though the equally distressed passengers languished in Africa.

Within two weeks after the repatriation of the crew, thirteen of the colonists petitioned the Gold Coast government for succor and begged that they be returned to their homes. They reflected upon the error they had made in trusting Sam and agreed now that they had been fleeced. Sam, they said, had clearly had no intention of fulfilling any of the promises he had made. Pathetically, they turned against the movement which had posed so bright a future for them for so long a time and now threw themselves on the mercy of the Governor.

But the Governor, too, had no funds, and the petitioners remained in Saltpond. Some in desperate need wrote relatives and friends in the United States, and, little by little, many accumulated enough money to allow them passage home. But others, with no possibility of tapping such sources, moved out once again into the back country and attempted farming. Still others filtered out of the Gold Coast Colony altogether and took up residence in Nigeria and Liberia.

Of Sam, nothing more was heard. He fled, it was reported,

to Liberia, where he again began operations for a trading company. Others report that he was seized by the Gold Coast government and imprisoned at grim Cape Coast Castle.

Social movements do not, of course, just happen. They are produced by a variety of circumstances which precede them in time and by a complex, often inextricable, array of human interpretations of these circumstances. The events which ultimately give rise to the often cataclysmic decisions of people to rebel, to run away, to reform, to fight, take time to unfold. As a leading social psychologist has pointed out, "collective inter-action and other activities contributing to a social movement are not usually affairs that occur within a few episodes. Their scope extends far beyond the face-to-face encounters of a given number of individuals."

People do not make important decisions quickly, nor are these decisions, when they run counter to prevailing mores, reinforced in a moment. It takes convincing, and convincing takes the careful rationalization of the individual's decision to lay aside his prior beliefs and commitments, a process which is, at best, painful and tedious. The diffuse uneasiness and the lingering frustration which the Negroes of Okfuskee County began to feel after statehood took years to crystallize into action. The Sam movement represented, then, the final, fitful culmination of a longer period of private talks, of intense emotional interaction, of subtle, unconscious value judgments, of uncertain decision-making among those people who sensed this frustration and became aware that they could not relieve their tension in the more usual channels which their cultural milieu provided.

The situational factors contributing to the movement need hardly be belabored. Boley, Clearview and the other Negro communities in Oklahoma were experiments in racial self-determination. If the Negroes had not believed this when they first occupied these racial isolates, they soon became convinced of it. But with the passing years, the discrepancy between the aims and aspirations of the all-Negro communities and the actualities of their life-histories illustrated vividly the lengths to which the Negro would be permitted to go—the real

limits of his social tether—even if he did not come into direct
and open conflict with the white group.

The Negro community was a compromise between complete
integration which was then, as now, unfeasible in terms of
some white values and tormenting and humiliating subordina-
tion in biracial communities. The Negro in the all-Negro community was not yet ready, in 1904, to rebel against the stern
racial etiquette in the United States, but he nonetheless hoped
to find in his new form of residence a solution to a situation
which showed little promise of imminent improvement. The
all-Negro community was in no sense a retreat from the
American standards and values which the Negroes had learned
to cherish, nor was it yet an anachronistic revival of African-
ism, but rather it constituted an attempt to develop fully and
to exploit completely the American culture.

But this exploitation was refused to the Negro, not at once,
to be sure, but in invidious, piecemeal fashion. Disenfran-
chised slowly but certainly, the Negro was obliged with each
new onslaught to adjust his previous ethic. Such constant revision soon became vapid, and the Negro community relented
in the face of white hostility.

Faced with bitter ambiguity, no longer certain of the direction which they should take, Oklahoma Negroes fell upon
Sam as they had upon no other person in their history. To
them, Sam represented an escape which they believed was a
solution, but he also represented removal to a land where
they could continue their conceived roles as leaders, pioneers
and persons of prestige and importance. They were not skulk-
ing off to Africa as beaten men and women, but they were
instead returning proudly to their homeland, full of the ideas
that residence in America had taught them and equipped
with the skills which had made their nation famous. The
Americans believed they were on their way to save the
Africans, to "uplift" them, as the pioneers preached at their
landing at Saltpond.

Sam's organization of the movement could hardly be called
consciously masterful. Though his local clubs proved an innovation, their memberships constantly reinforcing their own
fervid belief in the wisdom of the return, they developed

almost without his urging. But his personal appeal was enormous and in his presence no one thought to question him seriously. The stage was perfectly set for him, and he came and reaped the rewards.

Whether or not Sam was a charlatan is in every sense unimportant. To the Negroes preparing for the voyage Sam was a savior. Nothing could convince them to the contrary. Though many of the professional Negroes of the area, those very persons who had contributed so heavily to the self-fulfillment ethic which ultimately proved the basis for the group's disillusionment, refused to accompany him, the Negro majority both locally and distantly supported the scheme. This was a grand experiment, a showdown experiment, in which the African, rejected in his adopted nation, was proudly packing and returning home.

Sam's claims for Africa were immodest at best and in some cases altogether false. The pioneers, to a man, agreed that Sam had lied and cheated them. But many felt no bitterness. The trip to Africa, they agreed, had been worth the hardships they endured.

The movement and its fantastic leader now live only in the few spastic recollections of a handful who survive. Its status now is that of a hollow monument to a "basic unrest of the Negro community," to a "dissatisfaction so deep that it amounts to a hopelessness of ever gaining full life in America."

In these terms, one old woman's remark becomes even more poignant.

"I will and do say to you that the Negro people here for the first in my long life came together and acted like they loved one another."

If only briefly, Sam had given them something to live for.

FOR FURTHER READING

The best general treatment of black thought in the late nineteenth and early twentieth centuries is *August Meier, Negro Thought in America, 1890–1915* (Ann Arbor, 1966). *S. P. Fullinwider, *The Mind and Mood of Black America*

(Homewood, Ill., 1969) is interesting if not wholly convincing. There are two biographies of W. E. B. Du Bois worth consulting: *Elliott Rudwick, W. E. B. Du Bois, Propagandist of the Negro Protest* (New York, 1968) and Francis Broderick, *W. E. B. Du Bois: Negro Leader in a Time of Crisis* (Stanford, 1959). Du Bois's works should be read, especially *Dusk of Dawn* (New York, 1968); *The Souls of Black Folk* (available in several paperback editions); and *Autobiography of W. E. B. Du Bois* (New York, 1968). There is no satisfactory biography of Booker T. Washington, but studies worth reading are: *Samuel R. Spencer, Jr., Booker T. Washington and the Negro's Place in American Life* (Boston, 1955), which is sympathetic to Washington; and Basil Mathews, *Booker T. Washington, Educator and Interracial Interpreter* (London, 1948). To understand Washington it is necessary to read his autobiography, *Up from Slavery* (available in several paperback editions). The early history of the NAACP is related in the scholarly *NAACP, 1909–1920* (Baltimore, 1967) by Charles F. Kellogg. Useful information on the development of black colleges and education can be found in Henry Bullock, *A History of Negro Education* (Cambridge, 1967) and Horace Mann Bond, *The Education of the Negro in the American Social Order* (New York, 1934). Alfred Sam's back-to-Africa movement is treated fully in William Bittle and Gilbert Geis, *The Longest Way Home* (Detroit, 1964). An interesting but sketchy work is Earl E. Thorpe, *The Mind of the Negro: An Intellectual History of Afro-Americans* (Baton Rouge, 1961). Information on the last years of Frederick Douglass is in *Benjamin Quarles, Frederick Douglass* (New York, 1968).

PART 2

URBANIZATION, CIVIL RIGHTS, AND BLACK NATIONALISM:

1910 to the Present

URBANIZATION

The dramatic shift of black Americans from the rural South to the cities is described in the selection from the Report of the President's Commission on Civil Disorders. Whereas nearly 90 percent of all blacks lived in the South in 1910, by the 1960s about half lived elsewhere. Whereas the black population was less urbanized than the white at the turn of the century, the position has been reversed by the 1960s. The black migration to the central cities coupled with the white movement to the suburbs meant that the central cities were increasingly black.

The report also described the formation of ghettos in the

cities and the conditions of living for their residents. Actually these conditions were not new to post-1910 America. Racial ghettos had been less well defined in the nineteenth century, but living conditions for blacks in the cities then were worse than for whites. Small ghettos did exist before 1910. In 1899 W. E. B. Du Bois published his famous *The Philadelphia Negro,* describing the situation in that city. The scene pictured by Du Bois was depressingly similar to that of the 1960s.

Evidence exists that the rural emigration was slowing down by the end of the 1960s; however, the white exodus from the large cities was continuing. Thus the trend still was toward an increasingly black central city. A trickle of blacks did move to the suburbs, and in the 1950s and 1960s there were signs that suburban ghettos were forming. Though they were perhaps more middle-class than their urban counterparts and had fewer social problems, they were ghettos with the potential of following the pattern of central city development.

A number of factors prompted the great migration to the cities. The deteriorating racial situation in the South described earlier was clearly a consideration, but most important were the economic factors. These were of a push-pull nature. Southern rural poverty, aggravated by floods, famine, and the boll weevil, pushed thousands off the farms. The changing job market pulled blacks, largely young male workers, to the North. Also, with the outbreak of World War I, immigration from other countries fell and northern factories searched for new sources of labor. Over one million immigrants had come to America in 1914; in 1916 and again in 1917 less than 300,000 arrived and in 1918 scarcely over 100,000 entered. Some black newspapers like the *Chicago Defender* and recruiting agents from northern industry, urged blacks to migrate, and letters from those who had already gone north urged others to follow.

Alarmed southern towns attempted vainly to legislate against labor recruiters. Alarmed white northerners resorted to violence to deter blacks from moving into their neighborhoods. In Chicago between 1917 and 1921 fifty-eight bombs were hurled at black homes or those of real estate men who sold to

black families. In other cases whites organized property owners' associations to keep blacks out.

In spite of hostility and in spite of overcrowded housing and
discrimination in the labor market, the migrants still came, for
the North offered more than the South. The black population
of Chicago alone more than doubled in the decade 1910–1920.
New York City had only 60,000 blacks in 1900 but over 300,000
in 1930, most of them living in Harlem, the black cultural
capital of America.

Although the movement of blacks was not always as dramatic as during the second decade of the twentieth century, it
continued in the years following World War I. In the 1940s
and after the end of World War II, the movement was heavily
to the West Coast cities. Los Angeles became an important
black center and experienced many of the same tensions that
eastern cities had years before.

It has been argued by some sociologists and historians that
certain black institutions, especially the family, have been ad-
versely affected by the ghetto experience. The fact that so
many of the migrants to industrial centers were young males
did affect both the communities they left behind and the cities
in which they settled, and the pressures of ghetto living often
strained family life.

Yet in the long run urbanization has led to advantages for
the black population. While approximately one half of all black
families were in the lower income brackets in the 1960s, and
many were below the poverty level, those in the rural South
were more apt to be poor than those in the urban North and
West. In spite of the widespread discrimination in the North
and West, job and educational opportunities were better there
and social mobility was more possible. Although proportionately more black families owned homes in the South than in
the North, it is doubtful whether actual housing conditions
were better in the South. They were probably worse. Proportionately more black families in the southern cities lived in
substandard housing than in the North. Nearly half of the
black population was still rural in the 1960s, and most of these
individuals lived in substandard housing. City community

services such as health and welfare, though inadequate, were better than those left behind in the country.

The fact was that most black families living on the land in the 1960s, practically all of whom were in the South, were faced with a low standard of living. Periodic government investigations and scholarly accounts revealed that not only did many of these families go to bed hungry each night, but also many suffered from acute malnutrition. The New Deal and post-World War II farm programs offered little or nothing to the southern black farmer, and in some cases worked against his interests. Few blacks were able to climb from sharecropping to middle-class farm ownership. Many working on farms were migratory workers who were largely untouched by the welfare state, and because of their low level of skills and education they were part of the nation's hard-core poor. The only answers for many were those of the past: continuation of rural poverty or movement to the cities. And in an advancing technological society, these migrants found new opportunities in the cities.

The concentration of blacks in the urban ghettos made possible the election of black officials. After the virtual elimination of the black voter from southern politics by 1910, the political resurgence of black Americans came in the North. In 1917 Edward Johnson was the first black elected to the New York State Assembly; two years earlier Oscar De Priest had become the first black alderman in Chicago. De Priest went on to become the first black congressman from the North (and the first in the nation since 1901) when Chicago's black population sent him to Washington in 1928. By the 1960s a number of blacks had been elected to state legislatures, until there were 104 in 24 states in 1966. Black congressmen included Senator Edward Brooke from Massachusetts, and blacks also held local offices. The first black mayors of large cities also appeared in the North: Richard Hatcher of Gary, Indiana, and Carl Stokes of Cleveland. As the black vote grew in the North, it was recognized in the 1960s by increased appointments to executive offices, including the cabinet, and to the Supreme Court. With the reduction of restrictions against black voting and the increased registration of blacks in the South, a political regeneration took place there in the 1960s, but the ghettos still furnished the main basis for potential political power.

In spite of the gains made by urbanites compared to those in the rural South, life in the ghetto fell woefully short of the ideals of the American dream. High rates of unemployment, especially among the young; poor education; and inadequate housing and public facilities led to mounting feelings of frustration and to the explosions of the 1960s. Nor did the civil rights movement and governmental programs seem to offer solutions. The ghetto seemed destined to continue, as America was unwilling to institute the changes necessary to make life more hopeful for the ghetto's residents.

9

*From the Kerner
Commission Report*

THE FORMATION
OF THE RACIAL GHETTOS

Major Trends in Negro Population

Throughout the twentieth century, and particularly in the last three decades, the Negro population of the United States has been steadily moving—from rural areas to urban, from South to North and West.

SOURCE: *Report of the National Advisory Commission on Civil Disorders* (Washington, D.C.: U.S. Government Printing Office, 1968), chs. 6, 7, 8, pp. 115–41.

In 1910, 2.7 million Negroes lived in American cities—28 percent of the nation's Negro population of 9.8 million. Today, about 15 million Negro Americans live in metropolitan areas, or 69 percent of the Negro population of 21.5 million. In 1910, 885,000 Negroes—9 percent—lived outside the South. Now, almost 10 million, about 45 percent, live in the North or West.

These shifts in population have resulted from three basic trends:

> A rapid increase in the size of the Negro population.
>
> A continuous flow of Negroes from Southern rural areas, partly to large cities in the South, but primarily to large cities in the North and West.
>
> An increasing concentration of Negroes in large metropolitan areas within racially segregated neighborhoods.

Taken together, these trends have produced large and constantly growing concentrations of Negro population within big cities in all parts of the nation. Because most major civil disorders of recent years occurred in predominantly Negro neighborhoods, we have examined the causes of this concentration.

The Growth Rate of the Negro Population

During the first half of this century, the white population of the United States grew at a slightly faster rate than the Negro population. Because fertility rates[1] among Negro women were more than offset by death rates among Negroes and large-scale immigration of whites from Europe, the proportion of Negroes in the country declined from 12 percent in 1900 to 10 percent in 1940.

By the end of World War II—and increasingly since then—major advances in medicine and medical care, together with the increasing youth of the Negro population resulting from higher fertility rates, caused death rates among Negroes to fall much faster than among whites. This is shown in Table 1. In addition, white immigration from outside the United States dropped dramatically after stringent restrictions were adopted in the 1920s. (See Table 2.)

[1] The "fertility rate" is the number of live births per year per 1,000 women aged 15 to 44 in the group concerned.

TABLE 1   *Death Rate/1,000 Population*

Year	Whites	Nonwhites	Ratio of nonwhite rate to white rate
1900	17.0	25.0	1.47
1940	10.4	13.8	1.33
1965	9.4	9.6	1.02

TABLE 2

20-year-period	Total immigration (millions)
1901–20	14.5
1921–40	4.6
1941–60	3.6

Thus, by mid-century, both factors which had previously off-set higher fertility rates among Negro women no longer were in effect.

While Negro fertility rates, after rising rapidly to 1957, have declined sharply in the past decade, white fertility rates have dropped even more, leaving Negro rates much higher in comparison. (See Table 3.)

TABLE 3   *Live Births Per 1,000 Women Aged 15–44*

Year	White	Nonwhite	Ratio of nonwhite to white
1940	77.1	102.4	1.33
1957	117.4	163.4	1.39
1965	91.4	133.9	1.46

The result is that Negro population is now growing significantly faster than white population. From 1940 to 1960, the white population rose 34.0 percent, but the Negro population rose 46.6 percent. From 1960 to 1966, the white population grew 7.6 percent, whereas Negro population rose 14.4 percent, almost twice as much.

Consequently, the proportion of Negroes in the total population has risen from 10.0 percent in 1950 to 10.5 percent in 1960, and 11.1 percent in 1966.[2]

In 1950, at least one of every ten Americans was Negro; in 1966, one of nine. If this trend continues, one of every eight Americans will be Negro by 1972.

Another consequence of higher birth rates among Negroes is that the Negro population is considerably younger than the white population. In 1966, the median age among whites was 29.1 years, as compared to 21.1 among Negroes. About 35 percent of the white population was under 18 years of age, compared with 45 percent for Negroes. About one of every six children under five and one of every six new babies are Negro.

Negro-white fertility rates bear an interesting relationship to educational experience. Negro women with low levels of education have more children than white women with similar schooling, while Negro women with four years or more of college education have fewer children than white women similarly educated. Table 4 illustrates this. This suggests that the difference between Negro and white fertility rates may decline in the future if Negro educational attainment compares more closely with that of whites, and if a rising proportion of members of both groups complete college.

TABLE 4

	Number of children ever born to all women (married or unmarried) 35–39 years old, by level of education (based on 1960 census)	
Education level attained	*Nonwhite*	*White*
Completed elementary school	3.0	2.8
Four years of high school	2.3	2.3
Four years of college	1.7	2.2
Five years or more of college	1.2	1.6

[2] These proportions are undoubtedly too low because the Census Bureau has consistently undercounted the number of Negroes in the U.S. by as much as 10 percent.

The Migration of Negroes from the South

THE MAGNITUDE OF THIS MIGRATION

In 1910, 91 percent of the nation's 9.8 million Negroes lived in the South. Twenty-seven percent of American Negroes lived in cities of 2,500 persons or more, as compared to 49 percent of the nation's white population.

By 1966, the Negro population had increased to 21.5 million, and two significant geographic shifts had taken place. The proportion of Negroes living in the South had dropped to 55 percent, and about 69 percent of all Negroes lived in metropolitan areas compared to 64 percent for whites. While the total Negro population more than doubled from 1910 to 1966, the number living in cities rose over fivefold (from 2.7 million to 14.8 million) and the number outside the South rose elevenfold (from 885,000 to 9.7 million).

Negro migration from the South began after the Civil War. By the turn of the century, sizable Negro populations lived in many large Northern cities—Philadelphia, for example, had 63,400 Negro residents in 1900. The movement of Negroes out of the rural South accelerated during World War I, when floods and boll weevils hurt farming in the South and the industrial demands of the war created thousands of new jobs for unskilled workers in the North. After the war, the shift to mechanized farming spurred the continuing movement of Negroes from rural Southern areas.

The Depression slowed this migratory flow, but World War II set it in motion again. More recently, continuing mechanization of agriculture and the expansion of industrial employment in Northern and Western cities have served to sustain the movement of Negroes out of the South, although at a slightly lower rate. (See Table 5.)

From 1960 to 1963, annual Negro out-migration actually dropped to 78,000 but then rose to over 125,000 from 1963 to 1966.

IMPORTANT CHARACTERISTICS OF THIS MIGRATION

It is useful to recall that even the latest scale of Negro migration is relatively small when compared to the earlier waves

TABLE 5

Period	Net Negro out-migration from the South	Annual average rate
1910–20	454,000	45,400
1920–30	749,000	74,900
1930–40	348,000	34,800
1940–50	1,597,000	159,700
1950–60	1,457,000	145,700
1960–66	613,000	102,500

of European immigrants. A total of 8.8 million immigrants entered the United States between 1901 and 1911, and another 5.7 million arrived during the following decade. Even during the years from 1960 through 1966, the 1.8 million immigrants from abroad were almost three times the 613,000 Negroes who departed the South. In these same 6 years, California alone gained over 1.5 million new residents from internal shifts of American population.

Three major routes of Negro migration from the South have developed. One runs north along the Atlantic Seaboard toward Boston, another north from Mississippi toward Chicago, and the third west from Texas and Louisiana toward California. Between 1955 and 1960, 50 percent of the nonwhite migrants to the New York metropolitan area came from North Carolina, South Carolina, Virginia, Georgia, and Alabama; North Carolina alone supplied 20 percent of all New York's nonwhite immigrants. During the same period, almost 60 percent of the nonwhite migrants to Chicago came from Mississippi, Tennessee, Arkansas, Alabama, and Louisiana; Mississippi accounted for almost one-third. During these years, three-fourths of the nonwhite migrants to Los Angeles came from Texas, Louisiana, Mississippi, Arkansas, and Alabama.

The flow of Negroes from the South has caused the Negro population to grow more rapidly in the North and West, as indicated in Table 6.

As a result, although a much higher proportion of Negroes still reside in the South, the distribution of Negroes throughout the United States is beginning to approximate that of whites, as Tables 7 and 8 show.

TABLE 6

	Total Negro population gains (millions)		Percentage of gain
Period	North & West	South	North & West
1940–50	1.859	0.321	85.2
1950–60	2.741	1.086	71.6
1960–66	2.119	0.517	80.4

TABLE 7

Percentage Distribution of the Population by Region— 1950, 1960, and 1966

	Negro			White		
	1950	1960	1966	1950	1960*	1966
United States	100	100	100	100	100	100
South	68	60	55	27	27	28
North	28	34	37	59	56	55
Northeast	13	16	17	28	26	26
Northcentral	15	18	20	31	30	29
West	4	6	8	14	16	17

* Rounds to 99.

TABLE 8

Negroes as a Percentage of the Total Population in the United States and Each Region 1950, 1960, and 1966

	1950	1960	1966
United States	10	11	11
South	22	21	20
North	5	7	8
West	3	4	5

Negroes in the North and West are now so numerous that natural increase rather than migration provides the greater part of Negro population gains there. And even though Negro migration has continued at a high level, it comprises a constantly declining proportion of Negro growth in these regions. (See Table 9.)

TABLE 9

Period	Percentage of total North and West Negro gain from Southern in-migration
1940–50	85.9
1950–60	53.1
1960–66	28.9

In other words, we have reached the point where the Negro populations of the North and West will continue to expand significantly even if migration from the South drops substantially.

FUTURE MIGRATION

Despite accelerating Negro migration from the South, the Negro population there has continued to rise. (See Table 10.)

Nor is it likely to halt. Negro birth rates in the South, as elsewhere, have fallen sharply since 1957, but so far this decline has been offset by the rising Negro population base remaining in the South. From 1950 to 1960, Southern Negro births generated an average net increase of 254,000 per year and, from 1960 to 1966, an average of 188,000 per year. Even if Negro birth rates continue to fall they are likely to remain high enough to support significant migration to other regions for some time to come.

The Negro population in the South is becoming increasingly urbanized. In 1950, there were 5.4 million Southern rural Negroes; by 1960, 4.8 million. But this decline has been more than offset by increases in the urban population. A rising proportion of interregional migration now consists of persons moving from one city to another. From 1960 to 1966, rural Negro population

TABLE 10

Date	Negro population in the South (millions)	Change from preceding date	
		Total	Annual average
1940	9.9	—	—
1950	10.2	321,000	32,100
1960	11.3	1,086,000	108,600
1966	11.8	517,000	86,200

in the South was far below its peak, but the annual average migration of Negroes from the South was still substantial.

These facts demonstrate that Negro migration from the South, which has maintained a high rate for the past 60 years, will continue unless economic conditions change dramatically in either the South or the North and West. This conclusion is reinforced by the fact that most Southern states in recent decades have also experienced outflows of white population. From 1950 to 1960, 11 of the 17 Southern states (including the District of Columbia) "exported" white population—as compared to 13 which "exported" Negro population. Excluding Florida's net gain by migration of 1.5 million, the other 16 Southern states together had a net loss by migration of 1.46 million whites.

The Concentration of Negro Population in Large Cities

WHERE NEGRO URBANIZATION HAS OCCURRED

Statistically, the Negro population in America has become more urbanized, and more metropolitan, than the white population. According to Census Bureau estimates, almost 70 percent of all Negroes in 1966 lived in metropolitan areas, compared to 64 percent of all whites. In the South, more than half the Negro population now lives in cities. Rural Negroes outnumber urban Negroes in only four states: Arkansas, Mississippi, North Carolina, and South Carolina.

Basic data concerning Negro urbanization trends . . . indicate that:

Almost all Negro population growth is occurring within metropolitan areas, primarily within central cities. From 1950 to 1966, the U.S. Negro population rose 6.5 million. Over 98 percent of that increase took place in metropolitan areas—86 percent within central cities, 12 percent in the urban fringe.

The vast majority of white population growth is occurring in suburban portions of metropolitan areas. From 1950 to 1966, 77.8 percent of the white population increase of 35.6 million took place in the suburbs. Central cities received only 2.5 percent of this total white increase. Since 1960, white central-city population has actually declined by 1.3 million.

As a result, central cities are steadily becoming more heavily

Negro, while the urban fringes around them remain almost entirely white. The proportion of Negroes in all central cities rose steadily from 12 percent in 1950, to 17 percent in 1960, to 20 percent in 1966. Meanwhile, metropolitan areas outside of central cities remained 95 percent white from 1950 to 1960 and became 96 percent white by 1966.

The Negro population is growing faster, both absolutely and relatively, in the larger metropolitan areas than in the smaller ones. From 1950 to 1966, the proportion of nonwhites in the central cities of metropolitan areas with 1 million or more persons doubled, reaching 26 percent, as compared with 20 percent in the central cities of metropolitan areas containing from 250,000 to 1 million persons and 12 percent in the central cities of metropolitan areas containing under 250,000 persons.

The 12 largest central cities—New York, Chicago, Los Angeles, Philadelphia, Detroit, Baltimore, Houston, Cleveland, Washington, D.C., St. Louis, Milwaukee, and San Francisco—now contain over two-thirds of the Negro population outside the South and almost one-third of the total in the United States. All these cities have experienced rapid increases in Negro population since 1950. In six—Chicago, Detroit, Cleveland, St. Louis, Milwaukee, and San Francisco —the proportion of Negroes at least doubled. In two others— New York and Los Angeles—it probably doubled. In 1968, seven of these cities are over 30 percent Negro, and one, Washington, D.C., is two-thirds Negro.

FACTORS CAUSING RESIDENTIAL SEGREGATION
IN METROPOLITAN AREAS

The early pattern of Negro settlement within each metropolitan area followed that of the immigrant groups. Migrants converged on the older sections of the central city because the lowest-cost housing was located there, friends and relatives were likely to be living there, and the older neighborhoods then often had good public transportation.

But the later phases of Negro settlement and expansion in metropolitan areas diverge sharply from those typical of white immigrants. As the whites were absorbed by the larger society, many left their predominantly ethnic neighborhoods and moved to outlying areas to obtain newer housing and better schools.

Some scattered randomly over the suburban area. Others established new ethnic clusters in the suburbs, but even these rarely contained solely members of a single ethnic group. As a result, most middle-class neighborhoods—both in the suburbs and within central cities—have no distinctive ethnic character, except that they are white.

Nowhere has the expansion of America's urban Negro population followed this pattern of dispersal. Thousands of Negro families have attained incomes, living standards, and cultural levels matching or surpassing those of whites who have "upgraded" themselves from distinctly ethnic neighborhoods. Yet most Negro families have remained within predominantly Negro neighborhoods, primarily because they have been effectively excluded from white residential areas.

Their exclusion has been accomplished through various discriminatory practices, some obvious and overt, others subtle and hidden. Deliberate efforts are sometimes made to discourage Negro families from purchasing or renting homes in all-white neighborhoods. Intimidation and threats of violence have ranged from throwing garbage on lawns and making threatening phone calls to burning crosses in yards and even dynamiting property. More often, real estate agents simply refuse to show homes to Negro buyers.

Many middle-class Negro families, therefore, cease looking for homes beyond all-Negro areas or nearby "changing" neighborhoods. For them, trying to move into all-white neighborhoods is not worth the psychological efforts and costs required.

Another form of discrimination just as significant is white withdrawal from, or refusal to enter, neighborhoods where large numbers of Negroes are moving or already residing. Normal population turnover causes about 2.0 percent of the residents of average U.S. neighborhoods to move out every year because of income changes, job transfers, shifts in life-cycle position, or deaths. This normal turnover rate is even higher in apartment areas. The refusal of whites to move into changing areas when vacancies occur there from normal turnover means that most of these vacancies are eventually occupied by Negroes. An inexorable shift toward heavy Negro occupancy results.

Once this happens, the remaining whites seek to leave, thus confirming the existing belief among whites that complete transformation of a neighborhood is inevitable once Negroes begin to enter. Since the belief itself is one of the major causes of the transformation, it becomes a self-fulfilling prophecy which inhibits the development of racially integrated neighborhoods.

As a result, Negro settlements expand almost entirely through "massive racial transition" at the edges of existing all-Negro neighborhoods, rather than by a gradual dispersion of population throughout the metropolitan area.

Two points are particularly important:

"Massive transition" requires no panic or flight by the original white residents of a neighborhood into which Negroes begin moving. All it requires is the failure or refusal of other whites to fill the vacancies resulting from normal turnover.

Thus, efforts to stop massive transition by persuading present white residents to remain will ultimately fail unless whites outside the neighborhood can be persuaded to move in.

It is obviously true that some residential separation of whites and Negroes would occur even without discriminatory practices by whites. This would result from the desires of some Negroes to live in predominantly Negro neighborhoods and from differences in meaningful social variables, such as income and educational levels. But these factors alone would not lead to the almost complete segregation of whites and Negroes which has developed in our metropolitan areas.

THE EXODUS OF WHITES FROM CENTRAL CITIES

The process of racial transition in central-city neighborhoods has been only one factor among many others causing millions of whites to move out of central cities as the Negro populations there expanded. More basic perhaps have been the rising mobility and affluence of middle-class families and the more attractive living conditions—particularly better schools—in the suburbs.

Whatever the reason, the result is clear. In 1950, 45.5 million whites lived in central cities. If this population had grown from 1950 to 1960 at the same rate as the nation's white population as a whole, it would have increased by 8 million. It actually rose only 2.2 million, indicating an outflow of 5.8 million.[3]

From 1960 to 1966, the white outflow appears to have been even more rapid. White population of central cities declined 1.3 million instead of rising 3.6 million—as it would if it had grown at the same rate as the entire white population. In theory, therefore, 4.9 million whites left central cities during these 6 years.

Statistics for all central cities as a group understate the relationship between Negro population growth and white outflow in individual central cities. The fact is, many cities with relatively few Negroes experienced rapid white-population growth, thereby obscuring the size of white out-migration that took place in cities having large increases in Negro population. For example, from 1950 to 1960, the 10 largest cities in the United States had a total Negro population increase of 1.6 million, or 55 percent, while the white population there declined 1.4 million. If the two cities where the white population increased (Los Angeles and Houston) are excluded, the nonwhite population in the remaining eight rose 1.4 million, whereas their white population declined 2.1 million. If the white population in these cities had increased at only half the rate of the white population in the United States as a whole from 1950 to 1960, it would have risen by 1.4 million. Thus, these eight cities actually experienced a white out-migration of at least 3.5 million, while gaining 1.4 million nonwhites.

THE EXTENT OF RESIDENTIAL SEGREGATION

The rapid expansion of all-Negro residential areas and large-scale white withdrawal have continued a pattern of residential segregation that has existed in American cities for decades. A recent study[4] reveals that this pattern is present to a high degree in every large city in America. The authors devised an

[3] The outflow of whites may be somewhat smaller than the 5.8 million difference between these figures, because the ages of the whites in many central cities are higher than in the Nation as a whole, and therefore the population would have grown somewhat more slowly.
[4] "Negroes in Cities," Karl and Alma Taeuber, Aldine Publishing Co., Chicago (1965).

index to measure the degree of residential segregation. The index indicates for each city that percentage of Negroes who would have to move from the blocks where they now live to other blocks in order to provide a perfectly proportional unsegregated distribution of population.

According to their findings, the average segregation index for 207 of the largest U.S. cities was 86.2 in 1960. This means that an average of over 86 percent of all Negroes would have had to change blocks to create an unsegregated population distribution. Southern cities had a higher average index (90.9) than cities in the Northeast (79.2), the North Central (87.7), or the West (79.3). Only eight cities had index values below 70, whereas over 50 had values above 91.7.

The degree of residential segregation for all 207 cities has been relatively stable, averaging 85.2 in 1940, 87.3 in 1950, and 86.2 in 1960. Variations within individual regions were only slightly larger. However, a recent Census Bureau study shows that in most of the 12 large cities where special censuses were taken in the mid-1960s, the proportions of Negroes living in neighborhoods of greatest Negro concentration had increased since 1960.

Residential segregation is generally more prevalent with respect to Negroes than for any other minority group, including Puerto Ricans, Orientals, and Mexican-Americans. Moreover, it varies little between central city and suburb. This nearly universal pattern cannot be explained in terms of economic discrimination against all low-income groups. Analysis of 15 representative cities indicates that white upper- and middle-income households are far more segregated from Negro upper- and middle-income households than from white lower-income households.

In summary, the concentration of Negroes in central cities results from a combination of forces. Some of these forces, such as migration and initial settlement patterns in older neighborhoods, are similar to those which affected previous ethnic minorities. Others—particularly discrimination in employment and segregation in housing and schools—are a result of white attitudes based on race and color. These forces continue to shape the future of the central city.

| | | | Estimate,* |
TABLE 11	1950	1960	1965
New York, N.Y.	10	14	18
Chicago, Ill.	14	23	28
Los Angeles, Calif.	9	14	17
Philadelphia, Pa.	18	26	31
Detroit, Mich.	16	29	34
Baltimore, Md.	24	35	38
Houston, Tex.	21	23	23
Cleveland, Ohio	16	29	34
Washington, D.C.	35	54	66
St. Louis, Mo.	18	29	36
Milwaukee, Wis.	3	8	11
San Francisco, Calif.	6	10	12
Boston, Mass.	5	9	13
Dallas, Tex.	13	19	21
New Orleans, La.	32	37	41
Pittsburgh, Pa.	12	17	20
San Antonio, Tex.	7	7	8
San Diego, Calif.	5	6	7
Seattle, Wash.	3	5	7
Buffalo, N.Y.	6	13	17
Cincinnati, Ohio	16	22	24
Memphis, Tenn.	37	37	40
Denver, Colo.	4	6	9
Atlanta, Ga.	37	38	44
Minneapolis, Minn.	1	2	4
Indianapolis, Ind.	15	21	23
Kansas City, Mo.	12	18	22
Columbus, Ohio	12	16	18
Phoenix, Ariz.	5	5	5
Newark, N.J.	17	34	47

Proportion of Negroes in Each of the 30 Largest Cities, 1950, 1960, and Estimated 1965

* Except for Cleveland, Buffalo, Memphis, and Phoenix, for which a special census has been made in recent years, these are very rough estimations computed on the basis of the change in relative proportions of Negro births and deaths since 1960.

SOURCE: U.S. Department of Commerce, Bureau of the Census, BLS Report No. 332, p. 11.

UNEMPLOYMENT, FAMILY STRUCTURE, AND SOCIAL DISORGANIZATION

Recent Economic Trends

The Negro population in our country is as diverse in income, occupation, family composition, and other variables as the white community. Nevertheless, for purposes of analysis, three major Negro economic groups can be identified.

The first and smallest group consists of middle and upper income individuals and households whose educational, occupational, and cultural characteristics are similar to those of middle and upper income white groups.

The second and largest group contains Negroes whose incomes are above the "poverty level" but who have not attained the educational, occupational, or income status typical of middle-class Americans.

The third group has very low educational, occupational, and income attainments and lives below the "poverty level."

A recent compilation of data on American Negroes by the Departments of Labor and Commerce shows that although incomes of both Negroes and whites have been rising rapidly,

> Negro incomes still remain far below those of whites. Negro median family income was only 58 percent of the white median in 1966.
>
> Negro family income is not keeping pace with white family income growth. In constant 1965 dollars, median nonwhite income in 1947 was $2,174 lower than median white income. By 1966, the gap had grown to $3,036.
>
> The Negro upper income group is expanding rapidly and achieving sizeable income gains. In 1966, 28 percent of all Negro families received incomes of $7,000 or more, compared with 55 percent of white families. This was 1.6 times the proportion of Negroes receiving comparable incomes in 1960, and four times greater than the proportion receiving such incomes in 1947. Moreover, the proportion of Negroes employed in high-skill, high-status, and well-paying jobs rose faster than comparable proportions among whites from 1960 to 1966.
>
> As Negro incomes have risen, the size of the lowest income group has grown smaller, and the middle and upper groups

have grown larger—both relatively and absolutely. (See Table 12.)

About two-thirds of the lowest income group—or 20 percent of all Negro families—are making no significant economic gains despite continued general prosperity. Half of these hardcore disadvantaged—more than 2 million persons —live in central-city neighborhoods. Recent special censuses in Los Angeles and Cleveland indicate that the incomes of persons living in the worst slum areas have not risen at all during this period, unemployment rates have declined only slightly, the proportion of families with female heads has increased, and housing conditions have worsened even though rents have risen.

TABLE 12

| | Percentage of Negro families | | | Percentage of white families |
| | 1947 | 1960 | 1966 | 1966 |
Group				
$7,000 and over	7	17	28	55
$3,000 to $6,999	29	40	41	33
Under $3,000	65	44	32	13

Thus, between 2.0 and 2.5 million poor Negroes are living in disadvantaged neighborhoods of central cities in the United States. These persons comprise only slightly more than 1 percent of the Nation's total population, but they make up about 16 to 20 percent of the total Negro population of all central cities, and a much higher proportion in certain cities.

Unemployment and Underemployment

THE CRITICAL SIGNIFICANCE OF EMPLOYMENT

The capacity to obtain and hold a "good job" is the traditional test of participation in American society. Steady employment with adequate compensation provides both purchasing power and social status. It develops the capabilities, confidence, and self-esteem an individual needs to be a responsible citizen, and provides a basis for a stable family life. As Daniel P. Moynihan has written:

The principal measure of progress toward equality will be that of employment. It is the primary source of individual or group identity. In America what you do is what you are: to do nothing is to be nothing; to do little to be little. The equations are implacable and blunt, and ruthlessly public.

For the Negro American it is already, and will continue to be, the master problem. It is the measure of white bona fides. It is the measure of Negro competence, and also of the competence of American society. Most importantly, the linkage between problems of employment and the range of social pathology that afflicts the Negro community is unmistakable. Employment not only controls the present for the Negro American but, in a most profound way, it is creating the future as well.

For residents of disadvantaged Negro neighborhoods, obtaining good jobs is vastly more difficult than for most workers in society. For decades, social, economic, and psychological disadvantages surrounding the urban Negro poor have impaired their work capacities and opportunities. The result is a cycle of failure—the employment disabilities of one generation breed those of the next.

Negro Unemployment

Unemployment rates among Negroes have declined from a post-Korean War high of 12.6 percent in 1958 to 8.2 percent in 1967. Among married Negro men, the unemployment rate for 1967 was down to 3.2 percent.[5]

Notwithstanding this decline, unemployment rates for Negroes are still double those for whites in every category, including married men, as they have been throughout the postwar period. Moreover, since 1954, even during the current unprecedented period of sustained economic growth, unemployment among Negroes has been continuously above the 6 percent "recession" level widely regarded as a sign of serious economic weakness when prevalent for the entire work force.

While the Negro unemployment rate remains high in relation to the white rate, the number of additional jobs needed

[5] Adjusted for Census Bureau undercounting.

to lower this to the level of white unemployment is surprisingly small. In 1967, approximately 3 million persons were unemployed during an average week, of whom about 638,000, or 21 percent were nonwhites. When corrected for undercounting, total nonwhite unemployment was approximately 712,000 or 8 percent of the nonwhite labor force. To reduce the unemployment rate to 3.4 percent, the rate prevalent among whites, jobs must be found for 57.5 percent of these unemployed persons. This amounts to nearly 409,000 jobs, or about 27 percent of the net number of new jobs added to the economy in the year 1967 alone and only slightly more than one-half of 1 percent of all jobs in the United States in 1967.

THE LOW-STATUS AND LOW-PAYING NATURE OF MANY NEGRO JOBS

Even more important perhaps than unemployment is the related problem of the undesirable nature of many jobs open to Negroes. Negro workers are concentrated in the lowest-skilled and lowest-paying occupations. These jobs often involve substandard wages, great instability and uncertainty of tenure, extremely low status in the eyes of both employer and employee, little or no chance for meaningful advancement, and unpleasant or exhausting duties. Negro men in particular are more than three times as likely as whites to be in unskilled or service jobs which pay far less than most. (See Table 13.)

This concentration in the least desirable jobs can be viewed another way by calculating the changes which would occur if Negro men were employed in various occupations in the same proportions as the male labor force as a whole (not solely the white labor force). (See Table 14.)

Thus, upgrading the employment of Negro men to make their occupational distribution identical with that of the labor force as a whole would have an immense impact upon the nature of their occupations. About 1.3 million nonwhite men—or 28 percent of those employed in 1966—would move up the employment ladder into one of the higher-status and higher-paying categories. The effect of such a shift upon the incomes of Negro men would be very great. Using the 1966 job distribution, the shift indicated above would produce about

$4.8 billion more earned income for nonwhite men alone if they received the 1965 median income in each occupation. This would be a rise of approximately 30 percent in the earnings actually received by all nonwhite men in 1965 (not counting any sources of income other than wages and salaries).

TABLE 13

Type of occupation	Percentage of male workers in each type of occupation, 1966		Median earnings of all male civilians in each occupation, 1965
	White	Nonwhite	
Professional, technical, and managerial	27	9	$7,603*
Clerical and sales	14	9	5,532*
Craftsmen and foremen	20	12	6,270
Operatives	20	27	5,046
Service workers	6	16	3,436
Nonfarm laborers	6	20	2,410
Farmers and farm workers	7	8	1,669*

* Average of two categories from normal Census Bureau categories as combined in data presented in The Social and Economic Conditions of Negroes in the United States (BLS No. 332).

TABLE 14

Type of occupation	Number of male nonwhite workers, 1966			
	As actually distributed*	If distributed the same as all male workers	Difference	
			Number	Per- centage
Professional, technical, and managerial	415,000	1,173,000	+758,000	+183
Clerical and sales	415,000	628,000	+213,000	+51
Craftsmen and foremen	553,000	894,000	+341,000	+62
Operatives	1,244,000	964,000	−280,000	−23
Service workers	737,000	326,000	−411,000	−56
Nonfarm laborers	922,000	340,000	−582,000	−63
Farmers and farm workers	369,000	330,000	−39,000	−11

* Estimates based upon percentages set forth in BLS No. 332, p. 41.

Of course, the kind of "instant upgrading" visualized in these calculations does not represent a practical alternative for national policy. The economy cannot drastically reduce the total number of low-status jobs it now contains, or shift large numbers of people upward in occupation in any short period. Therefore, major upgrading in the employment status of Negro men must come through a faster relative expansion of higher-level jobs than lower-level jobs (which has been occurring for several decades), an improvement in the skills of nonwhite workers so they can obtain a high proportion of those added better jobs, and a drastic reduction of discriminatory hiring and promotion practices in all enterprises, both private and public.

Nevertheless, this hypothetical example clearly shows that the concentration of male Negro employment at the lowest end of the occupational scale is greatly depressing the incomes of U.S. Negroes in general. In fact, this is the single most important source of poverty among Negroes. It is even more important than unemployment, as can be shown by a second hypothetical calculation. In 1966, there were about 724,000 unemployed nonwhites in the United States on the average, including adults and teenagers, and allowing for the Census Bureau undercount of Negroes. If every one of these persons had been employed and had received the median amount earned by nonwhite males in 1966 ($3,864), this would have added a total of $2.8 billion to nonwhite income as a whole. If only enough of these persons had been employed at that wage to reduce nonwhite unemployment from 7.3 percent to 3.3 percent—the rate among whites in 1966—then the income gain for nonwhites would have totaled about $1.5 billion. But if nonwhite unemployment remained at 7.3 percent, and nonwhite men were upgraded so that they had the same occupational distribution and incomes as all men in the labor force considered together, this would have produced about $4.8 billion in additional income, as noted above (using 1965 earnings for calculation). Thus the potential income gains from upgrading the male nonwhite labor force are much larger than those from reducing nonwhite unemployment.

This conclusion underlines the difficulty of improving the economic status of Negro men. It is far easier to create new jobs than either to create new jobs with relatively high status and earning power, or to upgrade existing employed or partly employed workers into such better-quality employment. Yet only such upgrading will eliminate the fundamental basis of poverty and deprivation among Negro families.

Access to good-quality jobs clearly affects the willingness of Negro men actively to seek work. In riot cities surveyed by the Commission with the largest percentage of Negroes in skilled and semiskilled jobs, Negro men participated in the labor force to the same extent as, or greater than, white men. Conversely, where most Negro men were heavily concentrated in menial jobs, they participated less in the labor force than white men.

Even given similar employment, Negro workers with the same education as white workers are paid less. This disparity doubtless results to some extent from inferior training in segregated schools, and also from the fact that large numbers of Negroes are only now entering certain occupations for the first time. However, the differentials are so large and so universal at all educational levels that they clearly reflect the patterns of discrimination which characterize hiring and promotion practices in many segments of the economy. For example, in 1966, among persons who had completed high school, the median income of Negroes was only 73 percent that of whites. Even among persons with an eighth-grade education, Negro median income was only 80 percent of white median income.

At the same time, a higher proportion of Negro women than white women participates in the labor force at nearly all ages except 16 to 19. For instance, in 1966, 55 percent of nonwhite women from 25 to 34 years of age were employed, compared to only 38 percent of white women in the same age group. The fact that almost half of all adult Negro women work reflects the fact that so many Negro males have unsteady and low-paying jobs. Yet even though Negro women are often better able to find work than Negro men, the unemployment rate among adult nonwhite women (20 years old and over) in 1967 was 7.1 percent, compared to the 4.3 percent rate among adult nonwhite men.

Unemployment rates are, of course, much higher among teenagers, both Negro and white, than among adults; in fact about one-third of all unemployed Negroes in 1967 were between 16 and 19 years old. During the first 9 months of 1967, the unemployment rate among nonwhite teenagers was 26.5 per cent; for whites, it was 10.6 percent. About 219,300 nonwhite teenagers were unemployed.[6] About 58,300 were still in school but were actively looking for jobs.

SUBEMPLOYMENT IN DISADVANTAGED NEGRO NEIGHBORHOODS

In disadvantaged areas, employment conditions for Negroes are in a chronic state of crisis. Surveys in low-income neighborhoods of nine large cities made by the Department of Labor late in 1966 revealed that the rate of unemployment there was 9.3 percent, compared to 7.3 percent for Negroes generally and 3.3 percent for whites. Moreover, a high proportion of the persons living in these areas were "underemployed," that is, they were either part-time workers looking for full-time employment, or full-time workers earning less than $3,000 per year, or had dropped out of the labor force. The Department of Labor estimated that this underemployment is 2½ times greater than the number of unemployed in these areas. Therefore, the "subemployment rate," including both the unemployed and the underemployed, was about 32.7 percent in the nine areas surveyed, or 8.8 times greater than the overall unemployment rate for all U.S. workers. Since underemployment also exists outside disadvantaged neighborhoods, comparing the full subemployment rate in these areas with the unemployment rate for the Nation as a whole is not entirely valid. However, it provides some measure of the enormous disparity between employment conditions in most of the Nation and those prevalent in disadvantaged Negro areas in our large cities.

The critical problem is to determine the actual number of

[6] After adjusting for Census Bureau undercounting.

those unemployed and underemployed in central-city Negro ghettos. . . . The outcome of this process is summarized in Table 15.

Therefore, in order to bring subemployment in these areas down to a level equal to unemployment alone among whites, enough steady, reasonably paying jobs (and the training and motivation to perform them) must be provided to eliminate all underemployment and reduce unemployment by 65 percent. For all three age groups combined, this deficit amounted to 923,000 jobs in 1967.

TABLE 15

| Group | Nonwhite subemployment in disadvantaged areas of all central cities, 1967 | | |
	Unemployment	Underemployment	Total subemployment
Adult men	102,000	230,000	332,000
Adult women	118,000	266,000	384,000
Teenagers	98,000	220,000	318,000
Total	318,000	716,000	1,034,000

The Magnitude of Poverty in Disadvantaged Neighborhoods

The chronic unemployment problems in the central city, aggravated by the constant arrival of new unemployed migrants, is the fundamental cause of the persistent poverty in disadvantaged Negro areas.

"Poverty" in the affluent society is more than absolute deprivation. Many of the poor in the United States would be well off in other societies. Relative deprivation—inequality— is a more useful concept of poverty with respect to the Negro in America because it encompasses social and political exclusions as well as economic inequality. Because of the lack of data of this type, we have had to focus our analysis on a measure of poverty which is both economic and absolute—the Social Security Administration's "poverty level"[7] concept. It is

[7] $3,335 per year for an urban family of four.

clear, however, that broader measures of poverty would substantiate the conclusions that follow.

In 1966, there were 29.7 million persons in the United States
—15.3 percent of the Nation's population—with incomes below
the "poverty level," as defined by the Social Security Administration. Of these, 20.3 million were white (68.3 percent), and
9.3 million nonwhite (13.7 percent). Thus, about 11.9 percent
of the Nation's whites and 40.6 percent of its nonwhites were
poor under the Social Security definition.

The location of the Nation's poor is best shown from 1964
data as indicated by Table 16.

TABLE 16

| | Percentage of those in poverty in each group living in— | | | |
| | Metropolitan areas | | | |
Group	In central cities	Outside central cities	Other areas	Total
Whites	23.8	21.8	54.4	100
Nonwhites	41.7	10.8	47.5	100
Total	29.4	18.4	52.2	100

SOURCE: Social Security Administration.

The following facts concerning poverty are relevant to an
understanding of the problems faced by people living in disadvantaged neighborhoods.[8]

In central cities 30.7 percent of nonwhite families of two or
more persons lived in poverty compared to only 8.8 percent of
whites.

Of the 10.1 million poor persons in central cities in 1964,
about 4.4 million of these (43.6 percent) were nonwhites, and
5.7 million (56.4 percent) were whites. The poor whites were
much older on the average than the poor nonwhites. The
proportion of poor persons 65 years old or older was 23.2
percent among whites, but only 6.8 percent among nonwhites.

Poverty was more than twice as prevalent among nonwhite
families with female heads as among those with male heads,

[8] Source: Social Security Administration; based on 1964 data.

57 percent compared to 21 percent. In central cities, 26 percent of all nonwhite families of two or more persons had female heads, as compared to 12 percent of white families.

Among nonwhite families headed by a female, and having children under 6, the incidence of poverty was 81 percent. Moreover, there were 243,000 such families living in poverty in central cities—or over 9 percent of all nonwhite families in those cities.

Among all children living in poverty within central cities, nonwhites outnumbered whites by over 400,000. The number of poor nonwhite children equalled or surpassed the number of white poor children in every age group. (See Table 17.)

Two stark facts emerge:

54 percent of all poor children in central cities in 1964 were nonwhites.

Of the 4.4 million nonwhites living in poverty within central cities in 1964, 52 percent were children under 16 and 61 percent were under 21.

Since 1964, the number of nonwhite families living in poverty within central cities has remained about the same; hence, these poverty conditions are probably still prevalent in central cities in terms of absolute numbers of persons, although the proportion of persons in poverty may have dropped slightly.[9]

		Number of Children Living	
TABLE 17		*in Poverty (Millions)*	
Age group	*White*	*Nonwhite*	*Percentage of total nonwhite*
Under 6	0.9	1.0	53
6 to 15	1.0	1.3	57
16 to 21	0.4	0.4	50
Total	2.3	2.7	54

[9] For the Nation as a whole, the proportion of nonwhite families living in poverty dropped from 39 percent to 35 percent from 1964 to 1966 (defining "family" somewhat differently from the definition used in the data above). The number of such families declined from 1.9 million to 1.7 million. However, the number and proportion of all nonwhites living in central cities rose in the same period. As a result, the number of nonwhite families living in so-called "poverty areas" of large cities actually rose from 1,561,000 in 1960 to 1,588,000 in 1966.

The Social Impact of Employment Problems in Disadvantaged Negro Areas

UNEMPLOYMENT AND THE FAMILY

The high rates of unemployment and underemployment in racial ghettos are evidence, in part, that many men living in these areas are seeking, but cannot obtain, jobs which will support a family. Perhaps equally important, most jobs they can get are at the low end of the occupational scale, and often lack the necessary status to sustain a worker's self-respect, or the respect of his family and friends. These same men are also constantly confronted with the message of discrimination: "You are inferior because of a trait you did not cause and cannot change." This message reinforces feelings of inadequacy arising from repeated failure to obtain and keep decent jobs.

Wives of these men are forced to work and usually produce more money. If the men stay at home without working, their inadequacies constantly confront them and tensions arise between them and their wives and children. Under these pressures, it is not surprising that many of these men flee their responsibilities as husbands and fathers, leaving home, and drifting from city to city, or adopting the style of "street-corner men."

Statistical evidence tends to document this. A close correlation exists between the number of nonwhite married women separated from their husbands each year and the unemployment rate among nonwhite males 20 years old and over. Similarly, from 1948 to 1962, the number of new Aid to Families with Dependent Children cases rose and fell with the nonwhite male unemployment rate. Since 1963, however, the number of new cases—most of them Negro children—has steadily increased even though the unemployment rate among nonwhite males has declined. The impact of marital status on employment among Negroes is shown by the fact that in 1967 the proportion of married men either divorced or separated from their wives was more than twice as high among unemployed nonwhite men as among employed nonwhite men. Moreover, among those participating in the labor force, there was a higher proportion of married men with wives present than with wives absent. (See Table 18.)

FATHERLESS FAMILIES

The abandonment of the home by many Negro males affects a great many children growing up in the racial ghetto. As previously indicated, most American Negro families are headed by men, just like most other American families. Yet the proportion of families with female heads is much greater among Negroes than among whites at all income levels, and has been rising in recent years. (See Table 19.)

TABLE 18	*Unemployment Rate and Participation in Total Labor Force, 25 to 54-Year-Old Nonwhite Men, by Marital Status, March, 1967*	
	Unemployment rate, nonwhite	*Labor force participation (percent), nonwhite*
Married, wife present	3.7	96.7
Other (separated, divorced, widowed)	8.7	77.6

TABLE 19	*Proportion of Families of Various Types**			
	Husband-Wife		*Female head*	
Date	*White*	*Nonwhite*	*White*	*Nonwhite*
1950	88.0	77.7	8.5	17.6
1960	88.7	73.6	8.7	22.4
1966	88.8	72.7	8.9	23.7

* In percent.

This disparity between white and nonwhite families is far greater among the lowest income families—those most likely to reside in disadvantaged big-city neighborhoods—than among higher income families. Among families with incomes under

$3,000 in 1966, the proportion with female heads was 42 percent for Negroes but only 23 percent for whites. In contrast, among families with incomes of $7,000 or more, 8 percent of Negro families had female heads compared to 4 percent of whites.

The problems of "fatherlessness" are aggravated by the tendency of the poor to have large families. The average poor, urban, nonwhite family contains 4.8 persons, as compared with 3.7 for the average poor, urban, white family. This is one of the primary factors in the poverty status of nonwhite households in large cities.

The proportion of fatherless families appears to be increasing in the poorest Negro neighborhoods. In the Hough section of Cleveland, the proportion of families with female heads rose from 23 to 32 percent from 1960 to 1965. In the Watts section of Los Angeles it rose from 36 to 39 percent during the same period.

The handicap imposed on children growing up without fathers, in an atmosphere of poverty and deprivation, is increased because many mothers must work to provide support. Table 20 illustrates the disparity between the proportion of nonwhite women in the child-rearing ages who are in the labor force and the comparable proportion of white women.

TABLE 20	*Percentage of Women in the Labor Force*	
Age group	*Nonwhite*	*White*
20 to 24	55	51
25 to 34	55	38
35 to 44	61	45

With the father absent and the mother working, many ghetto children spend the bulk of their time on the streets— the streets of a crime-ridden, violence-prone, and poverty-stricken world. The image of success in this world is not that of the "solid citizen," the responsible husband and father, but rather that of the "hustler" who promotes his own interests by exploiting others. The dope sellers and the numbers runners are the "successful" men because their earnings far outstrip those men who try to climb the economic ladder in honest ways.

Young people in the ghetto are acutely conscious of a system which appears to offer rewards to those who illegally exploit others, and failure to those who struggle under traditional responsibilities. Under these circumstances, many adopt exploitation and the "hustle" as a way of life, disclaiming both work and marriage in favor of casual and temporary liaisons. This pattern reinforces itself from one generation to the next, creating a "culture of poverty" and an ingrained cynicism about society and its institutions.

THE "JUNGLE"

The culture of poverty that results from unemployment and family disorganization generates a system of ruthless, exploitative relationships within the ghetto. Prostitution, dope addiction, casual sexual affairs, and crime create an environmental jungle characterized by personal insecurity and tension. The effects of this development are stark:

> The rate of illegitimate births among nonwhite women has risen sharply in the past two decades. In 1940, 16.8 percent of all nonwhite births were illegitimate. By 1950 this proportion was 18 percent; by 1960, 21.6 percent; by 1966, 26.3 percent. In the ghettos of many large cities, illegitimacy rates exceed 50 percent.

> The rate of illegitimacy among nonwhite women is closely related to low income and high unemployment. In Washington, D.C., for example, an analysis of 1960 census tracts shows that in tracts with unemployment rates of 12 percent or more among nonwhite men, illegitimacy was over 40 percent. But in tracts with unemployment rates of 2.9 percent and below among nonwhite men, reported illegitimacy was under 20 percent. A similar contrast existed between tracts in which median nonwhite income was under $4,000 (where illegitimacy was 38 percent) and those in which it was $8,000 and over (where illegitimacy was 12 percent).

> Narcotics addiction is also heavily concentrated in low-income Negro neighborhoods, particularly in New York City. Of the 59,720 addicts known to the U.S. Bureau of Narcotics at the end of 1966, just over 50 percent were Negroes. Over

52 percent of all known addicts lived within New York State, mostly in Harlem and other Negro neighborhoods. These figures undoubtedly greatly understate the actual number of persons using narcotics regularly—especially those under 21.

Not surprisingly, at every age from 6 through 19, the proportion of children from homes with both parents present who actually attend school is higher than the proportion of children from homes with only one parent or neither present.

Rates of juvenile delinquency, venereal disease, dependency upon [Aid to Families with Dependent Children] support, and use of public assistance in general are much higher in disadvantaged Negro areas than in other parts of large cities. Data taken from New York City contrasting predominantly Negro neighborhoods with the city as a whole clearly illustrate this fact. (See Table 21.)

		Social Distress—Major Predominantly Negro Neighborhoods in New York City and the City as a Whole		
TABLE 21				
	Juvenile delinquency[a]	*Venereal disease[b]*	*ADC[c]*	*Public assistance[d]*
Brownsville	125.3	609.9	459.0	265.8
East New York	98.6	207.5	148.6	71.8
Bedford-Stuyvesant	115.2	771.3	337.1	197.2
Harlem	110.8	1,603.5	265.7	138.1
South Bronx	84.4	308.3	278.5	165.5
New York City	52.2	269.1	120.7	60.8

[a] Number of offenses per 1,000 persons 7–20 years (1965).
[b] Number of cases per 100,000 persons under 21 years (1964).
[c] Number of children in aid to dependent children cases per 1,000 under 18 years, using 1960 population as base (1965).
[d] Welfare assistance recipients per 1,000 persons, using 1960 population as base (1965).

In conclusion: in 1965, 1.2 million nonwhite children under 16 lived in central city families headed by a woman under 65. The great majority of these children were growing up in poverty under conditions that make them better candidates for crime and civil disorder than for jobs providing an entry into American society. Because of the immense importance of this fact—the potential loss to the society of these young people—we describe these conditions in the [following note.]

CALCULATIONS OF NONWHITE SUBEMPLOYMENT IN
DISADVANTAGED AREAS OF ALL CENTRAL CITIES, 1967

In 1967, total unemployment in the United States was distributed as follows, by age and color:

TABLE 22

Group	Nonwhite	White	Total
Adult men (20 and over)	193,000	866,000	1,059,000
Adult women (20 and over)	241,000	837,000	1,078,000
Teenagers (16–19)	204,000	635,000	839,000
Total	638,000	2,338,000	2,976,000

Adjustments for the Census Bureau undercount of nonwhite males in the labor force amounting to 7.5 percent for the teenage group, 18 percent for the adult male group and approximately 10 percent for adult females result in the following revised total employment:

TABLE 23

Group	Nonwhite	White	Total
Adult men	228,000	866,000	1,094,000
Adult women	265,000	837,000	1,102,000
Teenagers	219,000	635,000	854,000
Total	712,000	2,338,000	3,050,000

These figures cover the entire United States. To provide an estimate of the number of unemployed in disadvantaged neighborhoods within central cities, it is necessary to discover what proportion of the nonwhite unemployed are in central cities and what proportion of those in central cities are within the most disadvantaged neighborhoods. The Department of Labor survey in nine large central cities covering the first 9 months of 1967 showed that these cities contained 27.3 percent of the total nonwhite labor force in the United States, and 26.4 percent of total nonwhite unemployment. Hence, it is reasonable to assume that nonwhite unemployment is concentrated in central cities to about the same degree as the nonwhite labor force. In turn, the nonwhite labor force is located in central cities in about the same proportion as the nonwhite population, or 57.1 percent in 1967. Thus central-city unemployment among nonwhites was presumably about 57.1 percent of the national figures:

	Nonwhite Unemployment in All Central Cities
TABLE 24	
[Rounded]	
Adult men	130,000
Adult women	151,000
Teenagers	125,000
Total	406,000

Within large central cities, about 62 percent of all nonwhite families lived in certain Census Tracts which have been designated "poverty areas." These tracts ranked lowest in United States cities over 250,000 persons in size, according to an index of "deprivation" based upon family income, children in broken homes, persons with low educational attainment, males in unskilled jobs, and substandard housing. On the assumption that conditions in these poverty areas are comparable to those in the nine disadvantaged areas surveyed by the Department of Labor in 1966, the number of unemployed nonwhites in disadvantaged areas of central cities is as follows:[10]

	Nonwhite Unemployment in Disadvantaged Areas of All Central Cities, 1967
TABLE 25	
Adult men	102,000
Adult women	118,000
Teenagers	98,000
Total	318,000

[10] The number of nonwhite unemployed in the more disadvantaged areas was 26 percent higher than it would have been had it been proportional to the total population residing there. Therefore, the proportion of central city nonwhite unemployed in poverty areas is assumed to equal 78.1 percent (62 percent times 1.26).

The number of underemployed nonwhites in these areas was about 2.5 times larger than the number of unemployed. But we have already accounted for some underemployment in the adjustment for undercounting—so we will assume non-white underemployment was 2.25 times adjusted unemployment for all three age and sex groups. The resulting rough estimates are as follows:

TABLE 26		*Nonwhite Subemployment in Disadvantaged Areas of All Central Cities, 1967*	
Group	*Unemployment*	*Underemployment*	*Total Subemployment*
Adult men	102,000	230,000	332,000
Adult women	118,000	266,000	384,000
Teenagers	98,000	220,000	318,000
Total	318,000	716,000	1,034,000

CONDITIONS OF LIFE IN THE RACIAL GHETTO

The conditions of life in the racial ghetto are strikingly different from those to which most Americans are accustomed —especially white, middle-class Americans. We believe it important to describe these conditions and their effect on the lives of people who cannot escape from the ghetto.[11]

Crime and Insecurity

Nothing is more fundamental to the quality of life in any area than the sense of personal security of its residents, and nothing affects this more than crime.

[11] We have not attempted here to describe conditions relating to the fundamental problems of housing, education, and welfare, which are treated in detail in later chapters.

In general, crime rates in large cities are much higher than in other areas of our country. Within such cities, crime rates are higher in disadvantaged Negro areas than anywhere else.

The most widely used measure of crime is the number of "index crimes" (homicide, forcible rape, aggravated assault, robbery, burglary, grand larceny, and auto theft) in relation to population. In 1966, 1,754 such crimes were reported to police for every 100,000 Americans. In cities over 250,000, the rate was 3,153, and in cities over 1 million, it was 3,630—or more than double the national average. In suburban areas alone, including suburban cities, the rate was only 1,300, or just over one-third the rate in the largest cities.

Within larger cities, personal and property insecurity has consistently been highest in the older neighborhoods encircling the downtown business district. In most cities, crime rates for many decades have been higher in these inner areas than anywhere, except in downtown areas themselves, where they are inflated by the small number of residents.

High crime rates have persisted in these inner areas even though the ethnic character of their residents continually changed. Poor immigrants used these areas as "entry ports," then usually moved on to more desirable neighborhoods as soon as they acquired enough resources. Many "entry port" areas have now become racial ghettos.

The difference between crime rates in these disadvantaged neighborhoods and in other parts of the city is usually startling, as a comparison of crime rates in five police districts in Chicago for 1965 illustrates. These five include one high-income, all-white district at the periphery of the city, two very low-income, virtually all-Negro districts near the city core with numerous public housing projects, and two predominantly white districts, one with mainly lower middle-income families, the other containing a mixture of very high-income and relatively low-income households. The table shows crime rates against persons and against property in these five districts, plus the number of patrolmen assigned to them per 100,000 residents, as follows:

TABLE 27

Incidence of Index Crimes and Patrolmen Assignments per 100,000 Residents in 5 Chicago Police Districts, 1965

Number	High-income white district	Low middle-income white district	Mixed high- and low-income white district	Very low-income Negro district No. 1	Very low-income Negro district No. 2
Index crimes against persons	80	440	338	1,615	2,820
Index crimes against property	1,038	1,750	2,080	2,508	2,630
Patrolmen assigned	93	133	115	243	291

These data indicate that:

Variations in the crime rate against persons within the city are extremely large. One very low-income Negro district had 35 times as many serious crimes against persons per 100,000 residents as did the high-income white district.

Variations in the crime rate against property are much smaller. The highest rate was only 2.5 times larger than the lowest.

The lower the income in an area, the higher the crime rate there. Yet low-income Negro areas have significantly higher crime rates than low-income white areas. This reflects the high degree of social disorganization in Negro areas described in the previous chapter, as well as the fact that poor Negroes as a group have lower incomes than poor whites as a group.

The presence of more police patrolmen per 100,000 residents does not necessarily offset high crime in certain parts of the city. Although the Chicago Police Department had assigned over three times as many patrolmen per 100,000 residents to the highest crime areas shown as to the lowest, crime rates in the highest crime area for offenses against both persons and property combined were 4.9 times as high as in the lowest crime area.

Because most middle-class Americans live in neighborhoods similar to the more crime-free district described above, they have little comprehension of the sense of insecurity that characterizes the ghetto resident. Moreover, official statistics normally greatly understate actual crime rates because the vast majority of crimes are not reported to the police. For example, studies conducted for the President's Crime Commission in Washington, D.C., Boston, and Chicago, showed that three to six times as many crimes were actually committed against persons and homes as were reported to the police.

Two facts are crucial to an understanding of the effects of high crime rates in racial ghettos; most of these crimes are committed by a small minority of the residents, and the principal victims are the residents themselves. Throughout the United States, the great majority of crimes committed by Negroes involve other Negroes as victims. A special tabulation made by the Chicago Police Department for the President's Crime Commission indicated that over 85 percent of the crimes committed against persons by Negroes between September 1965 and March 1966 involved Negro victims.

As a result, the majority of law-abiding citizens who live in disadvantaged Negro areas face much higher probabilities of being victimized than residents of most higher-income areas, including almost all suburbs. For nonwhites, the probability of suffering from any index crime except larceny is 78 percent higher than for whites. The probability of being raped is 3.7 times higher among nonwhite women, and the probability of being robbed is 3.5 times higher for nonwhites in general.

The problems associated with high crime rates generate widespread hostility toward the police in these neighborhoods. . . . Thus, crime not only creates an atmosphere of insecurity and fear throughout Negro neighborhoods but also causes continuing attrition of the relationship between Negro residents and police. This bears a direct relationship to civil disorder.

There are reasons to expect the crime situation in these areas to become worse in the future. First, crime rates throughout the United States have been rising rapidly in recent years. The rate of index crimes against persons rose 37 percent from

1960 to 1966, and the rate of index crimes against property rose 50 percent. In the first nine months of 1967, the number of index crimes was up 16 percent over the same period in 1966, whereas the U.S. population rose about 1 percent. In cities of 250,000 to 1 million, index crime rose by over 20 percent, whereas it increased 4 percent in cities of over 1 million.[12]

Second, the number of police available to combat crime is rising much more slowly than the amount of crime. In 1966, there were about 20 percent more police employees in the United States than in 1960, and per capita expenditures for police rose from $15.29 in 1960 to $20.99 in 1966, a gain of 37 percent. But over the six-year period, the number of reported index crimes had jumped 62 percent. In spite of significant improvements in police efficiency, it is clear that police will be unable to cope with their expanding workload unless there is a dramatic increase in the resources allocated by society to this task.

Third, in the next decade, the number of young Negroes aged 14 to 24 will increase rapidly, particularly in central cities. This group is responsible for a disproportionately high share of crimes in all parts of the Nation. In 1966, persons under 25 years of age comprised the following proportions of those arrested for various major crimes: murder, 37 percent; forcible rape, 64 percent; robbery, 71 percent; burglary, 81 percent; larceny, about 77 percent; and auto theft, 89 percent. For all index crimes together, the arrest rate for Negroes is about four times higher than that for whites. Yet the number of young Negroes aged 14 to 24 in central cities will rise about 63 percent from 1966 to 1975, as compared to only 32 percent for the total Negro population of central cities.[13]

[12] The problem of interpreting and evaluating "rising" crime rates is complicated by the changing age distribution of the population, improvements in reporting methods, and the increasing willingness of victims to report crimes. Despite these complications, there is general agreement on the serious increase in the incidence of crime in the United States.

[13] Assuming those cities will experience the same proportion of total United States Negro population growth that they did from 1960 to 1966. The calculations are derived from population projections in Bureau of the Census, *Population Estimates,* Current Population Reports, Series P–25, No. 381. Dec. 18, 1967, p. 63.

Health and Sanitation Conditions

The residents of the racial ghetto are significantly less healthy than most other Americans. They suffer from higher mortality rates, higher incidence of major diseases, and lower availability and utilization of medical services. They also experience higher admission rates to mental hospitals.

These conditions result from a number of factors.

POVERTY

From the standpoint of health, poverty means deficient diets, lack of medical care, inadequate shelter and clothing and often lack of awareness of potential health needs. As a result, almost 30 percent of all persons with family incomes less than $2,000 per year suffer from chronic health conditions that adversely affect their employment—as compared with less than 8 percent of the families with incomes of $7,000 or more.

Poor families have the greatest need for financial assistance in meeting medical expenses. Only about 34 percent of families with incomes of less than $2,000 per year use health insurance benefits, as compared to nearly 90 percent of those with incomes of $7,000 or more.[14]

These factors are aggravated for Negroes when compared to whites for the simple reason that the proportion of persons in the United States who are poor is 3.5 times as high among Negroes (41 percent in 1966) as among whites (12 percent in 1966).

MATERNAL MORTALITY

Mortality rates for nonwhite mothers are four times as high as those for white mothers. There has been a sharp decline in

[14] Public programs of various kinds have been providing significant financial assistance for medical care in recent years. In 1964, over $1.1 billion was paid out by various governments for such aid. About 52 percent of medical vendor payments came from Federal Government agencies, 33 percent from states, and 12 percent from local governments. The biggest contributions were made by the Old Age Assistance Program and the Medical Assistance for the Aged Program. The enactment of Medicare in 1965 has significantly added to this flow of public assistance for medical aid. However, it is too early to evaluate the results upon health conditions among the poor.

such rates since 1940, when 774 nonwhite and 320 white mothers died for each 100,000 live births. In 1965, only 84 nonwhite and 21 white mothers died per 100,000 live births—but the gap between nonwhites and whites actually increased.

INFANT MORTALITY

Mortality rates among nonwhite babies are 58 percent higher than among whites for those under 1 month old and almost three times as high among those from 1 month to 1 year old. This is true in spite of a large drop in infant mortality rates in both groups since 1940 (Table 28).

TABLE 28	*Number of Infants Who Died per 1,000 Live Births*			
	Less than 1 month old		*1 month to 1 year old*	
Year	White	Nonwhite	White	Nonwhite
1940	27.2	39.7	16.0	34.1
1950	19.4	27.5	7.4	17.0
1960	17.2	26.9	5.7	16.4
1965	16.1	25.4	5.4	14.9

LIFE EXPECTANCY

To some extent because of infant mortality rates, life expectancy at birth was 6.9 years longer for whites (71.0 years) than for nonwhites (64.1 years) in 1965. Even in the prime working ages, life expectancy is significantly lower among nonwhites than among whites. In 1965, white persons 25 years old could expect to live an average of 48.6 more years, whereas nonwhites 25 years old could expect to live another 43.3 years, or 11 percent less. Similar but smaller discrepancies existed at all ages from 25 through 55; some actually increased slightly between 1960 and 1965.

LOWER UTILIZATION OF HEALTH SERVICES

A fact that also contributes to poorer health conditions in the ghetto is that Negro families with incomes similar to those of whites spend less on medical services and visit medical specialists less often (Table 29).

TABLE 29	*Percent of Family Expenditures Spent for Medical Care, 1960–61*		
Income group	White	Nonwhite	Ratio, white to nonwhite
Under $3,000	9	5	1.8:1
$3,000 to $7,499	7	5	1.4:1
$7,500 and over	6	4	1.5:1

Since the lowest income group contains a much larger proportion of nonwhite families than white families, the overall discrepancy in medical care spending between these two groups is very significant, as shown by Table 30.

TABLE 30	*Health Expenses per Person per Year for the Period from July to December 1962*					
	Expenses					
Income by racial group	Total medical	Hospital	Doctor	Dental	Medicine	Other
Under $2,000 per family per year:						
White	$130	$33	$41	$11	$32	$13
Nonwhite	63	15	23	5	16	5
$10,000 and more per family per year:						
White	179	34	61	37	31	16
Nonwhite	133	34	50	19	23	8

These data indicate that nonwhite families in the lower income group spent less than half as much per person on medical services as white families with similar incomes. This discrepancy sharply declines but is still significant in the higher income group, where total nonwhite medical expenditures per person equal, on the average, 74.3 percent of white expenditures.

Negroes spend less on medical care for several reasons. Negro households generally are larger, requiring greater non-medical expenses for each household and leaving less money for meeting medical expenses. Thus, lower expenditures per person would result even if expenditures per household were the same. Negroes also often pay more for other basic necessities such as food and consumer durables, as discussed in the next part of this chapter. In addition, fewer doctors, dentists, and medical facilities are conveniently available to Negroes than to most whites—a result both of geographic concentration of doctors in higher income areas in large cities and of discrimination against Negroes by doctors and hospitals. A survey in Cleveland indicated that there were 0.45 physicians per 1,000 people in poor neighborhoods, compared to 1.13 per 1,000 in nonpoverty areas. The result nationally is fewer visits to physicians and dentists (Table 31).

	Percent of Population Making One or More Visits to Indicated Type of Medical Specialist from July 1963 to June 1964			
TABLE 31				
	Family incomes of $2,000–$3,999		Family incomes of $7,000–$9,999	
Type of medical specialist	White	Nonwhite	White	Nonwhite
Physician	64	56	70	64
Dentist	31	20	52	33

Although widespread use of health insurance has led many hospitals to adopt nondiscriminatory policies, some private hospitals still refuse to admit Negro patients or to accept doctors with Negro patients. And many individual doctors still discriminate against Negro patients. As a result, Negroes are more likely to be treated in hospital clinics than whites and they are less likely to receive personalized service. This conclusion is confirmed by the data in Table 32.

ENVIRONMENTAL FACTORS

Environmental conditions in disadvantaged Negro neighborhoods create further reasons for poor health conditions there. The level of sanitation is strikingly below that which is prevalent in most higher income areas. One simple reason is that residents often lack proper storage facilities for food—adequate refrigerators, freezers, even garbage cans, which are sometimes stolen as fast as landlords can replace them.

TABLE 32

Percent of All Visits to Physicians
from July 1963 to June 1964,
Made in Indicated Ways

Type of visit to physician	Family incomes of $2,000–$3,999		Family incomes of $7,000–$9,999	
	White	Nonwhite	White	Nonwhite
In physician's office	68	56	73	66
Hospital clinic	17	35	7	16
Other (mainly telephone)	15	9	20	18
Total	100	100	100	100

In areas where garbage collection and other sanitation services are grossly inadequate—commonly in the poorer parts of our large cities—rats proliferate. It is estimated that in 1965, there were over 14,000 cases of ratbite in the United States, mostly in such neighborhoods.

The importance of these conditions was outlined for the Commission as follows:[15]

> Sanitation Commissioners of New York City and Chicago both feel this [sanitation] to be an important community problem and report themselves as being under substantial pressure to improve conditions. *It must be concluded that slum sanitation is a serious problem in the minds of the urban poor and well merits, at least on that ground, the attention of the Commission.* A related problem, according to one Sanitation Commissioner, is the fact that residents of areas bordering on slums feel that sanitation and neighborhood cleanliness is a crucial issue, relating to the stability of their blocks and constituting an important psychological index of "how far gone" their area is.
>
> . . . There is no known study comparing sanitation services between slum and nonslum areas. The experts agree, however, that there are more services in the slums on a quantitative basis, although perhaps not on a per capita basis. In New York, for example, garbage pickups are supposedly scheduled for about six times a week in slums, compared to three times a week in other areas of the city; the comparable figures in Chicago are two to three times a week versus once a week.

[15] Memorandum to the Commission dated Nov. 16, 1967, from Robert Patricelli, minority counsel, Subcommittee on Employment Manpower and Poverty, U.S. Senate.

The point, therefore, is not the relative quantitative level of services but the peculiarly intense needs of ghetto areas for sanitation services. This high demand is the product of numerous factors including: (1) higher population density; (2) lack of well managed buildings and adequate garbage services provided by landlords, number of receptacles, carrying to curbside, number of electric garbage disposals; (3) high relocation rates of tenants and businesses, producing heavy volume of bulk refuse left on streets and in buildings; (4) different uses of the streets—as outdoor living rooms in summer, recreation areas—producing high visibility and sensitivity to garbage problems; (5) large numbers of abandoned cars; (6) severe rodent and pest problems; (7) traffic congestion blocking garbage collection; and (8) obstructed street cleaning and snow removal on crowded, car-choked streets. Each of these elements adds to the problem and suggests a different possible line of attack.

Exploitation of Disadvantaged Consumers by Retail Merchants

Much of the violence in recent civil disorders has been directed at stores and other commercial establishments in disadvantaged Negro areas. In some cases, rioters focused on stores operated by white merchants who, they apparently believed, had been charging exorbitant prices or selling inferior goods. Not all the violence against these stores can be attributed to "revenge" for such practices. Yet it is clear that many residents of disadvantaged Negro neighborhoods believe they suffer constant abuses by local merchants.

Significant grievances concerning unfair commercial practices affecting Negro consumers were found in 11 of the 20 cities studied by the Commission. The fact that most of the merchants who operate stores in Negro areas are white undoubtedly contributes to the conclusion among Negroes that they are exploited by white society.

It is difficult to assess the precise degree and extent of exploitation. No systematic and reliable survey comparing consumer pricing and credit practices in all-Negro and other neighborhoods has ever been conducted on a nationwide basis. Differences in prices and credit practices between white middle-income areas and Negro low-income areas to some extent reflect differences in the real costs of serving these two markets (such as differential losses from pilferage in supermarkets), but the exact extent of these cost differences has never been estimated accurately. Finally, an examination of exploitative consumer practices must consider the particular structure and functions of the low-income consumer durables market.

INSTALLMENT BUYING

This complex situation can best be understood by first considering certain basic facts:

Various cultural factors generate constant pressure on low-income families to buy many relatively expensive durable goods and display them in their homes. This pressure comes in part from continuous exposure to commercial advertising, especially on television. In January 1967, over 88 percent of all Negro households had TV sets. A 1961 study of 464 low-income families in New York City showed that 95 percent of these relatively poor families had TV sets.

Many poor families have extremely low incomes, bad previous credit records, unstable sources of income or other attributes which make it virtually impossible for them to buy merchandise from established large national or local retail firms. These families lack enough savings to pay cash, and they cannot meet the standard credit requirements of established general merchants because they are too likely to fall behind in their payments.

Poor families in urban areas are far less mobile than others. A 1967 Chicago study of low-income Negro households indicated their low automobile ownership compelled them to patronize neighborhood merchants. These merchants typically provided smaller selection, poorer services and higher prices than big national outlets. The 1961 New York study also indicated that families who shopped outside their own neighborhoods were far less likely to pay exorbitant prices.

Most low-income families are uneducated concerning the nature of credit purchase contracts, the legal rights and obligations of both buyers and sellers, sources of advice for consumers who are having difficulties with merchants and the operation of the courts concerned with these matters. In contrast, merchants engaged in selling goods to them are very well informed.

In most states, the laws governing relations between consumers and merchants in effect offer protection only to informed, sophisticated parties with understanding of each other's rights and obligations. Consequently, these laws are little suited to protect the rights of most low-income consumers.

In this situation, exploitative practices flourish. Ghetto residents who want to buy relatively expensive goods cannot do so from standard retail outlets and are thus restricted to local stores. Forced to use credit, they have little understanding of the pitfalls of credit buying. But because they have unstable incomes and frequently fail to make payments, the cost to the merchants of serving them is significantly above that of serving middle-income consumers. Consequently, a special kind of merchant appears to sell them goods on terms designed to cover the high cost of doing business in ghetto neighborhoods.

Whether they actually gain higher profits, these merchants charge higher prices than those in other parts of the city to cover the greater credit risks and other higher operating costs inherent in neighborhood outlets. A recent study conducted by the Federal Trade Commission in Washington, D.C., illustrates this conclusion dramatically. The FTC identified a number of stores specializing in selling furniture and appliances to low-income households. About 92 percent of the sales of these stores were credit sales involving installment purchases, as compared to 27 percent of the sales in general retail outlets handling the same merchandise.

The median income annually of a sample of 486 customers of these stores was about $4,200, but one-third had annual incomes below $3,600, about 6 percent were receiving welfare payments, and another 76 percent were employed in the lowest paying occupations (service workers, operatives, laborers and domestics), as compared to 36 percent of the total labor force in Washington in those occupations.

Definitely catering to a low-income group, these stores charged significantly higher prices than general merchandise outlets in the Washington area. According to testimony by

Paul Rand Dixon, Chairman of the FTC, an item selling wholesale at $100 would retail on the average for $165 in a general merchandise store and for $250 in a low-income specialty store. Thus, the customers of these outlets were paying an average price premium of about 52 percent.

While higher prices are not necessarily exploitative in themselves, many merchants in ghetto neighborhoods take advantage of their superior knowledge of credit buying by engaging in various exploitative tactics—high-pressure salesmanship, "bait advertising," misrepresentation of prices, substitution of used goods for promised new ones, failure to notify consumers of legal actions against them, refusal to repair or replace substandard goods, exorbitant prices or credit charges, and use of shoddy merchandise. Such tactics affect a great many low-income consumers. In the New York study, 60 percent of all households had suffered from consumer problems (some of which were purely their own fault). About 23 percent had experienced serious exploitation. Another 20 percent, many of whom were also exploited, had experienced repossession, garnishment, or threat of garnishment.

GARNISHMENT

Garnishment practices in many states allow creditors to deprive individuals of their wages through court action, without hearing or trial. In about 20 states, the wages of an employee can be diverted to a creditor merely upon the latter's deposition, with no advance hearing where the employee can defend himself. He often receives no prior notice of such action and is usually unaware of the law's operation and too poor to hire legal defense. Moreover, consumers may find themselves still owing money on a sales contract even after the creditor has repossessed the goods. The New York study cited earlier in this chapter indicated that 20 percent of a sample of low-income families had been subjected to legal action regarding consumer purchases. And the Federal Trade Commission study in Washington, D.C., showed that, on the average, retailers specializing in credit sales of furniture and appliances to low-income consumers resorted to court action once for every $2,200 of sales. Since their average sale was $207, this amounted to using the courts to collect from one of every 11 customers. In contrast, department stores in the same area used court action against approximately one of every 14,500 customers.[16]

VARIATIONS IN FOOD PRICES

Residents of low-income Negro neighborhoods frequently claim that they pay higher prices for food in local markets than wealthier white suburbanites and receive inferior quality meat and produce. Statistically reliable information comparing prices and quality in these two kinds of areas is generally unavailable. The U.S. Bureau of Labor Statistics, studying food prices in six cities in 1966, compared prices of a standard list of 18 items in low-income areas and higher-income areas in each city. In a total of 180 stores, including independent and chain stores, and for items of the same type sold in the same types of stores, there were no significant differences in prices between low-income and high-income areas. However, stores in low-income areas were more likely to be small independents (which had somewhat higher prices), to sell low-quality produce and meat at any given price, and to be patronized by people who typically bought smaller-sized packages which are more expensive per unit of measure. In other words, many low-income consumers in fact pay higher prices, although the situation varies greatly from place to place.

Although these findings must be considered inconclusive, there are significant reasons to believe that poor households generally pay higher prices for the food they buy and receive lower-quality food. Low-income consumers buy more food at local groceries because they are less mobile. Prices in these small stores are significantly higher than in major supermarkets because they cannot achieve economies of scale and because real operating costs are higher in low-income Negro areas than in outlying suburbs. For instance, inventory "shrinkage" from pilfering and other causes is normally under 2 percent of sales but can run twice as much in high-crime areas. Managers seek to make up for these added costs by charging higher prices for food or by substituting lower grades.

[16] Assuming their sales also averaged $207 per customer.

These practices do not necessarily involve exploitation, but they are often perceived as exploitative and unfair by those who are aware of the price and quality differences involved but unaware of operating costs. In addition, it is probable that genuinely exploitative pricing practices exist in some areas. In either case, differential food prices constitute another factor convincing urban Negroes in low-income neighborhoods that whites discriminate against them.

FOR FURTHER READING

On the creation of the ghetto the reader should consult: *Gilbert Osofsky, *Harlem: The Making of a Ghetto* (New York, 1966); *Allan Spear, *Black Chicago* (Chicago, 1969); Seth Scheiner, *Negro Mecca* (New York, 1965); *Arna Bontemps and Jack Conroy, *Anyplace But Here* (New York, 1966); and the classic *Horace Cayton and St. Clair Drake, *Black Metropolis* (New York, 1962). On living conditions within the ghetto, see Robert Weaver, *The Negro Ghetto* (New York, 1948), but *Kenneth Clark, *Dark Ghetto* (New York, 1967) is more up to date. Arthur Waskow, *From Race Riot to Sit-In* (New York, 1966) deals with some of the urban riots since World War I.

General information on conditions of black social life and urban life in particular can be found in *Andrew Billingsley, *Black Families in White America* (Englewood Cliffs, N.J., 1968); *E. Franklin Frazier, *The Negro Family in the United States* (Chicago, 1966) and *The Black Bourgeoisie* (New York, 1962); Kenneth Clark and Talcott Parsons (eds.), *The Negro American* (Boston, 1966); and *Thomas Pettigrew, *A Profile of the Negro American* (Princeton, 1964). The controversial Moynihan report, *The Negro Family: The Case for National Action* (Washington, 1965), should not be read without consulting *Lee Rainwater and William Yancey (eds.), *The Politics of Controversy* (Boston, 1967). The study by *Gunnar Myrdal, *An American Dilemma* (New York, 1964) contains much useful information on the social and economic status of black Americans.

CIVIL RIGHTS AND
BLACK NATIONALISM

The Great Migration, through its consequences, helped produce the civil rights movement. With the resurgence of black politics and the rise of an educated middle class in the urban black community, a base for the movement grew in the North. Yet it cannot be simply understood as a byproduct of urbanization.

Actually the movement never totally died, even during the bleak early decades of the twentieth century. The NAACP and the Urban League worked against racism during those years. The NAACP began its long battle in the courts and achieved its first victory in 1915 when the Oklahoma grandfather clause disfranchising black voters was declared unconstitutional. The early legal victories were modest, but they became more important after World War II, culminating in the 1954 school desegregation decision. That decision declared that segregated schools were inherently unequal; hence they violated the equal protection clause of the Fourteenth Amendment. The Urban League, though rarely challenging segregation directly and unable to achieve spectacular victories as the NAACP did, tried to improve the living conditions of black urbanites.

In the 1920s and 1930s whites and blacks formed interracial committees to deal with some of the worst aspects of racial discrimination and to arouse public opinion against lynching. These committees, with limited goals and budgets, had only a slight effect on the basic structure of discrimination, but they made progress in a few communities. Also in the 1930s black groups tackled particular problems. In New York City, Adam Clayton Powell, Jr. organized demonstrations to change the hiring practices of white-owned businesses in Harlem, and "Don't buy where you can't work" campaigns were organized in other cities.

The New Deal was generally unwilling to tackle the problem of racism. Blacks did receive relief funds and some economic benefits from New Deal programs, but Franklin Roosevelt did little to push for federal antilynching laws or for civil rights. He gave these programs low priority and was unwilling to challenge southern white control of congressional committees. The New Deal programs permitted segregation to continue, as in FHA loans and public housing, and New Dealers were very slow to promote black workers in their agencies. Some, such as Aubrey Williams of the National Youth Administration, tried to equalize the benefits of their programs, and some of the agencies brought in special advisors, white and black, to work in the black community. Roosevelt did not even want to establish a federal fair employment practices commission during the war and did so only when A. Philip Randolph threatened to lead a march on Washington.

It was during the 1940s that the civil rights movement gained momentum, and during the decade following the 1954

Supreme Court decision on school desegregation it reached its zenith. Richard Dalfiume's essay discusses the mood among black Americans during the war years, a mood of increasing dissatisfaction with American professions of equality, which were not realized in practice. Out of it grew mass action, beginning with the Montgomery bus boycott led by Martin Luther King, Jr. in 1955 and the sit-in movement of the early 1960s. August Meier's essay discusses the tactics and activities of the various civil rights groups and notes that they were facing a crisis in the mid-1960s.

Certainly impatience and increased self-awareness, especially among the young, were major factors in the growth of the movement. There were other reasons, however. The traditional defense of white supremacy, so long supported by science and the major intellectual trends in western society, was challenged in the late 1920s and 1930s. Increasingly, anthropologists, biologists, political scientists, historians, and other academicians assailed the notion of white supremacy. There had always been intellectual critics of racism, but by the 1950s few intellectuals could be found to support it. The message of the massive Myrdal study, *An American Dilemma,* was that environment and history, not race, shape behavior.

International pressures were at work, too. Some white Americans began to see the hypocrisy of fighting a war against fascism abroad and maintaining racism at home. The end of western colonialism and the growing awareness of African history also destroyed old myths. Competition for third-world allies on occasion made the federal government move against discrimination in the United States.

Certainly economic forces played a role. Black Americans, who made on the average only 39 percent of what whites did in 1939, improved their lot when there was a labor shortage during the 1940s and early 1950s, especially during the war. The income gap was still wide in the mid-1950s, but it had narrowed. The discovery of the Negro market and the desire to exploit it led some firms to improve their employment practices. Television succumbed in the 1960s, and black faces appeared on TV ads and programs. Shortages in highly skilled occupations also opened new opportunities for blacks. The arts and sports, where talent rather than background counted, opened up after World War II. This proved economically successful; sports owners discovered that black talent drew big gates and profits, and were therefore willing to hire more black athletes.

Thus a combination of economic, intellectual, and political forces brought changes to white and black Americans in the postwar period. Under the blows of civil rights laws passed from 1957 to 1968, direct action by civil rights groups, and court and executive orders, the legal props for segregation were destroyed in the 1950s and 1960s. The Fifteenth Amendment, unenforced in the South since the first decade of the twentieth century, took on new meaning as the federal government began to protect the right to vote.

Private institutions that had traditionally excluded blacks began to modify their policies. Labor unions, for example, changed some of their exclusionary practices, and universities searched for black professors and students. Some housing projects were desegregated and others were planned from the beginning to be interracial. Black civil rights leaders and their white liberal allies achieved success in opening hospitals, schools, restaurants, and other institutions. The change from legal segregation was most noticeable in the South, but it also made its mark in the North and West.

In spite of the civil rights movement, racism remained. The movement had successfully assaulted legal segregation, passed many laws against discrimination, given new meaning to the right to vote, and aided many black families in finding jobs. The simple fact was, however, that as the 1960s came to a close approximately half of the black families remained below the poverty level or slightly above it. The income gap between whites and blacks was still substantial. In highly skilled occupations the gains were substantial, but for the lower classes they were hardly noticeable. Thus the achievements of the movement aided chiefly the middle class, the black elite. Moreover, court decisions and laws were generally unable to desegregate schools and housing, especially in the ghettos.

Aware of the slow pace of change, many black Americans turned to black nationalism in search of an identity in American society. As noted above, the roots of black nationalism go back to the nineteenth century. In the 1920s Marcus Garvey built the first mass movement based upon a nationalist appeal. Garvey drew his followers from the lower-class urbanites. The disillusionment following World War I, the race riots of 1919, the lynching of black veterans in uniform, and discrimination in jobs and housing in the northern cities made many look to Garvey rather than to the middle-class leadership of the NAACP. Though a number of black intellectuals and most organizational leaders were opposed to Garvey, the intellectuals of the Harlem Renaissance had a similar mood and turned away from middle-class values. Garvey's Universal Negro Improvement Association was unsuccessful, however, and after his deportation from the United States he had little direct influence on black America.

Like Marcus Garvey, the Black Muslims drew their strength from the lower-class urbanites. Arna Bontemps and Jack Conroy discuss in their essay the rise of the Muslims and the appeal of Malcolm X, who articulated so well the frustrations of black Americans. The number of actual followers of Elijah Muhammed was not large, but the appeal of nationalism could not be measured by membership in the Nation of Islam. Though many were unwilling to follow the theology of the Muslims or join the organization, the Black Muslims' indictment of white America struck a responsive chord. In the mid-1960s the mood of nationalism spread beyond the lower class into the middle class and especially among the youth and college students. The older civil rights organizations, such as the Urban League and the NAACP, and the new Southern Christian Leadership Conference were not so susceptible as the Student Nonviolent Coordinating Committee and the Congress of Racial Equality, but even they felt the pressure. The revolt against white liberal leadership and in some cases against black middle-class leadership puzzled many whites, but it was the logical outcome of the appeal of the black nationalists, who sought to control their own destiny and shape their own values.

The civil rights movement and black nationalism were not totally at odds. Some black power advocates argued that they too sought social justice in America, not permanent separation.

These spokesmen said the black power movement was in part the extension of cultural pluralism to the black community. They argued that white ethnic groups banded together to foster their own aims and the black community, which was already segregated, should also develop its own power base to achieve its goals. Therefore they rejected interracial leadership of the civil rights movement on tactical grounds and urged that a black led and controlled movement was the way to destroy white racism. These advocates of black power had come to the conclusion that segregation would not disappear in the near future and that this fact should be accepted. Yet there were other nationalists who went beyond tactical considerations and insisted they did not want to assimilate into white America. They pointed to the materialism and hypocrisy of white America and its imperialism overseas and said that it was better for the black community to keep its own culture and heritage, but to get its fair share of the wealth of America.

In the 1950s and 1960s some observers insisted that race relations had become America's number one social problem, and in 1968 the President's Commission on Civil Disorders claimed the problem was white racism. For black Americans white racism had always been the number one problem. Nor was there any sign of a let-up in the tension of the 1960s. The inability of white America to eliminate racism and the growing impatience of black America foretold a continuing social crisis.

10

The "Forgotten Years" of the Negro Revolution

RICHARD DALFIUME

A recent president of the American Sociological Society addressed himself to a puzzling question about what we know as the Civil Rights Revolution: "Why did social scientists—and sociologists in particular—not foresee the explosion of collective action of Negro Americans toward full integration into American society?" He pointed out that "it is the vigor and urgency of the Negro demand that is new, not its direction or supporting ideas." Without arguing the point further, the lack

SOURCE: *Journal of American History*, LV (June 1968), 90–106 (footnotes omitted). Reprinted by permission of the *Journal of American History*.

of knowledge can be attributed to two groups—the ahistorical social scientists, and the historians who, until recently, have neglected modern Negro history.

The search for a "watershed" in recent Negro history ends at the years that comprised World War II, 1939–1945. James Baldwin has written of this period: "The treatment accorded the Negro during the Second World War marks, for me, a turning point in the Negro's relation to America. To put it briefly, and somewhat too simply, a certain hope died, a certain respect for white Americans faded." Writing during World War II, Gunnar Myrdal predicted that the war would act as a "stimulant" to Negro protest, and he felt that "there is bound to be a redefinition of the Negro's status in America as a result of this War." The Negro sociologist E. Franklin Frazier states that World War II marked the point where "the Negro was no longer willing to accept discrimination in employment and in housing without protest." Charles E. Silberman writes that the war was a "turning point" in American race relations, in which "the seeds of the protest movements of the 1950s and 1960s were sown." While a few writers have indicated the importance of these years in the recent Negro protest movement, the majority have failed to do so. Overlooking what went before, most recent books on the subject claim that a Negro "revolution" or "revolt" occurred in 1954, 1955, 1960, or 1963. Because of the neglect of the war period, these years of transition in American race relations comprise the "forgotten years" of the Negro revolution.

To understand how the American Negro reacted to World War II, it is necessary to have some idea of the discrimination he faced. The defense build-up begun by the United States in 1940 was welcomed by Negroes who were disproportionately represented among the unemployed. Employment discrimination in the revived industries, however, was rampant. When Negroes sought jobs at aircraft factories where employers begged for workers, they were informed that "the Negro will be considered only as janitors and in other similar capacities. . . ." Government financed training programs to overcome the shortages of skilled workers discriminated against

Negro trainees. When government agencies issued orders against such discrimination, they were ignored.

Increasing defense preparations also meant an expansion of the armed forces. Here, as in industry, however, Negroes faced restrictions. Black Americans were assigned a minimal role and rigidly segregated. In the navy, Negroes could enlist only in the all-Negro messman's branch. The marine and the air corps excluded Negroes entirely. In the army, black Americans were prevented from enlisting, except for a few vacancies in the four regular army Negro units that had been created shortly after the Civil War; and the strength of these had been reduced drastically in the 1920s and 1930s.

Although the most important bread-and-butter issue for Negroes in this period was employment discrimination, their position in the armed forces was an important symbol. If one could not participate fully in the defense of his country, he could not lay claim to the rights of a full-fledged citizen. The NAACP organ, the *Crisis,* expressed this idea in its demand for unrestricted participation in the armed forces: "This is no fight merely to wear a uniform. This is a struggle for status, a struggle to take democracy off of parchment and give it life." Herbert Garfinkel, a student of Negro protest during this period, points out that "in many respects, the discriminatory practices against Negroes which characterized the military programs . . . cut deeper into Negro feelings than did employment discrimination."

Added to the rebuffs from industry and the armed services were a hundred others. Negroes, anxious to contribute to the Red Cross blood program, were turned away. Despite the fact that white and Negro blood is the same biologically, it was deemed inadvisable "to collect and mix caucasian and Negro blood indiscriminately." When Negro citizens called upon the governor of Tennessee to appoint some black members to the state's draft boards, he told them: "This is a white man's country. . . . The Negro had nothing to do with the settling of America." At a time when the United States claimed to be the last bulwark of democracy in a war-torn world, the legislature of Mississippi passed a law requiring different textbooks for

Negro schools: all references to voting, elections, and democracy were to be excluded from the black student's books.

The Negro's morale at the beginning of World War II is also partly explained by his experience in World War I. Black America had gone into that war with high morale, generated by the belief that the democratic slogans literally meant what they said. Most Negroes succumbed to the "close ranks" strategy announced by the crusading NAACP editor, W. E. B. Du Bois, who advocated subduing racial grievances in order to give full support to winning the war. But the image of a new democratic order was smashed by the race riots, lynchings, and continued rigid discrimination. The result was a mass trauma and a series of movements among Negroes in the 1920s which were characterized by a desire to withdraw from a white society which wanted little to do with them. When the war crisis of the 1940s came along, the bitter memories of World War I were recalled with the result that there was a built-in cynicism among Negroes toward the democratic slogans of the new war.

Nevertheless, Negroes were part of the general population being stimulated to come to the defense of democracy in the world. When they responded and attempted to do their share, they were turned away. The result was a widespread feeling of frustration and a general decline of the Negro's morale toward the war effort, as compared with the rest of American society. But paradoxically, the Negro's general morale was both low and high.

While the morale of the Negro, as an American, was low in regard to the war effort, the Negro, as a member of a minority group, had high morale in his heightened race consciousness and determination to fight for a better position in American society. The same slogans which caused the Negro to react cynically also served to emphasize the disparity between the creed and the practice of democracy as far as the Negro in America was concerned. Because of his position in society, the Negro reacted to the war both as an American and as a Negro. Discrimination against him had given rise to "a sickly, negative attitude toward national goals, but at the same time a vibrantly positive attitude toward racial aims and aspirations."

When war broke out in Europe in 1939, many black Americans tended to adopt an isolationist attitude. Those taking this position viewed the war as a "white man's war." George Schuyler, the iconoclastic columnist, was a typical spokesman for this view: "So far as the colored peoples of the earth are concerned," Schuyler wrote, "it is a toss-up between the 'democracies' and the dictatorships. . . . [W]hat is there to choose between the rule of the British in Africa and the rule of the Germans in Austria?" Another Negro columnist claimed that it was a blessing to have war so that whites could "mow one another down" rather than "have them quietly murder hundreds of thousands of Africans, East Indians and Chinese. . . ." This kind of isolationism took the form of anti-colonialism, particularly against the British. There was some sympathy for France, however, because of its more liberal treatment of black citizens.

Another spur to isolationist sentiment was the obvious hypocrisy of calling for the defense of democracy abroad while it was not a reality at home. The NAACP bitterly expressed this point:

> THE CRISIS is sorry for brutality, blood, and death among the peoples of Europe, just as we were sorry for China and Ethiopia. But the hysterical cries of the preachers of democracy for Europe leave us cold. We want democracy in Alabama and Arkansas, in Mississippi and Michigan, in the District of Columbia—*in the Senate of the United States.*

The editor of the Pittsburgh *Courier* proclaimed that Negroes had their "own war" at home "against oppression and exploitation from without and against disorganization and lack of confidence within"; and the Chicago *Defender* thought that "peace at home" should be the main concern of black Americans.

Many Negroes agreed with columnist Schuyler that "our war is not against Hitler in Europe, but against the Hitlers in America." The isolationist view of the war in Europe and the antagonism toward Great Britain led to an attitude that was rather neutral toward the Nazis and the Japanese, or, in some extreme cases, pro-Axis. Appealing to this latent feeling, isolationist periodicals tried to gain Negro support in their struggle against American entrance into the war. By 1940 there were also Negro cults such as the Ethiopian Pacific Movement, the World Wide Friends of Africa, the Brotherhood of Liberty for the Black People of America, and many others, which preached unity among the world's darker people, including Japanese. Many of these groups exploited the latent anti-semitism common among Negroes in the urban ghettos by claiming that the racial policies of Germany were correct.

Reports reached the public that some black Americans were expressing a vicarious pleasure over successes by the "yellow" Japanese and by Germany. In a quarrel with her employer in North Carolina, a Negro woman retorted: "I hope Hitler does come, because if he does he will get you first!" A Negro truck driver in Philadelphia was held on charges of treason after he was accused of telling a Negro soldier that he should not be in uniform and that "this is a white man's government and war and it's no damned good." After Pearl Harbor, a Negro sharecropper told his landlord: "By the way, Captain, I hear the Japs done declared war on you white folks." Another Negro declared that he was going to get his eyes slanted so that the next time a white man shoved him around he could fight back.

It is impossible to determine the extent of this kind of pro-Axis sentiment among Negroes, but it was widespread enough for the Negro press to make rather frequent mention of it. In 1942 and 1943 the federal government did arrest the members of several pro-Japanese Negro cults in Chicago, New York, Newark, New Jersey, and East St. Louis, Illinois. Although the numbers involved were small, the evidence indicated that Japanese agents had been at work among these groups and had capitalized on Negro grievances.

By the time of the Pearl Harbor attack, certain fundamental changes were taking place among American Negroes. Nowhere is this more evident than in a comparison of Negroes' reactions to World Wars I and II. The dominant opinion among them toward World War I was expressed by Du Bois. In World War II, most Negroes looked upon the earlier stand as a great mistake. The dominant attitude during World War II was that the Negro must fight for democracy on two fronts—at home as well as abroad. This opinion had first appeared in reaction to the discriminatory treatment of Negro soldiers; but with the attack on Pearl Harbor, this idea, stated in many different ways, became the slogan of black America.

American Negroes took advantage of the war to tie their racial demands to the ideology for which the war was being fought. Before Pearl Harbor, the Negro press frequently pointed out the similarity of American treatment of Negroes and Nazi Germany's treatment of minorities. In 1940, the Chicago *Defender* featured a mock invasion of the United States by Germany in which the Nazis were victorious because a fifth column of southern senators and other racists aided them. Later the *Crisis* printed an editorial which compared the white supremacy doctrine in America to the Nazi plan for Negroes, a comparison which indicated a marked similarity. Even the periodical of the conservative Urban League made such comparisons.

Many Negroes adopted a paradoxical stand on the meaning of the war. At the same time that it was labeled a "white man's war," Negroes often stated that they were bound to benefit from it. For example, Schuyler could argue that the war was not for democracy, but "Peace means . . . a continuation of the status quo . . . which must be ended if the Negro is to get free." And accordingly, the longer the war the better: "Perhaps in the shuffle we who have been on the bottom of the deck for so long will find ourselves at the top."

Cynicism and hope existed side by side in the Negro mind. Cynicism was often the attitude expressed after some outrageous example of discrimination. After Pearl Harbor, however, a mixture of hope and certainty—great changes favorable to the Negro would result from the war and things would never be the same again—became the dominant attitude. Hope was evident in the growing realization that the war provided the Negro with an excellent opportunity to prick the conscience of white America. "What an opportunity the crisis has been . . . for one to persuade, embarrass, compel and shame our government and our nation . . . into a more enlightened attitude toward a tenth of its people!" the Pittsburgh *Courier* proclaimed. Certainty that a better life would result from the war was based on the belief that revolutionary forces had been released throughout the world. It was no longer a "white man's world," and the "myth of white invincibility" had been shattered for good.

There was a growing protest against the racial status quo by black Americans; this was evidenced by the reevaluation of segregation in all sections of the country. In the North there was self-criticism of past acceptance of certain forms of segregation. Southern Negroes became bolder in openly questioning the sacredness of segregation. In October 1942, a group of southern Negro leaders met in Durham, North Carolina, and issued a statement on race relations. In addition to endorsing the idea that the Negro should fight for democracy at home as well as abroad, these leaders called for complete equality for the Negro in American life. While recognizing the "strength and age" of the South's racial customs, the Durham meeting was "fundamentally opposed to the principle and practice of compulsory segregation in our American society." In addition, there were reports of deep discontent among southern Negro college students and evidence that political activity among the blacks of the South, particularly on the local level, was increasing.

The American Negro, stimulated by the democratic ideology of the war, was reexamining his position in American society. "It cannot be doubted that the spirit of American Negroes in all classes is different today from what it was a generation ago," Myrdal observed. Part of this new spirit was an increased militancy, a readiness to protest loud and strong against grievances. The crisis gave Negroes more reason and opportunity to protest. Representative of all the trends of black thought and action—the cynicism, the hope, the heightened race consciousness, the militancy—was the March on Washington Movement (MOWM).

The general idea of exerting mass pressure upon the government to end defense discrimination did not originate with A. Philip Randolph's call for a march on Washington, D.C., in early 1941. Agitation for mass pressure had grown since the failure of a group of Negro leaders to gain any major concessions from President Franklin D. Roosevelt in September 1940. Various organizations, such as the NAACP, the Committee for

Participation of Negroes in the National Defense, and the Allied Committees on National Defense, held mass protest meetings around the country in late 1940 and early 1941. The weeks passed and these efforts did not seem to have any appreciable impact on the government; Walter White, Randolph, and other Negro leaders could not even secure an appointment to see the President. "Bitterness grew at an alarming pace throughout the country," White recalled.

It remained, however, for Randolph to consolidate this protest. In January 1941, he wrote an article for the Negro press which pointed out the failure of committees and individuals to achieve action against defense discrimination. "Only power can effect the enforcement and adoption of a given policy," Randolph noted; and "Power is the active principle of only the organized masses, the masses united for a definite purpose." To focus the weight of the black masses, he suggested that 10,000 Negroes march on Washington, D.C., with the slogan: "We loyal Negro-American citizens demand the right to work and fight for our country."

This march appeal led to the formation of one of the most significant—though today almost forgotten—Negro protest movements. The MOWM pioneered what has become the common denominator of today's Negro revolt—"the spontaneous involvement of large masses of Negroes in a political protest." Furthermore, as August Meier and Elliot Rudwick have recently pointed out, the MOWM clearly foreshadowed "the goals, tactics, and strategy of the mid-twentieth-century civil rights movement." Whites were excluded purposely to make it an all-Negro movement; its main weapon was direct action on the part of the black masses. Furthermore, the MOWM took as its major concern the economic problems of urban slum-dwellers.

Randolph's tactic of mass pressure through a demonstration of black power struck a response among the Negro masses. The number to march on Washington on July 1, 1941, was increased to 50,000, and only Roosevelt's agreement to issue an executive order establishing a President's Committee on Fair Employment Practices led to a cancellation of the march. Negroes then, and scholars later, generally interpreted this as a great victory. But the magnitude of the victory is diminished when one examines the original MOWM demands: an executive order forbidding government contracts to be awarded to a firm which practiced discrimination in hiring, an executive order abolishing discrimination in government defense training courses, an executive order requiring the United States Employment Service to supply workers without regard to race, an executive order abolishing segregation in the armed forces, an executive order abolishing discrimination and segregation on account of race in all departments of the federal government, and a request from the President to Congress to pass a law forbidding benefits of the National Labor Relations Act to unions denying Negroes membership. Regardless of the extent of the success of the MOWM, however, it represented something different in black protest. Unlike the older Negro movements, the MOWM had captured the imagination of the masses.

Although overlooked by most recent writers on civil rights, a mass militancy became characteristic of the American Negro in World War II. This was symbolized by the MOWM and was the reason for its wide appeal. Furthermore, older Negro organizations found themselves pushed into militant stands. For example, the NAACP underwent a tremendous growth in its membership and became representative of the Negro masses for the first time in its history. From 355 branches and a membership of 50,556 in 1940, the NAACP grew to 1,073 branches with a membership of slightly less than 450,000 in 1946. The editors of the Pittsburgh *Courier* recognized that a new spirit was present in black America. In the past, Negroes

> made the mistake of relying entirely upon the gratitude and sense of fair play of the American people. Now we are disillusioned. We have neither faith in promises, nor a high opinion of the integrity of the American people, where race is involved. Experience has taught us that we must rely primarily upon our own efforts. . . . That is why we protest, agitate, and demand that all forms of color prejudice be blotted out. . . .

By the time of the Japanese attack on Pearl Harbor, many in America, both inside and outside of the government, were worried over the state of Negro morale. There was fear that the Negro would be disloyal. The depth of white ignorance about the causes for the Negro's cynicism and low morale is obvious from the fact that the black press was blamed for the widespread discontent. The double victory attitude constantly displayed in Negro newspapers throughout the war, and supported by most black Americans, was considered as verging on disloyalty by most whites. White America, ignorant of the American Negroes' reaction to World War I, thought that black citizens should subdue their grievances for the duration.

During World War II, there was pressure upon the White House and the justice department from within the federal government to indict some Negro editors for sedition and interference with the war effort. President Roosevelt refused to sanction this, however. There was also an attempt to deny newsprint to the more militant Negro newspapers, but the President put an end to this when the matter was brought to his attention. The restriction of Negro newspapers from military installations became so widespread that the war department had to call a halt to this practice in 1943. These critics failed to realize that, although serving to unify black opinion, the Negro press simply reflected the Negro mind.

One of the most widely publicized attacks on the Negro press was made by the southern white liberal, Virginius Dabney, editor of the Richmond *Times Dispatch.* He charged that "extremist" Negro newspapers and Negro leaders were "demanding an overnight revolution in race relations," and as a consequence they were "stirring up interracial hate." Dabney concluded his indictment by warning that "it is a foregone conclusion that if an attempt is made forcibly to abolish segregation throughout the South, violence and bloodshed will result." The Negro press reacted vigorously to such charges. Admitting that there were "all-or-nothing" Negro leaders, the Norfolk *Journal and Guide* claimed they were created by the "nothing-at-all" attitude of whites. The Chicago *Defender* and Baltimore *Afro-American* took the position that they were only pointing out the shortcomings of American democracy, and this was certainly not disloyal. The NAACP and the Urban League claimed that it was patriotic for Negroes to protest against undemocratic practices, and those who sought to stifle this protest were the unpatriotic ones.

The Negro masses simply did not support a strategy of moderating their grievances for the duration of the war. After attending an Office of Facts and Figures conference for Negro leaders in March 1942, Roy Wilkins of the NAACP wrote:

> . . . It is a plain fact that no Negro leader with a constituency can face his members today and ask full support for the war in the light of the atmosphere the government has created. Some Negro educators who are responsible only to their boards or trustees might do so, but the heads of no organized groups would dare do so.

By 1942, the federal government began investigating Negro morale in order to find out what could be done to improve it. This project was undertaken by the Office of Facts and Figures and its successor, the Office of War Information. Surveys by these agencies indicated that the great amount of national publicity given the defense program only served to increase the Negro's awareness that he was not participating fully in that program. Black Americans found it increasingly difficult to reconcile their treatment with the announced war aims. Urban Negroes were the most resentful over defense discrimination, particularly against the treatment accorded black members of the armed forces. Never before had Negroes been so united behind a cause: the war had served to focus their attention on their unequal status in American society. Black Americans were almost unanimous in wanting a show of good intention from the federal government that changes would be made in the racial status quo.

The government's inclination to take steps to improve Negro morale, and the Negro's desire for change, were frustrated by the general attitude of white Americans. In 1942, after two years of militant agitation by Negroes, six out of ten white Americans felt that black Americans were satisfied with things the way they were and that Negroes were receiving all of the opportunities they deserved. More than half of all whites interviewed in the Northeast and West believed that there should be separate schools, separate restaurants, and separate neighborhoods for the races. A majority of whites in all parts of the country believed that the Negro would not be treated any better after the war than in 1942 and that the Negro's lesser role in society was due to his own shortcomings rather than anything the whites had done. The white opposition to racial change may have provided the rationale for governmental inactivity. Furthermore, the white obstinance must have added to the bitterness of black Americans.

Although few people recognized it, the war was working a revolution in American race relations. Sociologist Robert E. Park felt that the racial structure of society was "cracking," and the equilibrium reached after the Civil War seemed "to be under attack at a time and under conditions when it is particularly difficult to defend it." Sociologist Howard W. Odum wrote from the South that there was "an unmeasurable and unbridgeable distance between the white South and the reasonable expectation of the Negro." White southerners opposed to change in the racial mores sensed changes occurring among "their" Negroes. "Outsiders" from the North, Mrs. Franklin Roosevelt, and the Roosevelt Administration were all accused of attempting to undermine segregation under the pretense of wartime necessity.

Racial tensions were common in all sections of the country during the war. There were riots in 1943. Tensions were high because Negro Americans were challenging the status quo. When fourteen prominent Negroes, conservatives and liberals, southerners and northerners, were asked in 1944 what they thought the black American wanted, their responses were almost unanimous. Twelve of the fourteen said they thought that Negroes wanted full political equality, economic equality, equality of opportunity, and full social equality with the abolition of legal segregation. The war had stimulated the race consciousness and the desire for change among Negroes.

Most American Negroes and their leaders wanted the government to institute a revolutionary change in its race policy. Whereas the policy had been acquiescence in segregation since the end of Reconstruction, the government was now asked to set the example for the rest of the nation by supporting integration. This was the demand voiced by the great majority of the Negro leaders called together in March 1942 by the Office of Facts and Figures. *Crisis* magazine summarized the feelings of many black Americans: Negroes have "waited thus far in vain for some sharp and dramatic notice that this war is not to maintain the status quo here."

The White House, and it was not alone, failed to respond to the revolutionary changes occurring among the nation's largest minority. When the Fraternal Council of Negro Churches called upon President Roosevelt to end discrimination in the defense industries and armed forces, the position taken was that "it would be very bad to give encouragement beyond the point where actual results can be accomplished." Roosevelt did bestir himself over particularly outrageous incidents. When Roland Hayes, a noted Negro singer, was beaten and jailed in a Georgia town, the President dashed off a note to his attorney general: "Will you have someone go down and check up . . . and see if any law was violated. I suggest you send a northerner."

Roosevelt was not enthusiastic about major steps in the race relations field proposed by interested individuals within and without the government. In February 1942 Edwin R. Embree of the Julius Rosenwald Fund, acutely aware of the growing crisis in American race relations, urged Roosevelt to create a commission of experts on race relations to advise him on what steps the government should take to improve matters. FDR's answer to this proposal indicates that he felt race relations was one of the reform areas that had to be sacrificed for the present in order to prosecute the war. He thought such a commission was "premature" and that "we must start winning the war . . . before we do much general planning for the future." The President believed that "there is a danger of such long-range planning becoming projects of wide influence in escape from the realities of war. I am not convinced that we can be realists about the war and planners for the future at this critical time."

After the race riots of 1943, numerous proposals for a national committee on race relations were put forward; but FDR refused to change his position. Instead, the President simply appointed Jonathan Daniels to gather information from all government departments on current race tensions and what they were doing to combat them. This suggestion for what would eventually become a President's Committee on Civil Rights would have to wait until a President recognized that a revolution in race relations was occurring and that action by the government could no longer be put off. In the interim, many would share the shallow reasoning of Secretary of War Stimson that the cause of racial tension was "the deliberate effort . . . on the part of certain radical leaders of the colored race to use the war for obtaining . . . race equality and inter-racial marriages. . . ."

The hypocrisy and paradox involved in fighting a world war for the four freedoms and against aggression by an enemy preaching a master race ideology, while at the same time upholding racial segregation and white supremacy, were too obvious. The war crisis provided American Negroes with a unique opportunity to point out, for all to see, the difference between the American creed and practice. The democratic ideology and rhetoric with which the war was fought stimulated a sense of hope and certainty in black Americans that the old race structure was destroyed forever. In part, this confidence was also the result of the mass militancy and race consciousness that developed in these years. When the expected white acquiescence in a new racial order did not occur, the ground was prepared for the civil rights revolution of the 1950s and the 1960s; the seeds were indeed sown in the World War II years.

11

Negro Protest Movements and Organizations

AUGUST MEIER

After the Second World War, the general drift of American public opinion toward a more liberal racial attitude that had begun during the New Deal became accentuated as a result of the revolution against Western Imperialism in Asia and Africa that engendered a new respect for the nonwhite peoples of the world, and as a result of the subsequent competition for the support of the uncommitted nations connected with the Cold War. In this context of changing international trends and

source: *Journal of Negro Education*, XXXII (Fall 1963), 435–50 (footnotes omitted). Reprinted by permission of the *Journal of Negro Education* and the author.

shifting American public opinion, the campaign for Negro rights has, since mid-century, broadened rapidly and has, in fact, in certain fundamental respects changed its character. Thus there has been a shift in emphasis from legalism to direct action. At the same time the scope of the attack has widened. Meanwhile the civil rights movement has become both more and more a Negro movement, and more and more a mass movement. Finally the movement has become infused with a new militance, a new sense of urgency, a new psychology of immediatism as, despite increasing Southern resistance, the racial barriers have begun to crumble in an accelerating fashion.

Pre-eminent among the civil rights organizations in 1950 was the NAACP. Often interlocked with NAACP leadership, though in a number of places operating independently, were the voters' leagues that had arisen in the South after the Supreme Court outlawed the white primary (1944); together with the NAACP they had raised the number of Negro registered voters in twelve southeastern states from about 233,000 in 1940 to about 1,110,000 by 1952. Playing second fiddle to the NAACP, but holding the key to future strategy, was the tiny Congress of Racial Equality. The nationalist movements were only a speck on the horizon, for since Garvey the alienated lowest class of urban Negroes tended to find hope and dignity in the pentecostal churches and in such chiliastic sects as those of Daddy Grace, Elder Macheaux and Father Divine.

At mid-century the NAACP could look back upon a forty-year history of deliberate but definite advance. Often regarded as conservative today, its program of agitation, and political and legal action, and its insistence upon attacking segregation and other forms of discrimination, was originally considered radical in contrast to the accommodating ideology of Booker T. Washington, then in the ascendancy. Leaving the task of enlarging employment opportunities to the conciliatory methods of the more conservative Urban League, the NAACP had tried to attain the Negro's full constitutional rights through political pressure and the courts. By 1950, in fact, the NAACP could pride itself upon an imposing series of Supreme Court victories, particularly in the fields of due process and equal protection in criminal cases, residential segregation, and voting. Taken together, *Smith v. Allwright* (1944), invalidating the white primary, and *Shelly v. Kraemer* (1948), declaring restrictive covenants unenforceable, seemed to open a new era. As early as 1946 the NAACP had made its first dent in the system of transportation segregation, and the McLaurin and Sweatt decisions in 1950, though applicable only to graduate and professional schooling, suggested that the separate-but-equal principle itself would soon be completely overturned. During the early 1950s the NAACP's Legal Defense and Educational Fund concentrated on both interstate and intrastate transportation, discrimination in publicly owned recreational facilities, and segregation in the public schools. By the middle of the decade the Supreme Court had made clearcut decisions in support of the NAACP's position in each of these areas, thus firmly establishing the basic legal principles supporting desegregation.

Due to a rise in membership fees, the NAACP had lost nearly half its members in 1948; in 1950 the total was just under 200,000. Since then there has been a gradual rise, the number doubling to nearly 400,000 in 1962. Income for the Association rose more rapidly: between 1954 and 1958 its revenues increased from $465,000 to $1,000,000. Today the NAACP spends at the rate of well over a million dollars annually, while the National Legal Defense Fund (founded in 1939 and since 1955 a completely separate institution legally and administratively) spends almost as much. Significantly the major increase in membership in the late 1940s and early 1950s was in the South, so that by 1955 fully half of the NAACP members lived there. The legislative attack on the NAACP in the South after the 1954 Supreme Court decision (the Association is still under injunction not to operate in Alabama), the economic reprisals taken against NAACP leaders and parents who tried to register their children in previously all-white schools, and the harrassment and violence to which the Association's leaders were subjected in the white South's campaign against the organization, did not lead to a decline in membership—in fact Negroes rallied to it just because it was under such bitter attack.

During the late 1940s and early 1950s branch activity in the North concentrated largely on obtaining passage of fair employment and fair housing acts; in the border states and upper South the principal emphasis was on litigation to secure the use of public recreational facilities; and in the South generally this period witnessed considerable voter registration activity. During the second half of the decade Southern branches were engaged in extensive litigation against the South's massive resistance to school desegregation and subsequently against the more subtly drawn pupil-placement laws. Throughout the country during the late fifties there was a heavy accent on voter registration: it was felt that in the ballot lay the key to obtaining civil rights legislation and a sympathetic policy on the part of public officials. Increased income for the association made it possible to employ staff specialists first in labor, since 1958 in housing and voter registration, and quite recently in education. Both these, by advising branches on how to work their fields, and the burgeoning field staff (which grew from less than half a dozen in 1950 to twenty-seven in 1963), vastly stimulated NAACP activity on all fronts. The effort to eliminate discriminatory practices by trade unions had become a major concern by the middle of the decade; political and legal pressures were employed to see that publicly financed housing would be open to all; and recently the attack on de facto school desegregation in the North has become a major concern. Prior to 1960 nonviolent direct action was a more peripheral matter for NAACP branches—but in 1958 and 1959 NAACP college and youth chapters in Oklahoma City and St. Louis engaged in successful sit-ins, and elsewhere, as in Louisville and Baltimore, adult branches sponsored direct action. Nevertheless, looking back over the decade of the 1950s it is clear that the NAACP's chief concerns had been to increase the number of voters and to attack segregation in all its manifestations with both legal and political pressures.

Established in 1942, CORE was much younger than the NAACP, and in 1950 was still a small, chiefly white organization, confined to the North and a few border communities, and lacking even a single paid staff member. Contrary to popular impression, the use of nonviolent direct action was not a product of the postwar era, but of the depression, for CORE's origins lay in the activities of the Fellowship of Reconciliation, a Quaker social-action organization. This group of religious pacifists combined Gandhi's technique of *satyagraha* with the sit-*down* tactics of the Detroit automobile strikers, to produce the sit-*in*. F.O.R.'s synthesis of union tactics (including picketing) with Gandhian nonviolence was tested on a limited scale beginning around 1940. Then, in order to attract people whose interests lay in race relations rather than in philosophical pacifism, some of the F.O.R. leaders founded CORE.

CORE's membership and activity had been in the North during the 1940s, and in the border states at the turn of the decade and early 1950s. In 1956 CORE employed a paid field worker for the first time, and began its work in the Deep South, both by nibbling at the edges and, more daringly, engaging in activity in South Carolina. Like the NAACP, CORE always aimed at the attainment of full citizenship in all areas. But at first it was chiefly concerned with public accommodations. Though back in the early 1950s St. Louis CORE pioneered in the technique—later so effectively employed and popularized by the Philadelphia ministers—to obtain employment through selective buying campaigns, this did not become a major emphasis until fairly recently, and not until 1959–1960 did CORE use direct action to secure desegregation of privately owned apartment houses. Today in the North CORE concentrates on unemployment and housing, with some work in school desegregation; in the South it concentrates on places of public accommodation and to a lesser extent on voter registration.

CORE pioneered in the use of *satyagraha* in this country, but it was the Montgomery bus boycott of 1955–1956 that dramatically brought it to the attention of the nation, and the Negro community in particular. And it has been Martin Luther King, whom the bus boycott catapulted into prominence, who has now become the leading symbol of this strategy. Even before a court decision (obtained by NAACP lawyers) had spelled success for the Montgomery Improvement Association, a similar movement had started in Tallahassee, and afterwards one was undertaken in Birmingham where, following the state's injunction against the NAACP, a group of ministers headed by Fred Shuttlesworth had established the Alabama Christian Movement for Human Rights. About the same time there appeared the Tuskegee Civic Association, which undertook a three-year-long boycott of local merchants in response to the state's legislature gerrymander that placed practically all Negro voters outside of the town's limits—a campaign crowned with success when the Supreme Court ruled the gerrymander illegal in 1960.

The happenings in Montgomery, Tallahassee, Birmingham and Tuskegee were widely heralded as indicating the emergence of a "New Negro" in the South—militant, no longer fearful of white hoodlums, police and jails, and willing to use his collective economic weight to attain his ends. Seizing upon the new mood, King in 1957 established the Southern Christian Leadership Conference—an organization of affiliates rather than a membership organization like NAACP and CORE. Ideologically committed to a thoroughgoing philosophical pacifism of the Gandhian persuasion, SCLC's program includes not only the now-familiar demonstrations but also citizenship training schools which prepare leaders to go out into local communities and push voter-registration. SCLC's budget comes chiefly from contributions—its income for the year ending August 31, 1961, was nearly $200,000; its budget this year [1963] is almost two and a half times as much—approximately $375,000.

The NAACP thought it saw the beginning of the end in the 1954 Supreme Court decision. And truly, it was only the *beginning* of the end. Impressive as it was to cite the advances —especially legal advances—made in the post-war years, in spite of state laws and supreme court decisions something was clearly wrong. Negroes were still disfranchised in most of the Deep South; Supreme Court decisions in regard to transportation facilities were still largely ignored there; discrimination in employment and housing was the rule, even in states with model civil rights laws; and after 1954 the Negro unemployment rate grew constantly due to recessions and automation.

And then, as we have noted, there was the rise of Southern white militance in response to the 1954 decision, best represented by the White Citizens' Councils.

At the very time that legalism was thus proving itself a limited instrument, Negroes were gaining a new self-image of themselves as a result of the rise of the new African nations; King and others were demonstrating that nonviolent direct action could be effective in the South; and the new laws and court decisions, the gradually increasing interest of the federal government, the international situation, and the evident drift of white public opinion, had developed in American Negroes a new confidence in the future. In short there had occurred what has appropriately been described as a revolution in expectations. Negroes no longer felt that they had to accept the humiliations of second-class citizenship, and consequently these humiliations—somewhat fewer though they now were—appeared to be more intolerable than ever. This increasing impatience—and disillusionment—of Negroes accounted for the rising tempo of nonviolent direct action in the later 1950s which culminated in the student sit-ins and the Freedom Rides of 1960–1961.

Symptomatic of this impatience and disillusionment was the stepped-up campaign against trade-union discrimination. During the 1930s the CIO unions had made a new departure in establishing nondiscriminatory policies. However, the Civil Rights Committee of the merged AFL-CIO made little, if any, significant progress. While the chief charges of discrimination were still directed at the old AFL unions, notably in the building trades, there was also increasing dissatisfaction with the policies of the industrial unions. For example, even the United Automobile Workers—known for its liberalism until 1962—had no Negroes among its chief executives and policy makers. Beginning in 1958 the NAACP openly attacked its allies in the labor movement for abdicating their responsibility in regard to erasing the color line within the trade unions. In the spring of 1960, A. Philip Randolph established the Negro American Labor Council, to fight against discrimination from within the AFL-CIO. With a board consisting chiefly of staff people from the AFL-CIO unions, the NALC is made up of affiliates in a number of cities; a year after its formation it claimed between seven and ten thousand members. It lacks a paid staff, but it has been a valuable platform for agitation and a mighty symbol of the Negro worker's discontent.

Many date the new departure in the tactics of the civil rights movement from the Montgomery bus boycott in 1955—and the impact of this event is not to be minimized. But it seems to me that the really decisive break with the past came with the college student sit-ins that started spontaneously at Greensboro in 1960. This was so for several reasons. For one thing these sit-ins involved the use of nonviolent direct action on a massive, Southwide scale, never before attempted. Secondly, they involved tens of thousands of students, thousands of whom were arrested—an involvement of numbers of people heretofore inconceivable. Thirdly, it began a period—in which we are still living—in which the spearhead of the civil rights struggle has come from the youth. Of course the adults in the Negro community rallied to the aid of the students and supplied essential legal and financial assistance. But it has been the youth who have been the chief dynamic force in revamping the strategy of the established civil rights organizations— who in turn felt it necessary to do something in order to retain leadership in the movement.

The NAACP almost immediately swung into action, and the national office deliberately speeded up the formation of youth councils and college chapters with the specific purpose of engaging in demonstrations, while national staff members went to regional NAACP conferences that spring and knocked heads together in a strong effort to obtain local NAACP participation and support for this type of mass action. In fact, much of the sit-in activity during 1960 was carried on by NAACP youth councils and college chapters. Like the NAACP, SCLC sought to get on the student bandwagon, and it sponsored the Raleigh Conference at which the Student Nonviolent Coordinating Committee was established—though SNCC and SCLC later drifted apart. SNCC is theoretically a coordinating committee of affiliated youth groups in the Southern and border states; actually, for the most part a small group in Atlanta engages in action of its own choosing, and enlists the aid of people in the local communities where it decides to work. SNCC has been extraordinarily effective. Though it has the most modest budget of any of the civil rights organizations (it operated last year on $120,000), and its field secretaries work on a subsistence basis, and although it has been less publicized than the other organizations, it has probably supplied the major drive for the civil rights movement in the South. CORE in 1960 seemed to be in the doldrums, its techniques appropriated by more vigorous and lusty successors. But in 1961, following the Freedom Rides to Alabama and Mississippi, CORE re-emerged as in many ways the most imaginative and resourceful of the civil rights organizations in the application of the tactics in which it had pioneered.

The events of 1960 and 1961 ushered in a period of intense competitive rivalry for prestige and power in the civil rights field. It has been a four-way struggle—between SCLC, NAACP, SNCC and CORE (though even the Urban League has set forth upon more aggressive policies). Of the four it may be said that SNCC has probably been the most dynamic force, closely seconded by CORE. While various SCLC affiliates have taken the lead in nonviolent direct action in their communities, especially where local NAACP branches are dominated by conservative leadership, King, functioning chiefly as a symbolic or "spiritual" leader, has ordinarily moved into situations which others have begun to lend the magic of his image to the support of the local movement. Moreover, in many communities there have sprung up local organizations, established very often by ministers of working-class churches, taking various names, and unattached to any national body. Sometimes these are "umbrella" organizations, including within them local units of national organizations; at times they are entirely independent of, though not necessarily inimical to the NAACP or other established groups. As the oldest and therefore the most bureaucratic of the civil rights organizations, in many localities dominated by older, conservative leaders, the NAACP has quite naturally been on the defensive in a number of places. But it is impossible to generalize about the NAACP. While some branches have resisted the direct action techniques, others have embraced them wholeheartedly. There are cases of militant cliques ousting conservative leadership within NAACP branches; in Philadelphia for example the older leaders found their homes picketed with signs calling them "Uncle Toms." While the NAACP can scarcely take credit for initiating the direct action techniques, it is clearly invalid to stereotype it as run by a conservative Black Bourgeoisie wedded to legalism. Pushed and shoved by the exclusively action-oriented groups, the NAACP has pretty effectively met the challenge posed by them. In fact at the 1963 annual convention militants among the rank and file and the "radicals" on the paid staff triumphed against the more conservative elements. The convention enthusiastically endorsed direct action as the major NAACP tactic for the future, granted greater autonomy to the youth, and called upon the national board to adopt procedures for removing do-nothing conservative leadership from the branches.

However, the NAACP's predominance in the civil rights field, not seriously contested as late as 1960, has been broken. Often in fact one gets the impression that the rivalry among the different groups is not due so much to differences in philosophy, tactics or degree of militancy as much as to a power struggle for hegemony in the civil rights movement. Painful as these conflicts have been, the rivalry of civil rights groups has actually proven to be an essential ingredient of the dynamics of the civil rights movement over the past three and a half years; for in their attempt to outdo each other, each organization puts forth stronger effort than it otherwise would, and is constantly searching for new avenues along which to develop a program. And despite all rivalries, when the chips are down, the different organizations usually do manage to cooperate. Especially significant has been the growing cooperation this past spring [1963] between CORE and SNCC. The best example of this cooperation amidst rivalry is the fact that all of these organizations, along with others, worked together in sponsoring the August 28th March on Washington.

Two of the most significant aspects of the civil rights movement since 1960 are that it has become increasingly a Negro movement and at the same time increasingly a mass movement.

The two developments are not unrelated; and both of them, of course, had their origins well before 1950. The NAACP membership and branch leadership have always been almost entirely Negro; but at the start most of the staff and executive board were liberal whites. In 1921 the NAACP employed its first Negro executive secretary, James Weldon Johnson; in 1933 its legal staff came under Negro direction when Charles Houston took over; and today only two NAACP staff members are white (though the NAACP Legal Defense Fund's chief counsel has been a white man, Jack Greenberg, since Thurgood Marshall was elevated to the bench). Constitutional changes made in 1947 and 1962 have permitted greater membership participation in the election of the national board; one result of this has been a decline in the number of whites on it—today only a dozen whites remain out of a membership that in the coming months will reach a maximum of sixty. CORE started off as a predominantly white liberal middle-class organization; as late as 1960 perhaps only one third of its membership was Negro, and at that time its four chief executive officers, as well as its national chairman, were white. With the selection of James Farmer as national director in 1961, CORE's image changed markedly in the Negro community, and it was thereby able to attract far more Negro support. Today, of CORE's four chief executive officers two are white and two are Negro. While the majority of Northern CORE members are still white there has been growing Negro participation in that section, and in the South CORE's membership is almost entirely Negro. The climax to these developments came at CORE's 1963 convention, the first one at which a majority of the delegates were Negroes. The Southern Negro delegates really set the tone for the convention, and moved into positions of leadership. And for the first time in CORE's history a Negro was selected as national chairman. Randolph's March on Washington Movement during the Second World War adumbrated current tendencies in its insistence upon an all-Negro membership and leadership; Negroes, he said, must fight their own battle for citizenship rights. More recently, organizations like SCLC, the Alabama Christian Movement for Human Rights, the Tuskegee Civic Association, the Negro

American Labor Council, and the newer local groups have been Negro organizations from the start. SNCC has avoided any form of organic union with the predominantly white Northern Student Movement for Civil Rights—though it and Northern white students generally have been a prime source of SNCC's financial support; and while SNCC has a number of white field secretaries, it consciously projects itself as a Negro-led organization. There has been in fact a growing insistence that Negroes must take the initiative and leadership in achieving their freedom; that white liberals tend to be compromisers who cannot be fully trusted, though their financial support and participation in direct action is welcomed.

CORE's experience has shown clearly that in order to attract large numbers of Negroes to the civil rights movement Negro leadership is essential. And white liberals—and radicals—in the Movement have accepted this fact. The NAACP had originally appealed to the elite Negroes, and during the 1930s some of the younger intellectuals like Ralph Bunche attacked it for doing nothing about the problems of the masses. The Association modified its program somewhat, and during the 1940s and 1950s made an increasing appeal to working-class people, as its growing membership testifies. Actually it would be impossible to make any generalizations about the sources of NAACP branch membership and leadership today, because the variations from branch to branch are so considerable. At the risk of a great deal of oversimplification, and on the basis of general impression rather than careful investigation, one might say that in the South leadership tends to come from ministers, in the West from professional people, and in the Northeast from lower-middle-class people such as postal workers. Leadership thus generally tends to be more middle-class rather than either lower-class or upper-class. The nature of the membership of a branch, like its leadership, depends to a great extent upon specific local conditions and personalities. In some branches the more elite people in the community set the tone; in others the professional and business people show no interest and blue-collar workers predominate. CORE, originally composed of white-collar middle-class people, since 1960 has found more blue-collar skilled and even semi-skilled

workers joining its ranks, both in the North where it has moved
into the area of obtaining employment for working-class Negroes, and in the South. The youthful sit-inners of 1960–1961
were chiefly people of working-class origins—that is they
tended to be upward-mobile members of the Negro lower-
middle and upper-lower classes—though their leadership was
more likely to be drawn from people of middle-class origins.
From the beginning the bus boycotts in the South were mass
movements, and the same is true of newer movements like
the Albany Movement and the selective buying campaigns
being undertaken in a number of cities, though it should be
pointed out that all classes of the community are involved in
these efforts and that the middle and even upper classes are
disproportionately represented in the leadership.

A striking development of the past few months has been the
involvement of lower-lower-class people, many of whom are
unemployed or chronically so. It is this group that apparently
was responsible for the brick and bottle throwing in Birmingham and Jackson. Even more significantly some individuals of
this class, heretofore avoiding participation in demonstrations
sponsored by the direct-action groups, have begun to join in
with the nonviolent direct actionists, but unlike them have not
remained nonviolent in the face of attacks from white hoodlums, but have become involved in fracases with them in places
like Cambridge, Maryland, and Nashville. In the North this
group is chiefly concerned with obtaining jobs; in the South,
despite a high rate of unemployed it is becoming involved in
the struggle for public accommodations, though this is very possibly a result of the growing tendency to package demands
for desegregation of lunch counters and other facilities with
demands for jobs.

There are those who believe that overt violence on the part
of Negro demonstrators is on the rise, and that in hardcore
areas of the South, Gandhian techniques will not work and that
disillusionment with nonviolent tactics will set in. This line of
thinking and the recent outbreaks are reminiscent of the
events at Monroe, North Carolina, in 1959, and recall Robert
Williams' assertion that federal intervention would not occur
until Negroes struck back at their attackers. Moreover, there is

the possibility that the dire predictions in the daily press about possible racial violence may act in the nature of a self-fulfilling prophecy. Whether or not extensive violence occurs, astute leadership in the civil rights organizations will undoubtedly employ its possibility as a means of forcing quicker action from the white community.

In any event one must conclude that there has emerged a real thrust for achieving "Freedom Now" from the working-class people—that is from the lower and lower-middle-class people. SNCC, highly critical of the Black Bourgeoisie and white liberals alike, regards itself as the vanguard of the Negro masses—and to a remarkable extent that is exactly what the youthful demonstrators of the years since 1960 have proven to be. And this thrust from the working class—especially from working-class youth—has been largely responsible for the recent dynamics behind the civil rights movement. In fact the competition for prestige and power among the major civil rights organizations is in large part a competition for control over the masses of working-class Negroes. It is likely that a large part of the increasing militancy of middle and upper-class Negroes is derived from the new militancy of the working classes. As Bayard Rustin has said of Birmingham, here was a "black community [that] was welded into a classless revolt. A. G. Gaston, the Negro millionaire who with some ministers and other upper-class elements had publicly stated that the time was not ripe for such a broad protest, finally accommodated himself, as did the others, to the mass pressure from below and joined the struggle."

Now until recently it seemed quite possible that the un-skilled, lowest-class urban Negroes might turn to the escapist nationalist ideology of the Black Muslims, for this sect offered a sense of dignity and a future to those whom the civil rights movement seemed to neglect. More than anything else the increasing unemployment joined with the revolution in ex-pectations created a climate in which the Black Muslims thrived. The Black Muslims are simply one of several na-tionalist movements—but the only one of any size: estimates of their number vary, but it is almost certainly below 100,000, though there are many sympathizers and admirers. Historically nationalism of the extreme variety typified by the Black Muslims has been usually found among the most dispossessed of the Negro masses (the principal exception being the large-scale interest in colonization exhibited by the Negro elite during the 1850s), though there are certain tiny groups of nationalist intellectuals, like the avowedly black Marxist Monroe Defense Committee, and the Liberation Committee for Africa.

Just as the Garvey Movement was the lower-lower-class counterpart of the New Negro of the 1920s, so the Black Muslims are the counterpart of the new "New Negro" of the 1960s. The literature about this movement is so extensive that it would be superfluous to discuss its program here. However, despite the stark contrast between the integrationist aims of the civil rights organizations, and the separatist ideology of the Black Muslims, it is important to recognize that the two have much in common. Both are manifestations of a militant rejection of white doctrines of Negro inferiority and white policies of discrimination; both are essentially a quest for recognition of the Negroes' human dignity. Both reflect the new self-image of American Negroes arising out of the rise of the new African state. Both exhibit dissatisfaction with the traditional, accommodating, otherworldly Christianity of the Negro masses, which offered rewards in heaven rather than on earth. And both are indications of Negro rejection of the philosophy of gradualism, and both exhibit a rejection of the liberal white paternalism. In part perhaps because they have sensed the increasing attraction of the direct-action activities of the civil rights organizations which have been moving more vigorously into the area of employment discrimination; in part perhaps because they thought the moment opportune to make a bid for leadership of the entire Negro community, since March 1963 the Black Muslims seem to have made a turn to the right. There is now less emphasis upon separatism, more emphasis on the generalized abstractions of justice and freedom, and support is even urged for the programs of other groups which are working for freedom and justice for the race.

The influence of the Black Muslims on the civil rights movement is somewhat speculative. Negroes of all classes approve of their dramatic indictment of the American race system, and of their ability to place white men on the defensive. Their renown may have contributed to some extent to the tendency to assert pride in being black, or even of being black nationalists, that has enjoyed some vogue among Negro activists in recent years. Their activity may also have contributed not a little to the intensified activity of the more traditional organizations like the NAACP and Urban League, and may have helped alert the civil rights organizations generally to the importance of doing something vigorous about employment discrimination. Certainly fear of the Black Muslims has accelerated the efforts of influential whites to satisfy the demands of the civil rights organizations.

The new thrust from the Negro masses, the complex patterns of rivalry and cooperation among the various civil rights organizations, the increasing power of the Negro vote in the urban centers, the growing realization of the Negro's economic power that has derived from the successful boycotts, the obvious sensitivity of the government to foreign criticism of our racial system, have together resulted in a broadening and intensification of the Negro protest movement. Year by year and month by month the Negroes of the United States have been growing more militant, more immediatist. Civil rights organizations now make several demands together in a package, rather than fighting on single issues, as before, and are no longer satisfied with tokenism. The result is that the rate of change is being accelerated, and the Kennedy administration has been brought to seriously commit itself to sponsor major legislative remedies. But the dynamics of the situation are such that whatever Kennedy does will not be enough—both because Negro demands increase with every advance, and because the President is subject to counter-pressures from interest groups inimical to civil rights. Large-scale violence may or may not come about as a result of large-scale unemployment, Southern white intransigence, and increased Negro militance. But two things are certain—Negro militancy is bound to increase, and an accelerated tempo of advancement in civil rights appears inevitable.

The preceding pages were completed early in July [1963]. Over the past two months the Negro protest movement has been characterized by varied, and in a sense, contradictory tendencies. There appears to be a waxing nationalist spirit, and yet also evidence of increasing white support and participation; a growing belief that unity with white labor and greater socialization of the economy will be necessary to assure freedom and equality, and at the same time increasing evidence that white moderates—most notably churchmen and businessmen—are becoming involved.

The rising spirit of nationalism would appear to be the product of two forces. One is the growing sense of confidence and self-respect as advances are made. Evidence of this is to be found, for example, in a burgeoning interest among Negroes in Negro history. The other source of this nationalist spirit is the disillusionment with the pace of change, the continuing tendency of the Kennedy administration to compromise with Southern racists, the shock of increasing police brutality and white violence in the Deep South. All these combine to give Negroes a greater sense of isolation and alienation at the very time that white support for the cause of civil rights is increasing. One manifestation of this trend is the sentiment for an all-Negro "Freedom Now" political party. Oddly enough it would appear that this idea has been projected chiefly by the Socialist Workers Party (the Trotskyites), who are deliberately attempting to capitalize upon this nationalist sentiment in order to destroy the Democratic Party and thereby create, they hope, a truly revolutionary situation.

Universal among civil rights leaders is the belief, growing over the past year, that there can be no really meaningful solution to the civil rights question without a solution to the nation's economic problems. Mass unemployment lends urgency to the Negro protest at the same time that it makes the attainment of desegregation and equal rights a largely empty gain for the masses. Some civil rights leaders foresee an "inevitable" shift toward the left and toward increasing socialization in the American economic system; and they suggest that potentially the Negro protest movement can play an important role in eliminating poverty for whites as well as for Negroes. Moreover, as a result of the March on Washington there has been something of a rapprochement between the civil rights organizations and the more "progressive" elements among the former CIO unions, and if this proves fruitful there will certainly be sharply increased pressure on the national administration to take more radical steps to eliminate unemployment.

On the other hand the March on Washington also actively involved in civil rights, for the first time, a number of white moderates—a few even from the South—who had heretofore displayed no interest. In addition to the March itself, the shock of the outrages in Birmingham both in the spring and in recent weeks, has served to arouse moderate elements hitherto unconcerned. An even more remarkable manifestation of this trend is the $1.5 million raised among businessmen this past summer by Stephen Currier of the Taconic Foundation for the recently established Council for United Civil Rights Leadership and its allied Committee for Welfare, Education and Legal Defense.

Thus the future direction of the civil rights movement is uncertain. It seems likely that the Urban League and NAACP will probably continue to be—relatively speaking—conservative forces, while SNCC obviously will continue to be the most radical. (It is undoubtedly sound strategy that there continue to be diverse approaches among Negro protest organizations.) It is predictable that the white moderates are also likely to act as something of a relatively conservative influence. The joining of disparate elements in the two major current civil rights coalitions will inevitably mean a degree of instability within them. For the Council for United Civil Rights Leadership ranges from the "moneybags" represented by Stephen Currier to the parsimonious SNCC people, while the March on Washington Movement ranges from churchmen who dread the idea of "revolution" to the SNCC activists who revel in the idea that they are "revolutionists." Strictly speaking the civil rights movement (including SNCC) is not properly labelled revolutionary, for the vast majority of Negro activists do not desire to overturn the social structure—however much they say they want to do this—but rather they want to be included in it on a basis of equality. The Negro protest movement therefore is more properly described as a reform movement. Of course the differences between the radical and conservative elements in the civil rights movement are not by any means a matter of mere semantics. There is a marked difference between eminent clergymen getting themselves arrested for trespassing—and getting bailed right out—at the Gwynn Oak Amusement Park in Maryland, July 4, [1962], and the type of radical civil disobedience that would create a breakdown in the government of Alabama which SNCC is now recommending.

Negro protest organizations are therefore posed with knotty problems of strategy. It is apparent that, unlike Africa, the Negro protest movement in this country must depend upon substantial numbers of white allies for its success. Should, then, the major effort be made to hold and increase the support from the white moderates, as the abolitionists and other successful reform movements in this country's history were eventually able to do? Or should the stress be laid upon forging an alliance with the working-class whites and upon striving toward a more socialized economy? Indubitably the threat of an all-Negro party will push the Kennedy administration further along the road to civil rights; but would a successful party of this type, if it resulted in the victory of a reactionary Republican in 1964, serve to advance or retard the cause of civil rights? Should radical civil disobedience as proposed by SNCC be undertaken, at the risk of alienating considerable white support, but generating considerable international publicity and pressure? It is likely that all of these approaches will be attempted, and that like the competing civil rights organizations each of the competing strategies will play a part in the achieving of racial democracy in the United States.

12

Political Nationalism: The Garvey Movement

C. ERIC LINCOLN

The name of Marcus Garvey is one of the best known in recent Negro history, yet it is one that the Negro leadership would like very much to forget. Few Negroes have elicited such consummate scorn from their fellows as did this belligerent little man, caricatured by a contemporary as:

A Jamaican of unmixed stock, squat, stocky, fat and sleek, with protruding jaws, and heavy jowls, small bright pig-like eyes and rather bulldog-like face. Boastful, egotistic, tyranni-

SOURCE: C. Eric Lincoln, *The Black Muslims in America* (Boston: Beacon Press, 1961), pp. 56–66 (footnotes omitted). Copyright © 1961 by C. Eric Lincoln. Reprinted by permission of the publisher.

cal, intolerant, cunning, shifty, smooth and suave, avaricious
. . . gifted at self-advertisement, without shame in self-lauda-
tion . . . without regard for veracity, a lover of pomp and
tawdry finery and garish display.

Yet, for all the castigations of his many critics, Garvey enjoyed the admiration of hundreds of thousands of lower-class
Negroes, who followed him with enthusiasm and money, and
who received from him a new estimate of their worth and
their future. His movement fired the imaginations of a people
desperate for a new hope and a new purpose, however un-
realistic. "Its spirit of race chauvinism had the sympathy of the
overwhelming majority of the Negro people, including those
who opposed its objectives. For this was the potent spirit of
race pride that informed the 'New Negro'" of the 1920s—a
period of cultural renaissance and racial militancy among the
Negro intelligentsia.

The Garvey movement must inevitably be seen against the
background of the post-World War I era, a crucial and difficult
time for Negroes in the United States. They had helped to win
a war for democracy overseas, only to return to the customary
bigotry at home. They had risked death fighting beside the
white man in the trenches of France, only to die in America
at the white man's hand. In the first year after the war, seventy
Negroes were lynched, many of them still in uniform. Fourteen
Negroes were burned publicly by white citizens; eleven of
these martyrs were burned alive. During the "Red Summer"
of 1919, there were no fewer than twenty-five race riots across
the country. A riot in the nation's capital lasted three days; in
Chicago, thirty-eight people were killed and 537 injured during thirteen days of mob rule.

Along with the actual physical violence, there was intimidation everywhere. The Ku Klux Klan had been revived; and
New York, Illinois, Indiana, Michigan and several New England states had been added to its traditional roster of Southern
states. There was an increasing competition between Negroes
and whites for housing and jobs. Despair and militancy were
the alternate moods of the Negro veterans who had fought "to
make the world safe for democracy." They were disillusioned

about the share of democracy America had reserved for them, but they were determined to bid for their rights—loud and clear.

In the summer of 1914, Marcus Garvey had returned home to Jamaica from a visit to London, his mind seething with plans for a new Universal Negro Improvement Association. Ironically, his sense of mission had been triggered by a reading of *Up From Slavery,* the autobiography of Booker T. Washington, who had been despised by many Negroes for his life pattern of compromise and accommodation.

> I read *Up From Slavery* . . . and then my doom . . . of being a race leader dawned upon me. . . . I asked: "Where is the black man's Government? Where is his King and his kingdom? Where is his President, his country, and his ambassador, his army, his navy, his men of big affairs?" I could not find them, and then I declared, "I will help to make them."

And he did. Putting aside Washington's reminiscences of restraint and gratitude for white favors, he originated a movement devoted to extreme black nationalism and self-improvement. As a result, he came to share with Washington the bitter contempt of Negro intellectuals—though for the opposite reason.

The manifesto of the UNIA called attention to "the universal disunity existing among the people of the Negro or African race." It challenged "all people of Negro or African parentage" to subscribe to the UNIA program, which read in part:

> To establish a Universal Confraternity among the race; to promote the spirit of race pride and love; to reclaim the fallen of the race . . . to strengthen the imperialism [self-determination] of independent African States . . . to establish Universities, Colleges and Secondary Schools for the further education and culture of the boys and girls of the race to conduct a world-wide commercial and industrial intercourse.

The motto of the Association was: "One God! One Aim! One Destiny!"—a motto which has recently been adopted by the rabid Ras Tafarian cult, which also emanates from Jamaica.

In 1916, Marcus Garvey "came screaming out of the British West Indies onto the American Stage." He landed in New York, where at first little attention was paid to his street-corner speeches. Undaunted, he set out to tour thirty-eight states in order to study conditions of Negro life in America. When he returned to New York a year later, he had formulated certain opinions which were later to shape the largest mass movement in the history of the American Negro. Important among these conclusions was the amazing discovery that the "so-called Negro leaders . . . had no program, but were mere opportunists who were living off their so-called leadership while the poor people were groping in the dark." He seems to have concluded that too much of the leadership was concentrated in the hands of mulattoes and that these "part-white Negroes" could not be trusted. He was exceedingly disturbed that Negro leadership depended so heavily upon white philanthropy—an impossible paradox. He was most contemptuous because this dependent leadership seemed willing "to turn back the clock of progress" at the whim of the white benefactors.

The New York division of the UNIA soon became the headquarters of a world-wide organization. By midsummer of 1919, Garvey claimed to have two million members in thirty branches. His newspaper, *The Negro World*, was printed in French and Spanish, as well as in English; at its peak, it claimed a circulation of more than 200,000, "reaching the mass of Negroes throughout the world." The paper devoted itself mainly to a recapitulation and reinterpretation of the Negro's contribution to history. It recalled "the stirring heroism of such leaders of American slave rebellions as Denmark Vesey, Gabriel Prosser, and Nat Turner. The struggles of Zulu and Hottentot warriors against European rule, the histories of Moorish and Ethiopian empires, and the intrepid exploits of Toussaint L'Ouverture . . . were not neglected in the effort to make Negroes conscious and proud of their racial heritage." Readers were encouraged to speak out on racial matters, and Garvey himself "delighted in references to the greatness of colored civilizations at a time when white men were only barbarians and savages."

At the First International Convention of the UNIA, held in New York in August 1920, no fewer than twenty-five countries were represented. A mammoth parade—led by the African Legion, the Black Cross Nurses and other organizations of the UNIA—wound through Harlem and on to Madison Square Garden, where Garvey set the tone of the month-long convention with an opening address to 25,000 Negroes:

> We are the descendants of a suffering people; we are the descendants of a people determined to suffer no longer. . . . We shall now organize the 400,000,000 Negroes of the world into a vast organization to plant the banner of freedom on the great continent of Africa. . . . If Europe is for the Europeans, then Africa shall be for the black peoples of the world. We say it; we mean it. . . .

Later, the UNIA delegates drafted a "Declaration of the Rights of the Negro Peoples of the World," which was adopted on August 13, 1920. The declaration spelled out the Negro's rights in terms of political and judicial equality, racial self-determination and an independent Africa under a Negro government. It alleged that the League of Nations (which had just been organized in Switzerland) "seeks to deprive Negroes of their liberty." The League, it said, is "null and void as far as the Negro is concerned."

The convention also approved a flag for the movement: "red for the blood of the race, nobly shed in the past and dedicated to the future; black to symbolize pride in the color of its skin; and green for the promise of a new and better life in Africa." An order of nobility was created; honorary orders were established; salaries were voted for the leadership; and Garvey was elected Provisional President of the African Republic. Gabriel Johnson, mayor of Monrovia, capital of the free African Republic of Liberia, was named secretary of state in the Provisional Cabinet at a salary of $12,000 a year. So impressed was Johnson that, on his return home, he announced that his office in Garvey's Provisional Government gave him diplomatic precedence over the President of Liberia.

When the convention ended, the Garvey movement had attained world significance. " 'Up, you mighty race,' Garvey thundered, 'you can accomplish what you will,' and the Negro people responded with an enthusiastic determination born of centuries of frustration and despair." They poured a million dollars into the UNIA's Black Star Steamship Line—organized to link the black peoples of the world in commerce and trade, and to transport America's black millions back to their African "home." They gloried in the cooperative possession of grocery stores, laundries, restaurants and hotels. They took an unconcealed pride in staffing the Universal Black Cross Nurses, the Universal African Motor Corps, the Black Eagle Flying Corps and other UNIA auxiliaries with "Black men and women." An unarmed but smartly uniformed Universal African Legion paraded spectacularly through the streets of Harlem, and the admiring Negroes massed along the route whispered knowingly about the liberation of Africa by force of arms. Uncritical Negroes everywhere, and especially the despairing millions in the crowded slums of black America, acclaimed Garvey as the true leader of a new race.

Garvey's political ambitions were never made wholly explicit. The Ku Klux Klan and the fanatical Anglo-Saxon Clubs of that era assumed that he intended to lead all the Negroes in America to Africa; for this reason, they gave him their open support. But Garvey declared, "We do not want all the Negroes [to settle] in Africa. Some are no good here, and naturally will be no good there." His real intentions seem to have been not unlike those of modern Zionism. He wanted to build a state, somewhere in Africa, to which Negroes would come from all over the world, bringing with them a wealth of technical and professional skills. Within a few years, he hoped, the new state would gain such prestige and power that it would be recognized as a symbol of accomplishment and protection for Negroes all over the world. For Garvey was convinced, as is Elijah Muhammad, that the Negro can hope for neither peace nor dignity while he lives in a white society. Like Muhammad, he saw only one solution: the establishment of a separate nation "so strong as to strike fear" into the hearts of the oppressor white race.

But, unlike the Zionists, Garvey did not rest his ambitions here. The eventual liberation of all Africa was never far from his thinking. Presumably his black state, when it became sufficiently powerful, would begin a revolution that would free all Africa, for he spoke mysteriously of the hour of "Africa's Redemption": "It is in the wind. It is coming. One day, like a storm, it will be here." He told a white audience that "you will find ten years from now, or 100 years from now, Garvey was not an idle buffoon but was representing the new vision of the Negro. . . ." In what was perhaps a prophetic warning, he declared: "We say to the white man who now dominates Africa that it is to his interest to clear out of Africa now, because we are coming . . . 400,000,000 strong." And again, "We shall not ask England or France or Italy or Belgium, 'Why are you here?' We shall only command them, 'Get out of here.' "

Garvey's beachhead on the African continent was to be Liberia, the little country founded on the west coast by American slaves in 1847. The Liberian government had promised to "afford the association every facility legally possible in effectuating in Liberia its industrial, agricultural, and business projects." Specified settlements were laid out by the Liberian government and set aside for colonization, but Liberia's Acting President Edwin Barclay felt it necessary to warn Garvey that "the British and French have enquired. . . . But it is not always advisable nor politic to openly expose our secret intentions. . . . We don't tell them what we think; we only tell them what we like them to hear—what, in fact, they like to hear."

Garvey's movement was essentially political and social; he did not rest his doctrines and program upon any religious premise. Yet he did not neglect the wellspring of religious fervor—and discontent—in the Negro community. Then as now, many Negroes resented the white man's presumption in depicting God and Jesus as Caucasians, in filling the Christian churches and Bibles with pictures of a white God, a white Savior and an all-white heavenly host. Garvey seized on this resentment and carried it to a logical extreme. Since whatever is white cannot be beneficial to the black man, he pointed out, a white God cannot be the God of the Negro people. This was the God of the white man. The Negro's God must be black.

To promulgate a black religion, Garvey named as chaplain general of the UNIA a former Episcopal rector, the Reverend George Alexander McGuire. In the Episcopalian fold, Bishop

McGuire had long been a nettlesome critic, first agitating in vain for independent status for the Negro congregations, then organizing an Independent Episcopalian Church. This group followed him into the Garveyite movement and became the nucleus of a new, UNIA-sponsored African Orthodox Church. In his new position, McGuire was ordained a bishop by Archbishop Vilatte of the Syrian Orthodox Church, thus bringing to the African Orthodox Church direct apostolic succession from one of the oldest bodies in Christendom.

Under Garvey's aegis, Bishop McGuire set out to reorder the religious thinking of the vast membership of the UNIA. He established a cathedral and a seminary (named Endich, after an alleged Ethiopian mentioned in the New Testament) for the training of a new order of black priests. The liturgy, based on the Episcopalian ritual, was colorful and impressive. And the new church set high moral demands, seeking "to be true to the principles of Christianity without the shameful hypocrisy of the white churches." But the church was distinguished primarily by its appeal to race consciousness. "Forget the white gods," the bishop demanded. "Erase the white gods from your hearts." By 1924, after four years of his ministry, the Black Madonna and Child had become a standard picture in the homes of the faithful, and the worship of a Black Christ was openly advocated.

In August 1924, at the fourth annual convention of the UNIA, Bishop McGuire issued a public appeal to Negroes "to name the day when all members of the race would tear down and burn any pictures of the white Madonna and the white Christ found in their homes." The Negro clergy was loud in protest, and the Negro press derided the idea of a "black Jesus." But the African Orthodox Church had long since spread its missions through several states and into Canada, Cuba and Haiti. On both fronts, religious and political, Garvey's black nationalism was riding high.

From the start, however, Garvey had not been without his troubles. His movement had been kept under constant surveillance by New York State Assistant District Attorney Edwin P. Kilroe, whose interest bordered on harassment. The federal government was hardly sympathetic to Garvey's international ambitions; and abroad, the various colonial governments viewed him with outright alarm. His newspaper—in its English, French and Spanish editions—had been quickly suppressed throughout the colonial world. In America the newspaper was among several Negro organs cited by the U.S. Department of Justice in a 1919 report on alleged radicalism and sedition among American Negroes. The following year the Lusk Committee, investigating sedition in New York State, cited the *Negro World* as one of the most radical elements of the New Negro press. Both the committee and the Department of Justice portrayed Garvey as a dangerous agitator, inimical to the interests of his own people and of the country as a whole; but neither group was able to substantiate its charges.

Meanwhile, the governments of Great Britain and France became increasingly alarmed over the implications of the Garvey movement and spared no effort to keep it out of Africa— even to the extent of bringing indirect pressure to bear on the Republic of Liberia, which had agreed to provide for the settlement of about a hundred thousand Garvey followers in that country. The UNIA had been enthusiastically welcomed there, and the mayor of Monrovia had accepted a post as secretary of state in Garvey's provisional government. Garvey sent several missions to Liberia, one as late as June 1924, to prepare for the settlement of his followers, who were scheduled to begin arriving in October 1924.

In the summer of 1924, the pressure from the British and French (who governed the territories surrounding Liberia) took effect. The Liberian government, under President Charles D. B. King, sent a diplomatic note to the United States announcing that it was "irrevocably opposed both in principle and fact to the incendiary policy of the Universal Negro Improvement Association, headed by Marcus Garvey." The lands promised to Garvey were leased instead to the Firestone Rubber Corporation, and when the new Garvey mission arrived, the members were arrested for immediate deportation. Thereupon, the Liberian president was lionized by the British for his "courage and statesmanship." The British press hailed him for putting "his foot down very firmly on such misguided movements for the people of his own race, as that sponsored . . . by

Marcus Garvey and other agitators." The French government made him a Chevalier of the French Legion of Honor.

At home, Garvey was encountering increasing resistance within the Negro community. The emerging black bourgeoisie and the Negro intellectuals would have no part of him. Their attempt to mold the public image of Negroes as an intelligent, sophisticated people was undermined by his constant harangues and the spectacle of thousands of his followers parading in flamboyant uniforms through the streets of New York City. At first they simply ignored his movement; but as its notoriety increased, it drew the fire of most of the well-known Negro leaders, including A. Philip Randolph, Chandler Owen and W. E. B. Du Bois. Du Bois criticized the UNIA as "bombastic and impractical," although he later admitted that competition from Garvey had greatly hampered the development of his own Pan-African Congresses. The NAACP also criticized Garvey's movement, as did the National Urban League.

Nor did Garvey spare his critics. He characterized such leaders as Du Bois, James Weldon Johnson and Eugene Kinkle Jones as "weak-kneed and cringing . . . sycophant to the white man." He warned that "the 'Uncle Tom' Negroes must give way to the 'New Negro,' who is seeking his place in the sun."

Thus Garvey's troubles closed down upon him. His own lack of business acumen had kept him embroiled in legal wrangles over the Black Star Line and other commercial ventures of the UNIA. Now the apprehensions of the ruling powers on three continents were joined with those of America's conservative Negro leadership in a demand that the dangerous little Jamaican be cut down to size. The *Messenger* magazine, edited by Chandler Owen and A. Philip Randolph, led the Negro intellectuals in a direct attack. "Garvey must go!" became the rallying cry of many individuals who could agree on no other single issue.

Early in 1922, at the urging of the Negro press, Garvey had been indicted for using the mails to defraud in the promotion of stock in the UNIA's Black Star Steamship Line. But the government's case was weak, and the federal authorities made no move to prosecute. In January 1923, however, the calm was shattered by the murder of James W. H. Eason, an early

Garvey admirer who had split with the movement the previous year and was now rumored to have offered himself as a key prosecution witness in the mail-fraud case. There was no evidence linking Garvey or the UNIA to the crime, which remains unsolved, but the hostility of the responsible Negro leadership was whetted. Less than a week after the murder, a "Committee of Eight"—all prominent American Negroes, most of them active in the NAACP—sent an open letter to the U.S. Attorney General. The letter condemned Garveyism as a philosophy seeking "to arouse ill-feeling between the races" and urged that he "use his full influence completely to disband and extirpate the vicious movement, and that he vigorously and speedily push the government's case against Marcus Garvey for using the mails to defraud."

Garvey responded with a bitter denunciation of the "good old darkies" who had treacherously sought to curry favor with the white man at the expense of their "fellow Negroes whose only crime has been that of making an effort to improve the condition of the race." But in May the government brought the case to trial and won a conviction. Garvey was fined and sentenced to imprisonment for the maximum term of five years. He remained at liberty for seventeen months while his lawyers vainly appealed the decision, but in February 1925 he was taken to the federal penitentiary at Atlanta, Georgia. In December 1927 his sentence was commuted by President Coolidge; but Garvey had never become an American citizen, and since he had been convicted of a felony, the law required that he be immediately deported. From abroad he labored hard to keep his movement in the United States alive, but it quickly faded, and his death in London in 1940 was scarcely mentioned in the American press.

Garveyism is not dead. William L. Sherrill, once Garvey's representative to the League of Nations, still maintains UNIA headquarters in Detroit and serves as president of the straggling movement. The African Orthodox Church also survives, but its membership has dwindled to less than seven thousand. Various nationalistic cults in America, Africa and Jamaica still celebrate "Garvey Day" each August 1 with appropriate speeches and ceremony. And Garvey's own stature continues to grow as more and more observers concede that, for all his faults, he had a profound awakening effect on the American Negro community. Yet Garveyism lives on not really as a movement but as a symbol—a symbol of the militant Negro nationalism which so many black Americans see as their only alternative to eternal frustration and despair.

13

Registered with Allah

ARNA BONTEMPS AND JACK CONROY

The Asiatic black man is the original man, and ruler of the universe, the eight inhabited planets and this planet earth. Islam is the true religion. A religion which can be proved by mathematics in a limit of time. The Muslims have the wisdom. We're not afraid of the devil, this so-called white man. We talk right up to them. They're afraid of you if you've got the Truth. Just tell 'em, "White man, you're a devil. You were grafted from the original black man." He'll say, "Yes, you're

SOURCE: Arna Bontemps and Jack Conroy, *Anyplace But Here* (New York: Hill and Wang, Inc., 1966), pp. 216–241. Copyright 1945, © 1966 by Arna Bontemps and Jack Conroy. Originally published as *They Seek a City*. Reprinted by permission of the publisher.

*right." He'll admit it, 'cause you got the power. Just say,
"You're a beast; you've got one-third animal blood." He won't
deny it, 'cause it's true. When they were driven from the Holy
City of Mecca, they lived in the caves of Europe and mingled
with the beasts. Christianity is the religion of the so-called
white man. Have you ever noticed that the very things he
teaches us that the devil does is the very things he is doing?
He is the devil.*

    *—from a sermon by a minister of Chicago Temple No. 2,
Lost-Found Nation of Islam.*

Sometime before 1930 a Negro, or at any rate a dark-skinned
man, appeared in the "Paradise Valley" Negro neighborhood
of Detroit, selling silks and raincoats from door to door. He
soon made it clear that he was not to be regarded as an ordinary itinerant peddler. He introduced himself to prospective
customers in this manner:

    I am W. D. Fard, and I came from the Holy City of Mecca.
More about myself I will not tell you yet, for the time has not
yet come. I am your brother. You have not yet seen me in my
royal robes.

He proclaimed that his mission was to secure "freedom, justice, and equality" for his "uncle" living in the "wilderness of
North America, surrounded and robbed completely by the cave
man." "The uncle of W. D. Fard" became a symbolical term
for all Negroes of North America, while the white man was
referred to as a "cave man," a "satan," a "blue-eyed devil" or a
"Caucasian devil." Sometimes he would be called familiarly
or contemptuously a "cavy" or "common ca."

While Fard maintained that he was racially identical to
North American Negroes, he also claimed to have been born in
Mecca, the son of a wealthy member of the tribe of Koreish to
which the prophet Mohammed belonged. He was reputed to
have been educated in England or at the University of California; to have been trained for a diplomatic career in the
service of the kingdom of Hejaz. A less respectful report is that
he was jailed at least once in California as a narcotics pusher
before he arrived in Detroit. Though it had been surmised from
his talk that he must have been a follower of Noble Drew Ali
at some time or other, Elijah Muhammad, Fard's right-hand

disciple who was destined to head the Black Muslim movement in Chicago, denied that the two ever met. Fard has been pictured as light-colored for a Negro, with an Oriental cast of countenance. This description, if accurate, would lend credence to his contention that he was of Arabian descent.

Fard at times in his apocryphal career used various other names. Among these were Walli Farrad, Professor Ford, Farrad Mohammed, and F. Mohammed Ali. After his disappearance in 1933 or 1934, his followers deified him as the God Allah. Fard himself is said to have told Elijah Muhammad, "I am Mahdi; I am God."

While pursuing his trade as a peddler, Fard never lost an opportunity to lecture Negroes into whose homes he was invited. One of his converts said of him:

> He has told us that the silks he carried were the same kind our people used to make in their home country, Arabia, and that he had come from there. So we all asked him to tell us about our own country. If we asked him to eat with us, he would eat whatever we had on the table, but after the meal he would begin to talk like this:
> "Now, don't eat this food. It is poison to you. The people in your own country do not eat it. Since they eat the right kind of food they have the best health all the time. If you would live just like the people in your home country, you would never be sick any more."
> So we wanted him to tell us more about ourselves and our home country and about how we could be free from rheumatism, aches, and pains.

Fard began to arrange meetings in the homes of those willing to listen to him, and before long had gathered a small but devoted band of followers. His excoriations of the "white devil and his so-called spook civilization" became more and more virulent. He extended his condemnation to the Christian religion, though he frequently quoted from the Bible. In his *Secret Ritual of the Nation of Islam*, Part 2, Section II, Fard declared:

> Me and my people have tried this so-called mystery God for bread, clothing, and a home. And we have received nothing but hard times, hunger, naked, and out of doors. Also was beat and killed by the ones that advocated that kind of God.

Most of Fard's converts had arrived recently from the South, and were inclined to agree with his contentions about the outrages perpetrated by the "white devils" who were running everything to the disadvantage of the black man. Challar Sharrieff, who had rejected the "slave" name of Charles Peoples, told of hearing the prophet explain:

> The Bible tells you that the sun rises and sets. This is not so. The sun stands still. All your lives you have been thinking that the earth never moved. Stand and look toward the sun and know that it is the earth you are standing on that is moving.

This was indeed a revelation to Sharrieff. He went on:

> Up to that day I always went to the Baptist church. After I heard the sermon from the prophet, I was turned around completely. When I went home and heard that dinner was ready, I said: "I don't want to eat dinner. I just want to go back to the meetings." I wouldn't eat any meals, but I goes back that night and I goes to every meeting after that. Just to think that the sun above me never moved at all and that the earth we are on was doing the moving. That changed everything for me.

The Negroes of Detroit could see all about them justifications for Fard's accusations against the white man and his civilization. As the depression tightened its grip, numbers of them were laid off while white men were retained. In other instances, Negroes of long service were replaced by white newcomers. "Hard times, hunger, naked, and out of doors" assumed an immediate significance for the "original" black men. When they were obliged to apply for public assistance, the more sensitive Negroes keenly felt the humiliation attached. It was not hard to convince them that they were objects of special discrimination. Fard and his rapidly increasing band of disciples made considerable hay in the Negro community. It has been estimated that 8,000 Detroiters joined the cult during its first four years.

After Fard had succeeded in establishing permanent headquarters in the first Temple of Islam, he "registered" all the members, promising to restore their "righteous" or "original"

names to replace the "slave" names forcibly fastened on them
by the "Caucasian devil." To obtain his "righteous" name, the
applicant for membership was required to write Fard a letter
asking that he be freed of his "slave" name. While waiting
for his "righteous" name the acolyte was designated by his
first name and a simple "X." It was pointed out later that the
"X" stood for "unknown," as in algebra. It was assumed that
Fard knew the "righteous" names by virtue of the spirit of
Allah within him, or that they would be made known to him
by divine revelation at an appropriate time. There were complications in this system of nomenclature, however. At one time
the prophet reportedly bestowed three different surnames on
as many brothers, not being aware of their common parentage.
When confronted with this discrepancy, he blandly asserted
that he had perceived that each of the brothers had a different
father.

The rapid growth of the first temple in Detroit was accompanied by the birth of various subsidiary departments. The
Fruit of Islam (FOI), a semimilitary defense corps, was trained
in the use of boxing, karate, and judo. It was charged, but
emphatically denied, that they also drilled with rifles. The
Muslim Girls Training Corps Class instructed young women in
the domestic arts and taught them the behavior expected of a
Muslim wife and mother. Fard's especial pride, though, was the
University of Islam, to which the children of Muslim families
were sent rather than to the public schools.

At the university (in reality an elementary school with some
high school subjects) pupils were taught the "knowledge of
our own" as distinct from that of the "spook civilization of the
Caucasian devils." Courses were offered in "higher mathematics," astronomy, and what was termed the "general knowledge
and ending of the spook civilization." All this specialized knowledge was deemed necessary to combat the "tricknollogy"
learned by the "Caucasian devils" in their schools. The "higher
mathematics" consisted mainly of a variety of "problems"
usually embodying a symbolical meaning obscure or unintel-
ligible to the uninstructed and containing a dizzying number
of digits. The symbolism perhaps was designed to counter the
"tricknollogy" of the "blue-eyed devil." Several of these prob-

lems were read at each meeting of the cult as well as in classes of the University of Islam. This is a characteristic problem:

> A lion, in a cage, walking back and forth sixty feet per minute, seeking a way out of the cage. It took him nearly four centuries to find the door. Now, with modern equipment, he is walking three thousand feet per minute and he has three thousand miles by two thousand miles to go yet. How long will it take him to cover this territory of said three thousand by two thousand miles at the above walking rate? He also has seventeen million keys, which he turns at the rate of sixteen and seventeen one-hundredths per minute. How long will it take him to turn the whole seventeen million? Sixty minutes equals one hour, twenty-four hours equals one day, three hundred and sixty-five days equals one year. The above figures do not include rusty locks.

An obliging cult member shed some light on this problem by identifying the lion as the "original" black man, or Asiatic, held in bondage four centuries within a trap fabricated by the "Caucasian devil." The seventeen million keys represent a like number of "Asiatics" enslaved in the "wilderness of North America." "Modern equipment," naturally, means the teaching of Islam by which the "original" man is enabled to progress rapidly toward emancipation. "Rusty locks" are recalcitrant "Asiatics" who have not yet accepted Islam.

Here are three more problems:

> (1) What is the physical standard of a devil against the original? How many ounces of brains does an original have? What is the exact percentage of tricknollogy used by the devil in the so-called spook civilization? How long has the devil on the planet been using tricknollogy? Tell us how and who invented the devil.
>
> (2) The total atoms equal 10,000,000,000,000,000,000,-000,000,000,000,000,000,000,000,000,000,000,-000,000,000,000,000. How many atoms are there in North America?
>
> (3) The uncle of W. D. Fard lives in the wilderness of North America, surrounded and completely robbed by the cave man. He is working sixteen hours out of twenty-four hours for very little pay. He has eight in his family to support,

besides other little bills to meet each month. On top of that, a
cave man came along and sold him an old touring car, which
travels downhill at the rate of forty-eight miles an hour. If it
is shown by actual test that a force of two hundred fifty
pounds is required to maintain this rate at downhill speed,
what horsepower must the engine deliver at the wheels?
Thirty-three thousand pounds equals one horsepower.

At one time attendance officers of the Detroit Board of Education attempted to break up the University of Islam and to
compel its students to attend the public schools, claiming that
the university's teaching standards were below an acceptable
level even for the elementary grades. This move precipitated
violent resistance. Fearful of causing race riots, the courts released almost all of those arrested for physical interference
with the school board's orders.

More serious difficulties arose over the question of human
sacrifice. It was rumored in Detroit that Fard had stipulated
the sacrifice of four "Caucasian devils" as a prerequisite of the
pious Muslim's eventual return to the Holy City of Mecca. On
November 21, 1932, the people of Detroit became acutely conscious of the cult through its first widely publicized human
sacrifice. Robert Kariem, a prominent cultist whose "slave"
name had been Robert Harris, erected an altar in his home and
invited his roomer, John J. Smith, to offer himself as a human
sacrifice so that he might become "the Savior of the world."
Smith agreed, according to Harris, and at nine P.M.—the appointed time—Harris plunged a knife into his heart. The next
day the Detroit *News* commented:

> An Asiatic trend among Negro dole recipients of the Elm-
> wood district, noted at the time as a passing whim, today
> came back with horror to two women welfare workers on
> learning that the fanatical Robert Harris had intended them
> for human sacrifice as infidels. . . . Harris stated to the police
> that each of these was a "no-good Christian" and that they
> would have been sacrificed if he knew where he could find
> them.

By 1933 the Prophet of Islam had organized the Detroit
temple so efficiently that he felt able to recede into the back-

ground, appearing with less and less frequency to his followers during his final month in Detroit. This mysterious withdrawal only served to strengthen the belief that he was indeed the "Supreme Ruler of the Universe" (or, as he called himself, the God Allah) temporarily assuming a mundane form in order to fulfill a divine mission. Not all of his followers believed in Fard's divinity, and controversy over this question was one of the several causes of dissension in the movement. Another was the objections of some patriotic Muslims to what they judged to be Fard's disloyal attitude toward the United States government. One of these was Abdul Mohammed, who had been one of Fard's trusted lieutenants. Abdul refused to swear sole allegiance to the Moslem flag when he was ordered to do so, and seceded to form a small group of his own. As a direct consequence of internal disputes, the Chicago branch of the Nation of Islam came into being in late 1933 or early 1934.

Fard himself was last seen in Detroit at about the same time, or shortly before. He then disappeared altogether as far as any authoritative record is concerned. On one occasion Elijah Muhammad, his successor as head of the Lost-Found Nation of Islam but not heir to his divinity, stated that he had been with Fard at the airport when he was deported. The police record of a courtroom riot on March 5, 1935, involving members of the "Allah Temple of Islam" on South State Street, named the cultists' leader as "W. D. Fard, or Fard Mohammed, or Elijah Mohammed." An unsuccessful search was made for him. A newspaper account of the riot said that Noble Drew Ali had been the original prophet of the cult, described as "a secret organization of national proportions." Nothing that was disclosed definitely indicated that Fard was present at the riot, or, indeed, that he ever came to Chicago after leaving Detroit.

Fard's disappearance did not cause a real leadership hiatus. It had been apparent for some time that it had been his intention to place the Nation of Islam under the stewardship of Elijah Muhammad. Muhammad, whose "slave" name had been Elijah (or Robert) Poole, was born in 1897 in Sandersville, Georgia, the son of a Baptist preacher who tried to make a living for his wife and thirteen children as a sharecropper. At sixteen, having managed to struggle through the fourth grade in a ramshackle "colored" school, young Elijah left the parental nest. There followed a number of ill-paid and short-lasting jobs before he was married to Clara Evans. In 1923 the couple moved with their two children to Detroit, a Mecca of freedom and opportunity in the minds of many of Elijah's racial brethren held in bondage in the Egypt land called Dixie. Elijah said later that he has witnessed enough of the white man's cruel brutality in Georgia to last him 26,000 years. Detroit was somewhat less than the utopia he had envisioned. Prejudice and hard times had not been entirely left behind. Then a fortuitous meeting with W. D. Fard, probably when Elijah was working on the Chevrolet assembly line, brought a momentous change in the life and attitude of the transplanted Georgia boy. He always thereafter credited Fard with taking him out of "the gutters in the streets of Detroit" and teaching him the true knowledge of Islam. Elijah soon was an assiduous laborer in the temple vineyard. Fard at first bestowed upon him the "original" surname of Karriem, but later changed this to the more impressive cognomen of Muhammad in recognition of his yeoman service to the cause. When Fard dubbed him "Minister of Islam and Messenger of Allah," he was virtually choosing him as his successor.

After Fard's disappearance, Elijah's faction (those favorable to the deification of Fard), severed all connection with the parent group, assumed the name "Temple People," and set up headquarters in Chicago. The Detroit branch floundered uncertainly for a while without aggressive leadership, then came under the hegemony of Elijah. Both branches soon began to enjoy a moderate amount of prosperity.

In September 1942, FBI agents collared Elijah Muhammad and several other members of the Chicago temple. Some newspaper accounts gave Elijah's "real" name as Robert Poole. The Muslims were charged with evading the draft and influencing others to do so, and also with maintaining seditious relations with the Japanese government. The latter indictment more or less petered out. The Islamites would be likely to feel at least passive sympathy for any nation of colored people at war with the "blue-eyed Caucasian devils," but the government failed to prove that there was any active link between the Nation of Islam and the nation of Japan. The Muslims' aversion to any sort of registration other than that with Allah had antedated the war with Japan by a good many years.

The temple people had isolated themselves politically, socially and economically not only from white men but from Negroes who declined to reject Christianity as an evil ally of the "white devil." The economic confusion and upheaval attending the depression they explained by quoting Elijah's assertion that the white man's allotted rule of the world actually had ended in 1914, and that Allah was preparing to wipe out his "spook civilization." It had been existing on borrowed time. As we have seen, the Islamite's refusal to register for the draft indicated no new tendency. Cult members had always been particularly vociferous in their denunciations of President Franklin D. Roosevelt and the New Deal. In their opinion, the WPA and other alphabetical agencies spawned during the depression were subtle efforts on the part of white men to save what was left of their dying civilization by getting "original" black men to sign up and be given a number. They eschewed social security and relief case numbers as manifestations of the aptitude of the "white devil" in the devious art of "tricknollogy." They had no intention of giving the expiring "spook civilization" a revitalizing blood transfusion by embracing it or even collaborating with it. A typewritten piece of temple literature read:

> Roosevelt gave you a social security number just to hold you, and now he's getting ready to call in these numbers and give you a stamp. . . . He's going to put a stamp on you, the mark of the beast. You signed up with the devil and he gives you the filthy crumbs from his table like the rich man gave the man Lazarus.

Elijah Muhammad spent three years in the federal prison at Milan, Michigan. He does not seem to have languished idly there, but appears to have managed to maintain a connection with and a grip on the Black Muslim organization. (Muslim people for some reason objected to the "Black" attached to their name, even though they regarded black as emblematical of superiority. The term became so common, particularly after the Muslims engaged in public relations activities in the sixties, that they apparently ceased to resent it.)

After his release in 1946, Elijah vigorously resumed his organizational activities.

His imprisonment had the effect of glorifying him as a martyr to the cause of black men. It was easy for him to establish in the minds of many Negroes hitherto impervious to his exhortations that he had been persecuted for their sakes. There were at the time of Elijah's return to active control four temples in operation, those in Milwaukee and Washington, D.C., having been added to No. 1 in Detroit and No. 2 in Chicago. In the 1950s a period of spectacular expansion began. By the end of 1960 there were as many as sixty-nine temples or missions distributed throughout twenty-seven states extending from Massachusetts southward to Florida and westward to California. A comparatively small number of the buildings housing the temples or mosques were owned by the sect. Some of the Muslim groups met in rented quarters or even in the homes of members. Membership, of course, had zoomed accordingly. It has been variously estimated from the less than 7,000 (not even half as many as in 1960–61) cited in 1965 by Aubrey Barnette, a disillusioned dropout from Boston's Temple No. 11, to the undoubtedly overexuberant claim of 200,000 sometimes made by Muslim spokesmen. About 100,000 would seem to be a more credible figure. In addition to the hard-core, tithe-paying members there are many thousands of Negroes who secretly or openly admire the Islamites for their defiance of the white man and for the exemplary personal life to which they are pledged.

In the 1950s the Black Muslims discarded to a great extent their policy of secrecy about their doctrines and activities. Rather, they seemed to court publicity from the white man's media of communication. Elijah Muhammad held forth regularly on a network of radio stations. White reporters were invited to the annual conventions, being admitted to the hall after a thorough but polite frisking by the FOI. The 1956 convention, held in a Protestant church in Chicago, was the first large one to exhibit this new tolerance if not deference toward the opinions of the "blue-eyed white devils." The 1960 convention in the Chicago Coliseum, which was called the "Thirtieth Session," attracted an audience of about 2,000, which included six white men, one white woman, and an Indian. The messenger of Allah arrived an hour late, clad in a conservative blue suit and wearing the black velvet skull cap, adorned with jewels and a crescent, that had become his badge of office for such ceremonial occasions. In the course of his long oration he enlightened his audience, which often interrupted him with cries of approbation, with these rather startling cosmogonical revelations:

> Sixty-nine trillion years ago, what is now earth was called moon. That part which is now moon blasted off from the moon and went 12,000 miles away. What is now earth left its pocket and went 36,000 miles away. When the part that is now moon blasted off, it dropped water on the other part now earth, covering three-fourths of its surface. Hence the ocean. . . . Life has been going on for more than 66 trillion years. It has been here for 79 trillion years. Africa was then East Asia. The black man is of the tribe of Shabazz that came from Asia to the jungle of East Africa. There they became tough and hard. We are descendants of the Asiatic black people, according to the word of the Almighty Allah.

Elijah Muhammad also gave an account of a trip he had taken late in the previous year, accompanied by two of his sons, to Mohammedan sections of Asia and Africa, culminating in a pilgrimage to the Holy City of Mecca. He spoke of having been hospitably received everywhere. He found Cairo a "paradise" he was reluctant to leave. Taking exception to the Messenger's glowing account was one Talib Ahmad Dawud, leader of one of the several groups of "orthodox" Moslems in the United States that had branded Muhammad as an impostor and his cult as a fraud. Dawud had erroneously predicted that the Messenger of Allah would not be permitted to set foot on the soil of Saudi Arabia, much less make the traditional pilgrimage to Mecca. Dawud, a West Indian Negro who had been a musician with various jazz bands before being converted to Mohammedanism in 1940, was married to jazz singer Dakota Staton, also a Moslem. In 1950 Dawud took a large role in forming the Moslem Brotherhood, Inc., which set up temples in Philadelphia, Detroit, and Harlem and boasted of a membership of 100,000 "true" Moslems—a figure undoubtedly inflated. Dawud consistently jeered at Elijah Muhammad's assumption of divine authority, calling him "plain Elijah Poole of Sandersville, Georgia." At one time he and his wife tried unsuccessfully to legally enjoin the Lost-Found Nation of Islam from using the name "Muslim." He also inspired a series of anti-Elijah articles in the Chicago *New Crusader*. One of these alleged that W. D. Fard was in fact a white man, and produced a photograph to prove it. Plainly unfounded was the assertion that Fard was a Turkish agent for Hitler, and that Elijah Muhammad had met him in prison while doing his World War II stretch.

Despite the aspersions, it became evident that Elijah Muhammad's 1959 trip had had some impact upon the Moslem establishment in Cairo, Mecca, and elsewhere. The extent of his success in gaining recognition for his cult was difficult to gauge.

With the new candor about its doctrines and activities, the Lost-Found Nation of Islam outlined a rather elaborate mythology which borrowed in some of its latter aspects from the Christian Bible. The antihero or "devil" of this mythology is Yacub, who about 6,800 years ago was a dissident member of the original black tribe of Shabazz in the Holy City of Mecca. Precocious Yacub entered school when he was four; by the time he was eighteen he had graduated from all the existing colleges and universities. He was not overly modest about his capabilities, and his big talk irritated the Mecca authorities so much that they exiled him with 59,999 of his followers to the island of Patmos. Smarting under this rebuff, Yacub plotted revenge. He was a scientist skilled in genetics, and started a long series of breedings and crossbreedings that eventually developed a debased white man named Adam. Adam's descendants, at first walking on all fours and living in caves and trees (also mating with beasts), stayed on Patmos for six hundred years before they escaped to the mainland. They soon caused trouble for the "original" black men, over whom they at length gained mastery by resorting to underhanded dealings and low trickery. Tolerant Allah gave the white cave men six thousand years in which to perpetrate their knaveries and follies. When this time was up in 1914, he granted them an indefinite period of grace in which to reform. Unfortunately, they had not taken advantage of this benevolent reprieve, but recklessly persisted in their devilish ways. Prognostications of imminent doom became a regular feature of Muhammad's sermons in *Muhammad Speaks,* the cult's well-edited newspaper which began as a biweekly in 1960 and became a weekly in February 1965. On the front cover of the February 26, 1965, issue was emblazoned this lugubrious pronouncement by the Messenger: "FALLING, FALLING THE OLD WORLD!" In the accompanying article, beginning also on the front cover, Muhammad continued:

> America's burden in trying to protect herself from the attacking nations of the world is tremendous; one that she will not be able to carry. Therefore she must succumb to the powerful forces that are coming against her. The fall of a nation makes way for another. As the earth continues, all nations and their civilizations are limited upon it, except the original nation, which takes on renewal and changes. . . . Though in appearance America seems steadfast, she is moving toward an ultimate end.

The "so-called Negro," Muhammad went on, is due to inherit the earth—or what's left of it:

> Salvation must come to the so-called Negro. Everyone's eyes should be opened. The time of the ending of this world is now, and not yet to come, as you so foolishly think. The end is predicted and hinted in many places. Daniel (in the Bible) however gives you a better knowledge of it than in any other place. And, the Qur-an's prophecy is exact. Do not expect 10 more years. The fall will be within a few days.

This deference toward the "blue-eyed devil's" Scriptures is characteristic of the Messenger's curious ambivalence—making in one paragraph approving references to both the Holy Qur-an (Koran) and the Bible of the detested Christians.

With expansion both in membership and, presumably,

affluence, the Nation of Islam became more practical-minded and economics-oriented. Taking a leaf from Marcus Garvey's book as well as from that of Soviet planners, Elijah Muhammad evolved a grandiose blueprint for a Muslim center in Chicago which was to cost $20,000,000 financed in large part by weekly contributions sent in by the faithful. Solicitation for funds became a regular feature in *Muhammad Speaks,* which also ran a double-page spread picturing Muhammad's conception of the proposed educational center: a bulbous-domed mosque flanked on one side by an elementary school and high school and on the other by a college and university. Atop the mosque's dome was a golden star and crescent of the Islamites. The illustration, in color, had been executed by staff artist Eugene Majied, who, after noting that "an architect's drawing will be presented when suitable grounds are secured," continued:

> The Honorable Elijah Muhammad's idea as shown in the picture conveys to us the true, and noble aims of the man. He wants to see the so-called American Negro lifted up to something which bespeaks that of his own. The school, the Mosque, agriculture, manufacturing, engineering—these foundations will build for us that which we can call our own. Note that he has no crosses, which represent murder and death, but the Crescent, which represents Life. His Sign lives forever. Let ALL so-called Negroes help him, for ALL shall benefit from this great achievement. This is not for Muslims exclusively, but for the whole black nation. The Honorable Elijah Muhammad says: "Let the Negro build his tabernacle in the wilderness."

Majied's exhortation was supplemented by this appeal: "Send your contributions today to: Muhammad's Mosque No. 2 Educational Fund, 5335 Greenwood Avenue, Chicago, Illinois 60615."

(The reference to "suitable grounds" recalled a dispute over a five-acre tract the Black Muslims had bought in the Chatham-Avalon district of Chicago's far South Side for a reported $150,000. When it was learned that the Muslims intended to build their center on this site, both white and Negro residents of the community protested to such effect that the Chicago

Park Commission, which had made the sale to the Muslims in the first place, set aside the tract as a park in 1960. The Muslims sued and won a settlement amounting to $165,000, a sum larger than the original price. To complicate matters, the properties on Greenwood Avenue were scheduled for razing as part of the Hyde Park renewal project.)

In the meantime, various small business enterprises, mostly of the service type, had blossomed under the Nation of Islam aegis in several cities: restaurants, bakeries, dress shops, barbershops, groceries, and cleaning establishments. These were part of an ambitious three-year Economic Plan.

As was the case with Garvey's commercial ventures, there were skeptics who ridiculed and low-rated the Messenger's economic program. One of these was Aubrey Barnette, whose disillusionment had led him to resign as secretary of Muhammad's Temple of Islam No. 11 in Boston. His apostasy, he charged, had earned him a severe beating by a Muslim goon squad in August 1964. Visiting Chicago, Barnette says he discovered that the University of Islam was little more than an unaccredited grammar school. (The university previously had been castigated by Illinois State Senator Arthur R. Gottshalk as hate-breeding and substandard.) The only one of the several Muslim commercial enterprises that could be called a going concern, Barnette maintained, was the dress shop, and its solvency was mainly due to its monopoly on the ankle-length robes worn by Muslim sisters.

It had been the custom of the Messenger himself to preserve a dignified silence in the face of such animadversions, but no such restraint circumscribed his high-ranking functionaries. John Ali, national secretary of Muhammad's Mosques of Islam, paid his respects to dropout Barnette in an article captioned "Folly of the Paid Informer" in the February 26, 1965, issue of *Muhammad Speaks*. (Barnette was branded an "informer" because his exposé of the cult had appeared in the *Saturday Evening Post*.) Ali fervently avowed his loyalty at the conclusion of his article:

> No man in America, or anywhere in the world, loves his people more than Messenger Muhammad. No man in America or anywhere in the world has given or continues to give so

much of himself for his people as Messenger Elijah Muhammad. The garbage of the Aubrey Barnettes, the Malcolm Littles and other hypocrites, disbelievers and devils shall take its place in disgrace, regret and a lake of fire.

The "Malcolm Little" mentioned was being downgraded from Minister Malcolm X of Muhammad's Temple of Islam No. 7 in Harlem. Until his suspension by Elijah Muhammad late in 1964, he had figured as the most articulate and most intelligent spokesman for the Black Muslims and probably the aging Elijah Muhammad's heir apparent. His eloquence and nimble wit had made him welcome on television and radio shows and as a speaker before college groups. He once said, with pardonable complacency, that the New York *Times* in 1963 rated him as second in popularity on college campuses, only Barry Goldwater being more desirable.

Born Malcolm Little in Omaha, Nebraska, in 1925, Malcolm X was one of eleven children of a Baptist preacher who was also a militant and outspoken Garveyite. The elder Little's outspokenness provoked the Ku Klux Klan into burning down the family's home in Lansing, Michigan. After he accepted the Muslim dictum that all white men are congenital devils, Malcolm became convinced that his father's death beneath the wheels of a streetcar was not an accident as supposed but murder at the hands of white racists. They had first killed him and then laid him on the tracks to cover up their deed.

In his late teens Malcolm Little was a big-time vice lord in Harlem. His reddish hair and complexion caused him to be nicknamed "Big Red," and he blamed them on the ravishment of his grandmother by a "white devil" on the island of Grenada in the West Indies. "I hate every drop of that white rapist's blood that is in me," he said, after confessing that before he saw the true light of Islam he foolishly believed that his light color constituted some kind of status symbol. Malcolm was taking in as much as two thousand dollars a month from narcotics, bootlegging, policy, and prostitution. He wore two-hundred-dollar suits in which he kept a fat thousand-dollar roll for the benefit of less exacting lawmen willing to grant immunity for a price. Such whited sepulchers as rutting social workers and randy clergymen sought him when they craved a liaison with one of the colored whores he had in his stable. The hypocrisy of these pillars of society deepened his contempt for white men and their low-down ways. He also catered to the wishes of Negro men who wanted white women.

A jail cell was already familiar terrain to Malcolm when in 1947 he was committed to the maximum-security prison in Concord, Massachusetts. There he was visited by his brother Reginald, who had joined Muslim Mosque No. 1 in Detroit. Reginald converted his wayward brother, and upon his release Malcolm went to Chicago to see Messenger Elijah Muhammad. Elijah personally indoctrinated the acolyte so well that Malcolm X, formerly sinner Malcolm Little, was named assistant minister of Detroit Temple of Islam No. 1 in the summer of 1953. A month-long training session then ensued in the Messenger's home, a nineteen-room red brick mansion at 4847 Woodlawn Avenue in Chicago. Elijah Muhammad treated Malcolm like a son, and some time after his graduation from private lessons on Woodlawn Avenue the Messenger gave every evidence that he was proud of his brilliant protégé and had the utmost confidence in him. Sent to Philadelphia in March 1954, Malcolm had organized Temple No. 12 there before the first of June. His next post was as minister of Temple No. 7, then housed in a Harlem store front. Minister Malcolm X became a familiar figure on Harlem street corners, holding large audiences spellbound. In January 1958, with the blessing of the Messenger, he was married to Sister Betty X of the Harlem mosque, the ceremony being performed by a justice of the peace who was "an old hunchbacked white devil." The witnesses were "white devils" too.

More and more did Malcolm X emerge as the voice of Islam. The Messenger, growing old and plagued by failing health, dispatched him as his personal envoy on a tour of Africa and the Middle East in the summer of 1959. He was made editor of the *Messenger Magazine,* one of the several predecessors of *Muhammad Speaks.* "I thank Allah for my Brother Minister Malcolm," Elijah Muhammad told a Milwaukee audience.

For a long time Malcolm's devotion to Elijah made him impervious to such snide remarks as those made in 1957 by Thurgood Marshall, an NAACP leader who later was made a

Federal judge and then U.S. Solicitor General. Marshall declared that the Nation of Islam was "run by a bunch of thugs organized from prisons and jails and financed, I am sure, by some Arab group." As early as 1961, however, Malcolm recalled after his suspension, he had felt misgivings and had troubling doubts about the morals and the financial responsibility of his leader. Nasty rumors, at first whispered and then spoken aloud reached his ears. When in 1963 two ex-secretaries in Los Angeles accused the Messenger of getting them with child, Malcolm wrote to Elijah at his new home in Phoenix, Arizona, telling him he was being talked about. The Messenger had chosen the Arizona location because the climate was kinder to an asthmatic affliction which seemed to grow worse as he grew older. The upshot was that Malcolm was invited to fly to Phoenix for a conference. Elijah greeted him affectionately, and told him that his understanding of prophecy and of spiritual things would enable him to analyze correctly the situation when he explained:

> I'm David. When you read about how David took another man's wife, I'm that David. You read about Noah, who got drunk. That's me. You read about Lot, who went and laid up with his own daughter. I have to fulfill all those things.

Outside observers had thought for some time that self-interest eventually would compel Elijah Muhammad to cut the popular Malcolm X down to size. According to Malcolm, the Messenger's opportunity came as a result of the assassination of President Kennedy on November 22, 1963. Malcolm, along with other ministers, had been ordered by Muhammad to make no comment on the tragic event. But in the question-and-answer period of a meeting at the Manhattan Center in New York Malcolm observed that the President's murder was a case of the "chickens coming home to roost." He afterward insisted that he had meant by this that the murderous spirit vented in the slaying of an innocent black man might be expected to spread like a poison virus through the social and political structure until it destroyed even the white President.

Elijah reaction was to "suspend" Malcolm for ninety days. After some ineffective efforts to reason with the Messenger,

Malcolm formally broke off relations with the Lost-Found
Nation of Islam in March 1964, and founded the Muslim
Mosque, Inc. in New York City. Later in the year he journeyed
to Egypt and Saudi Arabia, studying Mohammedan doctrine
and listening to Islamic scholars. In Mecca he was received
by Crown Prince Faisal. For having made the pilgrimage there,
he was entitled to the honorary name of El Hajj Malik El-
Shabazz. In Ghana and Nigeria he conferred with government
officials, intellectuals, and diplomats from other African nations. The most significant experience of his trip, however, he
wrote about in a letter dated April 25 and mailed from Mecca
to a friend in New York City. In Mecca, he said, there were
more than 226,000 devout Moslems gathered for the annual
Hajj (pilgrimage). They had come from every part of the
world and were "of all colors and ranks." He continued:

> I have eaten from the same plate, drank from the same
> glass, slept on the same bed or rug, while praying to the same
> God . . . with fellow-Muslims whose skin was the whitest of
> white, whose eyes were the bluest of blue, and whose hair
> was the blondest of blond.

As an inevitable sequel he rejected in a letter dated September 22 "the 'strait-jacket world' created by my strong belief
that Elijah Muhammad was a messenger direct from God" in
the narrow-minded confines of which he had lived "for 12
long years." He emphatically disaffiliated himself from ". . .
Elijah Muhammad's racist philosophy which he has labeled
'Islam' only to fool and misuse gullible people as he fooled
and misused me."

When his plane landed in New York on May 21, 1964, he
was surrounded by "probably 50 or 60 reporters and photog-
raphers." He informed them of his change of heart about white
men, that he didn't now feel that all of them were "blue-eyed
devils." Malcolm soon proclaimed the birth of the Organization
of Afro-American Unity, and announced his intention of lifting civil rights into the area of human rights. The OAAU
would stress political and social action more than did the
spiritually oriented Nation of Islam. It would maintain, too,
that in places like Mississippi and Alabama where the govern-

ment is unable or unwilling to defend the Negro, he should defend himself with whatever weapons he might find available. To some this sounded like a declaration of war against the KKK. The agitation for a separate sovereign state for Negroes was to be discarded as impractical in the immediate situation. (The Nation of Islam had already abandoned its demands in that direction, substituting a milder proposal: "As long as we are not allowed to establish a state or territory of our own, we demand not only equal justice under the laws of the United States but equal employment opportunities—NOW!")

In July 1964 Malcolm attended the second meeting of the Organization of African Unity in Cairo, where the heads of thirty-three independent African states had gathered. He said that he intended to add a new dimension to the civil rights struggle in the United States, to attract international attention by having the United States cited at the United Nations for discriminatory practices. In a memorandum submitted to the conference he made this accusation:

> The American government is either unable or unwilling to protect the lives and property of your 22 million American brothers and sisters. We stand defenseless at the mercy of American racists who murder us at will for no reason other than we are black and of African descent. Our problems are your problems. We have lived for over 300 years in that American den of racist wolves in constant fear of losing life and limb.

Malcolm failed in his endeavor to have the United States cited, but he seems to have stimulated some interest in his organization and perhaps made some international ties. Later in the year he wrote from Mecca that he had been named United States representative of the World Muslim League, the supreme religious body of the Muslim world. He had been given the authority, he reported, to open a Muslim Center in New York City. Fifteen authorized teachers would be sent for the center, and fifteen scholarships for study at the Islamic University in Medina would be made available.

The defection of Malcolm X, who for some time had been in the public eye as the foremost spokesman of the Lost-Found

Nation of Islam, was a severe blow to the Muslims. Elijah Muhammad, a small and unprepossessing man with a reedy and undramatic voice, appeared to be getting more and more cautious and cagey. His denunciations of the "blue-eyed devils" became less and less vitriolic and his emphasis on a conventional means of emancipation—the three-year Economic Plan —more marked. It was a matter of common knowledge that the more impatient and hotheaded Islamites considered him about ready to fade out.

Nevertheless, those who foresaw an imminent collapse of the movement were not aware of its essentially strong and deep roots in the Negro community. In the despair-haunted slums where vice and crime flourished like a noxious weed the Muslims' exemplary conduct shone like good deeds in a naughty world. The brothers were always neatly and quietly arrayed; the sisters seemed enshrouded in untouchable chastity. If they inspired revulsion or fear, they also commanded respect. Becoming a dedicated Muslim seemed like taking Holy Orders. One had to renounce illicit sexual enjoyment, pork, gambling, liquor, dancing, movies, lying, dishonesty, and every other frailty, folly, or vice to which the human flesh is all too prone. The more enlightened might laugh at the sect's preposterous flights into the realm of science and other branches of knowledge, but these ludicrous aspects were not visible to the unlettered ghetto dweller. He could see only the living exemplars of what appeared to be the good and virtuous life to which all could ideally aspire. Though many of the poor were averse to active participation in any organization that might provoke the attention of the police or even the disapproval of the white man, their sympathies were with the proud and stiff-necked Muslims who had the nerve to look the "Caucasian devil" defiantly in the eye. A not uncommon attitude was: "I wouldn't join them, because I'm too pleasure-loving for that kind of life, but they're for my side and if the chips were down I'd have to be for them, too."

The press—even the Negro press—customarily viewed the activities of the Black Muslims with either jocosity or hostility. Take the question of violence. Though the tough FOI squads are trained to resist violence, they seldom have been the aggressors—and particularly not in brushes with the "Caucasian devil" and his police. Usually their skill in karate and other esoteric forms of combat is expended to settle internecine warfare or to discipline some erring brother who has strayed from the fold. A typical incident was that in Los Angeles on April 27, 1962. In a clash with the police that developed after two young Muslim brothers engaged in fisticuffs with two policemen who suspected them of having stolen men's suits, one Muslim was shot to death and six were wounded while one police officer was slightly wounded. (It was discovered after the carnage was over that one Muslim was merely handing a suit to the other so that he might take it to the dry cleaner's.) Several Muslims from a nearby temple got involved in the fracas. Chased by the policemen, they fled to sanctuary in the temple. In the meantime several squad cars arrived in response to a radioed appeal, and thirty police officers with drawn pistols invaded the temple. A meeting was just breaking up. The cops gunned down seven of the Muslims, dragged them to the sidewalk, and manacled them. Then they proceeded to stomp the handcuffed and wounded Islamites. One of them died. It was disclosed at the trial of nine Muslims indicted before the grand jury for assaulting and resisting the police that the only "weapon" used by the Islamites during the melee was a water jug with which the wounded policeman's elbow was struck. Though a number of witnesses testified to police brutality, no action was taken. The Muslims, expressing contempt for the white man's courts of law, refused to testify. A young policeman told of being surrounded by Muslims who were chanting, "Kill the white devils!" Or at least that's what he *thought* they were chanting. They were chanting in Arabic, which he couldn't understand.

This and other incidents tended to fortify the Muslim's contention that their characteristic role was as recipients of violence rather than instigators of it.

Just what direction would have been taken by Malcolm X and his Organization of Afro-American Unity can only be conjectured in the light of what happened. It was scarcely off the ground when he traveled to Selma, Alabama, where on February 4, 1965, he spoke before several hundred Negro students assembled to demonstrate for civil rights. He warned them that they might be forced to abandon their nonviolent tactics. "The white man," he said, "should thank God that Dr. King has held his people in check, because there are others who don't feel that way—others who are ready to lead a different kind of movement." This statement could be interpreted as indicating that Malcolm was announcing his availability as leader of such a movement.

On the afternoon of February 21, 1965, Malcolm X. Shabazz (as he then usually was called) entered the Audubon ballroom in upper Manhattan where about five hundred Negroes were waiting to hear him. It was a meeting of the Afro-American Unity group, and no whites had been invited.

Walking down the aisle toward the rostrum, Malcolm saluted his followers with the prescribed Muslim greeting: "As-salaam salaam" ("Peace be unto you").

"Wa-alaikum salaam" ("And unto you peace"), they chorused in response.

As Malcolm mounted the speaker's platform, what was later known to be a diversionary scuffle started near the rear of the hall. He had uttered only three words, "Brothers and sisters," when he was cut down by a burst of gunfire, apparently directed by three men who had taken advantage of the confusion to run down the center aisle. His body riddled by eleven bullets and two shotgun blasts, Malcolm died before he arrived at Presbyterian Medical Center.

A man accused of being one of the assassins with a shotgun was winged in the leg by one of Malcolm's bodyguards as he tried to flee. He proved to be Thomas Hagan, who had a previous police record as Talmadge Hayer. Hagan (or Hayer) declined to say whether he was a Black Muslim. In Chicago Elijah Muhammad denied any knowledge of him. Another suspect was nabbed, Norman 3X Butler. Identified as a Black Muslim "enforcer," he was out on bail for having shot and wounded a withdrawer from the Temple of Islam.

(The digit before Norman's "X" showed that there were others in his temple with the same first name. Distinct identity was preserved by prefixing a number. The name James is of such common occurrence that one member's name is James

67X. When the movement was smaller, "righteous" surnames—
for which the "X" stood until the head of Islam revealed them
by divination—were assigned rather frequently. Later on, it
was common for a member to use an "X" for years before the
"righteous" or "original" name was granted him.)

While Muhammad's organization would seem to be the
logical beneficiary of Malcolm's death, there were other
candidates. "A Harlem dope racket with supply lines stretch-
ing to Cuba and Red China was responsible," the New York
World-Telegram and Sun decided. This jibed with the paper's
previously stated theory that "left-wing extremists have been
peddling dope to finance their revolutionary activities." The
Ku Klux Klan was not overlooked as a possible culprit. And
what about the New York cops, in whose flesh the pyrotechnic
black nationalist had long been a festering thorn? In the
September 12, 1964, issue of the *Saturday Evening Post* Malcolm had written: "So, some of the followers of Elijah Muhammad would still consider it a first-rank honor to kill me. Also I
know that any day, any night, I could die at the hands of
some white devil racists." New York Assemblyman Percy
Sutton, Malcolm's attorney, said that Malcolm had told him
the day before that he knew he would be killed. He added
that the slain leader had intended to read in the meeting the
names of those who were intent on doing away with him.

Retaliation by Malcolm's followers was of course expected.
Its only immediate manifestation seemed to be the destruction
by a fire bomb of Muhammad's Temple of Islam No. 7, over
which the murdered man had once presided. When the annual Black Muslim convention was held in the Chicago Coliseum February 26–28, 1965, it was not only accompanied by a
heavy police guard but an augmented contingent of the FOI
kept constant vigil over every movement of the Messenger of
Allah. He repeatedly insisted he was not afraid. "I'm not to be
killed," he declared, ". . . and anyone who attempts to harm me
will come to a bad end." Though Elijah Muhammad expressed
serene confidence in Allah's protection, his police and cult
guards were not taking any chances they could avoid. A news-
paperman jokingly noted that only the top of Elijah's be-
jeweled fez was visible among the forest of heads belonging

to FOI elite guards. Chicago policemen were not stationed inside the Coliseum, but watched all the entrances and the immediate vicinity.

Fear of reprisal by partisans of Malcolm X was thought to be the main factor in reducing attendance to 3,000 or less, down from a high of about 6,000 the preceding year. Most interest was aroused on the second day when heavyweight champion Cassius Clay (renamed Muhammad Ali after his conversion to Islam) entertained with an exhibition bout. For the most part quiet prevailed. The only violence wreaked by the FOI was upon a young Negro named Willie Eugene Greer, who was severely beaten and thrown bleeding outside into the arms of Chicago policemen. Hospitalized for facial cuts and possible fractures of both legs and several ribs, Greer said he was not a member of the Black Muslims but was interested in their message to the extent that he had attended other meetings in the past. The official Muslim explanation of the incident was that Greer had been recognized as one who had made derogatory remarks about the Messenger of Allah on a former occasion. His ejection came on the third and last day when Elijah made his major address.

At the final session Elijah Muhammad spoke for more than three hours, and, as usual, imparted confidential information not to be had elsewhere. For example, he said that Allah (undoubtedly in his W. D. Fard incarnation) had talked to him many years ago about a trip to Mars during which he (Fard) had found the Martians to be about nine feet tall. Though their life expectancy was 1,200 years, they ranked below the American Negro in brain power. Allah at the same time advised any mortal from trying to make a trip to the moon. Landing would present no insuperable difficulties, but if the earthman drank any of the available water on the lunar surface his eyes would pop out of his head. Of more imminent concern to Elijah's hearers was the disclosure that more than two decades ago a group of businessmen had sunk $210,000,000 in the construction of a superplane that remained aloft a year at a time, traveling so fast that it is invisible. At the end of a year the plane merely drops down a tube into the atmosphere and siphons up enough oxygen to do it another year. Whatever

could be the use of such a marvel? Why, Muhammad darkly
hinted, the high-flying camarilla might just decide to use it to
wipe out the United States government in Washington before
the Black Muslims got around to it.

What had been Malcolm X's impact on his people and his
times, and how would it be projected into the future—reflected
in coming events? Few would venture a precise prediction, but
all could agree that Malcolm's martyrdom brought an immediate and, in some respects, spectacular response. His body,
lying in state for a week at the Unity Funeral Home, was
viewed by at least 30,000. Another 3,000 came to All Faith
Temple Church of God in Christ, where his bullet-ridden body,
swathed in the white cerements of Muslim ritual, reposed in a
bronze casket above which hung two murals picturing Jesus
Christ. The funeral obsequies (February 27, 1965) included a
fervent panegyric by Ossie Davis, Negro playwright and
actor. Malcolm, he said, had been one of Harlem's "brightest
hopes—extinguished now and gone from us forever." The
defector from the Black Muslims, Davis continued, had
stopped being "Negro" years before. The word had become
too puny and weak for him. "Malcolm was bigger than that.
Malcolm had become an Afro-American and he wanted—so
desperately—that we, that all his people, would become Afro-
Americans too."

To those who would turn away from him as "not a man but
a demon, a monster and a subverter and an enemy of the
black people," Davis recommended this answer:

> Did you ever talk to Brother Malcolm? Did you ever touch
> him or have him smile at you? Did you ever really listen to
> him? Did he ever do a mean thing? Was he ever himself asso-
> ciated with violence or any public disturbance? For if you did
> you would know him. And if you knew him, you would know
> why we must honor him: Malcolm was our manhood, our
> living black manhood! This was his meaning to his people.
> And, in honoring him, we honor the best in ourselves.
>
> However much we may have differed with him—or with
> each other about him and his value as a man, let his going
> from us serve only to bring us together, now. Consigning
> these mortal remains to earth, the common mother of all,

secure in the knowledge that what we place in the ground is no more now a man—but a seed which, after the winter of discontent—will come forth again to meet us. And we shall know him then for what he was and is—a Prince—our own black shining Prince!—who didn't hesitate to die, because he loved us so. . . .

FOR FURTHER READING

There is a growing literature on the civil rights movement. A good introduction is *Charles Silberman, *Crisis in Black and White* (New York, 1964). Other works include Howard Zinn, *The New Abolitionists* (Boston, 1964); William J. Brink and Louis Harris, *The Negro Revolution in America* (New York, 1964); *Louis Lomax, *The Negro Revolt* (New York, 1962); Alan Westin (ed.), *Freedom Now! The Civil Rights Struggle in America* (New York, 1964); Kenneth Clark (ed.), *The Negro Protest* (Boston, 1963); Loren Miller, *The Petitioners: The Story of the Supreme Court of the United States and the Negro* (New York, 1966); Anthony Lewis, *Portrait of a Decade* (New York, 1964); and Benjamin Muse, *Ten Years of Prelude: The Story of Integration Since the Supreme Court's 1954 Decision* (New York, 1964).

Early aspects of the movement are treated in Louis Rauchames, *Race, Jobs and Politics* (New York, 1953) and Herbert Garfinkel, *When Negroes March: The March on Washington Movement in the Organizational Politics for FEPC* (Glencoe Ill., 1959). An interesting discussion of black Americans' relation to Africa is Harold R. Isaacs, *The New World of Negro Americans* (New York, 1964). Martin Luther King, Jr.'s role and thought are depicted in his *Stride Toward Freedom* (New York, 1964) and *Where Do We Go from Here: Chaos or Community?* (New York, 1968).

A good collection of documents is *Francis L. Broderick and August Meier (eds.), *Negro Protest Thought in the Twentieth Century* (Indianapolis, 1965). Useful accounts by participants are Whitney Young, Jr., *To Be Equal* (New York, 1964) and James Farmer, *Freedom—When?* (New York, 1965).

Black nationalism, and the Black Muslims in particular, are covered in *E. U. Essien-Udom, *Black Nationalism: A Search for an Identity in America* (New York, 1964). The Garvey movement is covered in *E. David Cronon, *Black Moses: The Story of Marcus Garvey and the Universal Negro Improvement Association* (Madison, 1965) and the Black Muslims in *C. Eric Lincoln, *The Black Muslims in America* (Boston, 1963). Benjamin Muse discusses the trend to nationalism in *The American Negro Revolution: From Nonviolence to Black Power, 1963–1967* (Bloomington, Ind., 1968). Useful essays toward understanding black nationalism are the brilliant *Autobiography of Malcolm X* (New York, 1966); *Eldridge Cleaver, *Soul on Ice* (New York, 1969); *Stokely Carmichael and Charles V. Hamilton, *Black Power* (New York, 1967); and *Harold Cruse, *The Crisis of the Negro Intellectual* (New York, 1968).